THE LABOUR MARKET
AND INFLATION

*Other publications of the International
Institute for Labour Studies*

*

AUTOMATION ON SHIPBOARD
edited by G. J. Bonwick

COLLECTIVE BARGAINING IN AFRICAN COUNTRIES
*by B. C. Roberts and
L. Greyfié de Bellecombe*

EMPLOYMENT PROBLEMS OF AUTOMATION
AND ADVANCED TECHNOLOGY
edited by Jack Stieber

INDUSTRIAL RELATIONS AND ECONOMIC DEVELOPMENT
edited by Arthur Ross

THE LABOUR MARKET AND INFLATION

The Proceedings of a Symposium held at the
International Institute for Labour Studies
in Geneva, 24–26 October 1966, under the
Chairmanship of

PIERRE MASSÉ

EDITED BY

ANTHONY D. SMITH

WITH A PREFACE BY

R. W. COX

Director, International Institute
for Labour Studies

MACMILLAN

London · Melbourne · Toronto

ST MARTIN'S PRESS

New York

1968

MACMILLAN & CO LTD
Little Essex Street London WC2
and also at Bombay Calcutta and Madras
Macmillan South Africa (Publishers) Pty Ltd Johannesburg
The Macmillan Company of Australia Pty Ltd Melbourne
The Macmillan Company of Canada Ltd Toronto
St Martin's Press Inc New York

Library of Congress catalog card no. 68–10752

PRINTED IN GREAT BRITAIN BY
R. & R. CLARK, LTD., EDINBURGH

CONTENTS

v

AUTHORS OF PAPERS AND PARTICIPANTS

Chairman

Pierre Massé, Chairman of the French National Electricity Board and former French Planning Commissioner.

Participants

Pierre Le Brun, former Secretary, French General Confederation of Labour, Paris.

L. H. J. Crijns,[1] Chief of the Labour Problems Division, Commission of the European Economic Community, Brussels.

Sture Eskilsson, Assistant Director, Swedish Employers' Confederation, Stockholm.

D. Fehrs, Labour Problems Division, Commission of the European Economic Community, Brussels.

H. Giersch, Professor, and Head, Economics Department, Saarbrucken University, and Member of the Council of Economic Experts, Federal Republic of Germany.

R. P. Haveman, Labour Relations Adviser, Unilever N.V., Rotterdam.

Rt. Hon. Aubrey Jones, Chairman, National Board for Prices and Incomes of the United Kingdom, London.

Heinz Kienzl, Economic Adviser, Confederation of Austrian Trade Unions, Vienna.

Heinz Markmann, Department of Economic Planning, German Confederation of Trade Unions (DGB), Düsseldorf.

Franco Mattei, Director, Economic Policy Branch, General Confederation of Italian Industry, Rome.

Rudolf Meidner, Director, Research Department, Confederation of Swedish Trade Unions, Stockholm.

J. Pen, Professor, Faculty of Law, Groningen University, Netherlands.

Gösta Rehn, Director of Manpower and Social Affairs, Organisation for Economic Co-operation and Development, Paris.

C. T. Saunders, Research and Planning Division, United Nations Economic Commission for Europe, Geneva.

[1] Dr. Crijns was unable to attend the Symposium.

Authors of Papers and Participants

F. Sellier, Professor, Faculty of Law and Economic Sciences, University of Aix-en-Provence, France.

Bevan Stein, Head of the Prices and Incomes Section, National Accounts and Economic Forecasting Division, Organisation for Economic Cooperation and Development, Paris.

Adolf Sturmthal, Professor, Institute of Labor and Industrial Relations, University of Illinois, U.S.A.

Lloyd Ulman, Professor, and Director, Institute of Labor and Industrial Relations, University of California (Berkeley), U.S.A.

Nat Weinberg, Director, Special Projects Department, International Union, United Automobile, Aerospace and Agricultural Implement Workers of America, Detroit, U.S.A.

H. Zoeteweij, International Labour Office, Geneva.

Rapporteur

A. D. Smith, International Institute for Labour Studies, Geneva.

PREFACE

WHEN seven years ago the International Institute for Labour Studies was created with autonomous status by the ILO, one of its intended functions — alongside education and research — was to stimulate the discussion of current policy issues amongst practitioners and specialists in an atmosphere removed from the pressures and strains of negotiation and decision-making.

In its research, the Institute has come to have a special interest in prospective studies, that is, with searching out the main factors influencing future social conditions and the principal options in future social or labour policy.

The Institute, in October 1966, convened a Symposium on the labour market and inflation : a theme which seemed to meet both the criteria of current controversy and prospective interest. The groping and experimenting involved in attempts to apply incomes policies appear as first steps in a process which will profoundly shape the future of economic policy, of industrial relations and of politics.

The last of these terms — politics — is the broadest and in a sense includes the others. The practising politician's attitude towards politics has been expressed as 'who gets what, when, how'.[1] By this definition, income policies are of the essence of politics. Beyond the difficult problems of concepts, measurements and techniques inherent in the formulation of incomes policies or more limited wages policies, beyond the complex inter-relationships with other instruments of government economic policy, there bear in upon the shaping and application of these policies all the conflicting demands and expectations, more or less effectively organised and articulated, that activate politics. Incomes policies also may stimulate the creation of new procedures for political decision-making, portending long-term changes in the structures of political systems. Now new institutional forms are being tried out as vehicles for defining and defending the 'public interest' and securing the consent and collaboration of the organised particular interests.

The difficulties encountered in agreeing about and applying incomes policies thus invoke large questions about the extent to which

---

[1] Harold Lasswell, *Politics : who gets what, when, how*, Cleveland, Ohio, Meridian Books, 1958.

social goals are widely shared ; and the extent to which existing institutions need to be adapted to perform new functions. While being aware of these far-reaching implications the Institute, in convening this Symposium, tried to present the questions for discussion in a more limited and, hopefully, a more manageable way. It did not intend to open a discussion about incomes policies as such, much less to attempt to deal directly with the broader issues of political change I mention. It sought rather to take account of the growing literature on incomes policies and to add something through a piecemeal, incremental approach. Thus the questions put — which are spelled out in the Introduction — focus in the main on how to make existing decentralised methods of wage-fixing less inflation-prone.

For the same reason, participation in the Symposium was drawn from a number of countries in Europe and North America which share the cost inflation problem and are presumed to share also certain common institutional and political ideas, placing limits upon the kinds of measures which can be realistically contemplated to deal with this problem. In exploring for practical measures, it seemed best initially to adopt this criterion of relevancy.

The Institute, as a centre for studies, does not endorse or promote any particular ideas or proposals. There was no question, therefore, that the Symposium would try to agree upon recommendations. Those who took part did so as experienced and thoughtful individuals, not as representatives or officials. Indeed, in keeping with the aim of a completely free and uninhibited exchange, the discussions took place in private. At the close of the Symposium it was agreed that the authors would revise their papers for publication in so far as they felt desirable in the light of the discussion ; and that a summary report of what was said would be reconstituted from the tape-recording. This was done with the agreement of the participants. Using the papers and this record of the discussion, the general rapporteur of the Symposium, Mr. Anthony D. Smith, staff associate of the International Institute for Labour Studies, has prepared an analysis of the argument which appears as Chapter 13 in this volume. This is, of course, his analysis — not the formally approved report of an official meeting — for which he is entitled to the full merit and responsibility. I trust that this analysis by one observer-participant will prove to be a useful guide through a complex argument to both scholars and practitioners. Mr. Anthony Smith has also edited this volume as a whole.

The thanks of the Institute also go to Mr. H. Zoeteweij, of the

Preface

International Labour Office, who defined the *problématique* for the Symposium. The ILO publication *Prices, Wages and Incomes Policies in Industrialised Market Economies*, of which he is co-author with Professor H. Turner of Cambridge, was referred to frequently in the discussions.

Finally, the Institute expresses its appreciation to the authors of the papers included in this volume and the other participants in the discussion. Special thanks go to Mr. Pierre Massé, whose masterful chairmanship gave stimulus, discipline and coherence to the discussion of a difficult topic.

GENEVA,
20 April 1967

R. W. Cox
Director,
International Institute for
Labour Studies

INTRODUCTION

BY

ANTHONY D. SMITH

I. INFLATION, INCOMES POLICIES AND THE LABOUR MARKET

In most industrialised market economies, the post-war period has been one of steadily rising prices. Because of certain harmful internal and external effects of rising prices, these countries have sought methods which, whilst preserving full employment and maintaining economic growth, prevent or restrain price increases. That, by and large, prices have continued to rise — though full employment and economic growth have not always been maintained — suggests that their quest has been in vain. The papers and their discussion and analysis presented in this book, constitute one more attempt to improve our understanding of certain elements in the inflationary process and to find measures which, whilst treating these elements, leave full employment and economic growth undisturbed.

Naturally, as a prelude to their treatment, many attempts have been made to diagnose the fundamental causes of inflation. Broadly, two basic causes are generally identified : 'demand pull' and 'cost push'. The former set of forces are seen as causing inflation as a result of a continued rise in demand schedules after the point at which factor supplies become inelastic ; the latter set are thought to operate as a result of an 'autonomous' rise in factor prices. Unfortunately, the techniques of economic analysis have not really proved adequate to the task of determining the relative extent to which these two causes have been responsible for inflation. Consequently, decisions about the strategy for dealing with inflation have had to be based on crude evaluations of whether inflation is caused exclusively by demand pull, exclusively by cost push, or by a combination of both.

Adherents of the exclusively cost-push hypothesis are few enough for it to be ignored. However, there are some — who might be called economic 'determinists' — who believe that essentially 'demand pull' is at the root of inflation and that, accordingly, a solution has to be sought in an appropriate management of the level of demand. In short, factor and product prices can only be influenced by measures that affect demand and supply schedules ; attempts to achieve price stability by directly regulating wages or other factor incomes are doomed in the long run. Whilst the major precept of 'determinists' is that demand management holds the key to price stability, measures — such as active manpower policies — to increase factor supplies are in their view equally legitimate and likely to contribute towards success.

Most observers, however, believe that there are both demand-pull and cost-push elements in the post-war inflations experienced by industrialised countries, and policy has become based to an increasingly large extent on this conviction. In the absence of a reliable measure of the relative importance of 'demand pull' and 'cost push' forces, the assumption that the latter constitute an important element rests largely on empirical surveys of the manner in which decisions about wages and prices are in fact reached.[1] Such surveys confirm what is widely thought to be the case ; that many unions can claim, and many employers concede, substantial wage increases, and employers can increase profit 'mark ups', the cost of which can be passed on as higher prices, largely irrespective of the market situation. This Symposium is essentially concerned with examining certain aspects of the 'cost push' mechanism of wage determination, and exploring policies for their treatment.[2] Thus, it is based on the assumption that 'cost push' plays a role, probably an important one, in the inflationary process.

As stated, some policies have already been based on this assumption and therefore they seek to treat the problem by influencing factor prices directly rather than via demand and supply schedules. According to their coverage such policies are referred to as wage policies or incomes policies. It should be noted that these policies — especially incomes policies — can have objectives other than, or in addition to, the promotion of price stability — for instance, the redistribution of income ; and that they do not, in any case, seek to treat all cost-push elements — import prices and indirect taxes, for example, are outside their scope.

At this juncture, attention needs to be drawn to two features of

---

[1] See, for example, H. A. Turner and H. Zoeteweij, *Prices, Wages and Incomes Policies in Industrialised Market Economies*, ILO Studies and Reports, New Series No. 70, Geneva, 1966, chapter iii.

[2] This does not imply that profit mark-ups are considered less important, but only that the Symposium was limited to labour market phenomena.

such policies. Firstly, they have not been used in isolation but have been accompanied by policy measures of other kinds — budgetary, monetary and fiscal, etc. — which, in principle at least, seek to regulate the general level of demand in a way that helps to promote price stability. Secondly, the formulation and implementation of these policies, especially wage policies,[1] have encountered serious difficulties,[2] and none can be considered as having achieved substantial success over any length of time.

Certain difficulties are connected with wage-determination procedures, and the Symposium was essentially concerned with these. It was not intended that the Symposium would consider problems associated with price-determination procedures nor those that are posed in connection with the longer-term viability of wage or income policies (important though they are), beyond that required for placing the immediate subject-matter of the Symposium in proper perspective. That is, there was no intention to discuss in detail such questions as : whether or not the policy pursued should be a wage or incomes policy ; how factor shares in the national income ought to develop ; the means by which community support for the chosen policy can be enlisted ; and how the appropriate balance and integration of wage and incomes policies and other social and economic policies can be achieved.[3]

The topics designated for discussion in the Symposium, which are briefly described below, were singled out for treatment on two grounds. Firstly, a Symposium such as this could not make an effective contribution to the prevention of inflation, if its deliberations were thinly spread over the whole field of inflationary processes and anti-inflationary measures ; the examination of a set of difficulties associated with the operation of the labour market both limited the scope of the proceedings and provided a common focal point for the discussions. It is useful to limit discussion to the labour market — even if it is recognised that wages are not the only nor necessarily the main element of cost inflation — because of the special industrial relations features involved and because, more generally, the employment market shows a number of important aspects quite distinct from those of other factor or commodity markets.

Secondly, and more important, measures for dealing with inflation-

---

[1] No country has yet attempted a fully fledged incomes policy.
[2] For a discussion of these difficulties, see Turner and Zoeteweij, *op. cit.*, chapter vii.
[3] In the event, as pointed out below, some attention was inevitably devoted to such questions.

ary aspects of the labour market promise to help by two routes : they could assure some of the pre-conditions for successful wage and incomes policies ; but even in the absence of such policies, measures of the kind examined by the Symposium may still help to render the process of wage determination less inflation-prone.

Within the field of problems posed for wage and incomes policies by the institutions and operation of the labour market, it was intended that the Symposium would concentrate on two major questions. First, given that a wage policy normally involves a degree of centralisation in the sense that general criteria are established for sectional wage adjustments, can measures be taken in return for which unions might accept some restraint in the wage claims they put forward in the formal, centralised, wage bargaining negotiations ? Secondly, how can existing decentralised methods of wage determination be made less inflation-prone ?

It was intended that the Symposium would pay most attention to the second of these problems. In essence, this problem is concerned with methods for reducing wage drift — increases in wages additional to those formally determined by collective agreement, arbitration award or government decision. It should be clearly understood, however, that not all wage drift represents a breakdown or ineffectiveness of central control or 'guidance' of wages, and that, correspondingly, not all elements of wage drift should be considered as undesirable in this sense. In particular, a degree of wage drift arises as a result of very desirable changes in the composition of the labour force, as between the sexes, age groups and occupations. Similarly, higher rates of pay for overtime work, in so far as they represent a means of overcoming the rising disutility of labour and not a means of paying higher than basic wage rates, are not within the purview of these proceedings.

What, then, are the elements of wage drift, of which the inflationary impact, desirability and amenability to treatment should be the concern of the Symposium ? A simple model — even if too crude a one to be accepted as a faithful representation of the wage-drift mechanism — can be used to identify the major elements that need to be examined by the Symposium.[1]

It is useful to regard wage drift (of the type which concerns the Symposium) as being caused, initially, by two factors, one associated

---

[1] Although it was not a primary concern of the Symposium to erect any such model of the wage-drift *mechanism,* several *obiter dicta* on this aspect have been recorded in Chapter 13.

with the state of demand in the labour market ; the other with certain institutions of the labour market. In the former case, shortages of particular types of labour — even when there is no 'general' shortage that would call for demand-curbing measures — cause 'competitive bidding' for labour supplies, thereby giving rise to wage drift. Efforts to improve the geographical and occupational mobility of labour — the group of measures which have become known as active manpower policies — promise to mitigate or even avoid such shortages, and thereby diminish or eliminate wage drift from this source, and they merit the Symposium's attention on this score. Secondly, piece-work systems of remuneration are notorious for the way in which, between formal revisions of the rates, they cause earnings to rise — another form of wage drift. It was felt that the Symposium might consider the extent to which this form of inflationary pressure could be weakened by improved techniques for determining incentive rates and by considering the extent to which they could be replaced by alternative systems of remuneration.

But whatever the primary source of wage drift, the strong influence of tradition and concepts of social status on inter-occupational, inter-industry and other wage differentials is commonly regarded as a vehicle by which this initial and limited drift is matched by compensatory increases in the earnings of other workers. That is, the application of the 'comparability criterion' means that wage increases in some jobs, in some firms, in some industries and in some regions, give rise to strong pressures for wage increases in much broader sectors of the economy and thereby a rise in the general wage level. It was intended therefore that the Symposium should consider to what extent, in both the short and the long run, the crude comparability criterion could be replaced by such other methods of determining wage relativities as job evaluation schemes or a set of trade-union-preferred wage differentials.

Doubtless much — and perhaps most — can be done to eliminate wage drift by lessening the extent of, and improving the techniques for, incentive payment systems, by remedying structural labour shortages and by supplanting the crude comparability criterion with a more flexible system of wage differentials. However, it is possible that drift can only be adequately reduced and centrally determined wage rates or guidelines be implemented sufficiently rigorously, if more direct means of influencing the outcome of decentralised wage determination procedures can be found. In principle, there are several ways in which this might be accomplished. Perhaps the one most frequently discussed is the modification of the structure and powers of the trade union movement in order to allow its 'centre' to have more influence over wage negotiations at the periphery. But governments can also pursue policies — price and fiscal policies for example — which, if properly formulated, can have the effect of influencing wage determination procedures at the plant level in the required direction. These questions, too, were examined by the Symposium.

It would not be difficult to draw up a long list of a wide variety of measures which might be used to persuade unions to claim smaller wage increases than they would otherwise do. In fact, of course, most of these possibilities would be impracticable on account of their ramifications and costs in fields other than wages. From those measures which appear to merit further inspection, the Symposium restricted its attention to a few which have, as a common feature, their close connection with the operation of the labour market. More precisely, consideration was given to whether restraint in wage demands can be 'bought' by the wider use of long-term contracts, profit and capital-sharing schemes and investment-wage programmes, and whether, in fact, such systems have a less inflationary impact than the foregone wage rises.

II. THE PRESENTATION OF THE PROCEEDINGS

Ten papers, presented as Chapters 2 to 11 and dealing with individual topics within the field mapped out for the Symposium, were invited from some of the participants. Whilst all these papers contain general passages in which the basic philosophy of their authors, with respect to inflation and incomes policies, is set out, certain of them — those by Mr. Saunders, Mr. Weinberg (on the United States Guideposts), Prof. Pen, Dr. Crijns and Prof. Sellier — are rather more wide-ranging in their subject-matter than the others and, accordingly, have been presented first. In the case of those contributions dealing with more specific questions, juxtaposition has been given to papers dealing with related topics.

The discussion was divided into five parts, to each of which certain papers were more relevant than others. Thus, the papers presented by Mr. Saunders, Prof. Sellier and Mr. Weinberg (on the United States Guideposts) afforded a springboard for an initial discussion of the objectives, conditions and instruments of incomes policies,[1] a discussion which provided a framework for the rest of the proceedings. More germane to the objectives of the Symposium, there followed a discussion of ways in which wage claims can be reduced, based on an evaluation of certain schemes in the paper prepared by Prof. Pen.[2] The Symposium became more fully immersed in the operation of the labour market with discussions of the three remaining items : labour shortages and competitive bidding ; the inflationary impact of the wage structure ; and certain international aspects of collective bargaining and incomes policies.[3] These three discussions were based on the papers of, respectively, Mr. Le Brun and Dr. Markmann, Mr. Aubrey Jones and Mr. Eskilsson, Dr. Crijns and Mr. Weinberg (on International Trade Union Co-operation and National Stabilisation Policies). These discussions have been summarised, in the above order, and presented in an Annex.[4]

In addition to his introductory statement, presented as Chapter 1, Mr. Massé drew attention to some of the more significant themes in the debate in a closing statement which forms Chapter 12. Chapter 13, an analysis of the proceedings, is based on three sources : the papers presented at the Symposium ; the discussions ; and replies to a questionnaire which the participants were invited to take away and consider rather more leisurely. This questionnaire covered a variety of topics, including : the appropriate objectives of wage and incomes policies, and whether or not their operation should be limited to short-term problems ; the degree of compulsion required in implementing such policies ; and the importance of active manpower policies, the rationalisation of and union preferences for wage structures, profit-sharing and capital-sharing schemes, demand policies and price policies — as adjuncts or substitutes for wage or income policies.

Chapter 13 is divided into two parts. The first contains an evaluation of the proceedings relating to the subject-matter proper of the Symposium — 'The Labour Market and Inflation'. Inevitably, however, wider questions relating to inflation and to wage and incomes policies were touched upon, in greater or less detail, in the proceedings. In the first place, the papers included statements of the basic philosophy, in this field, of their authors. Secondly, participants were anxious to emphasise the ways in which discussions

---

[1] *Discussion*, pp. 178 to 201.   [2] *Discussion*, pp. 201 to 210.
[3] Respectively, *Discussion*, pp. 210 to 228, 228 to 237, and 237 to 240.
[4] Referred to as *Discussion*.

of items within the particular field of this Symposium have implications for the conduct or acceptability of a wider incomes policy. Thirdly, some participants took the opportunity which this platform offered to air views about aspects of incomes policies which they believe have been seriously neglected.[1] These wider questions are reviewed in the second part of Chapter 13.

[1] In particular, certain international implications of incomes policies were accorded more than usual attention.

Chapter 1

THE SETTING OF THE SYMPOSIUM
BY
PIERRE MASSÉ

THE Symposium on 'The Labour Market and Inflation', at which
I am greatly honoured to act as chairman, has been called to discuss,
essentially, methods of reducing inflationary wage pressure in conditions of full employment and economic growth. In other words,
it is connected with what is nowadays called an incomes policy and
measures to control or consciously influence the trend of wages. As
you know, it has not hitherto proved possible in France to secure
general agreement on this subject and I presume that the organisers
of this Symposium, in asking me to be chairman, have taken the view
that we often derive more knowledge — or at least more experience
— from failure than from success.

In order to appreciate the importance of this meeting it should, I
think, be placed in proper perspective, that is, against the general
background of contemporary economic growth. You may feel that
in attempting such a task I am being over-ambitious. But in my
view this is the only way of putting the question in its true perspective, for, as Prof. Pen rightly concludes in his paper, 'the fight against
inflation requires a comprehensive approach'.

Economic growth is now a more rapid, more widespread and more
conscious process than it used to be, which implies that there has
been a fairly drastic change since the conditions which existed in the
pre-war period. Yet we must be careful not to be too categorical
about this. The history of economic ideas shows just how much
doctrines have been affected by the environment in which they were
first proposed, whether they were propounded by Malthus, Marx or
Keynes. Let us not therefore become dogmatic about the nature of
growth, because the current trend has only existed for a mere twenty
years.

The assumption of continued rapid expansion undoubtedly affords
the most appropriate working hypothesis on which current policies
should be based. There are sound reasons for this. On the supply

I

side the return to capital has not declined along with accumulation, as it was mistakenly assumed it would in the nineteenth century. Improvements in quality as a result of technical progress, better education and more modern equipment have shown that this pessimistic forecast is a false one. On the demand side the spectre of long-term stagnation as a consequence of economic maturity has vanished as a result of all the goals and developments which are symbolised in the expression 'the new frontier'. These considerations are well known and there is no need for me to dwell on them.

Another point I feel should be made is that according to the most dependable studies of the development process carried out in France (by Berthet, Carré, Dubois and Malinvaud), such qualitatively and quantitatively identifiable factors as labour and capital account for only about half the growth which has occurred since the end of the war (an average of 5·1 per cent. per annum). Of course, the cause of the other half is to be found in the improvements in technology and management techniques and in changes in the size of firms and their markets, though the precise effects of these factors are difficult to measure. Such a result testifies to the importance of creativeness in the human spirit's struggle against the bonds of nature, and affords hope that this ill-defined but very vital 'progress' will not suddenly peter out. It is very desirable that economic growth models should try to take account of all the factors which fall into this class.

However, the Western economies — and probably others too — suffer a serious weakness that stems from the unsystematic and haphazard nature of the machinery for distributing incomes. Admittedly in the past twenty years we have managed to avoid the major slumps of the previous era. Even the terminology of economics bears witness to the change that has taken place, a 'recession' now implying not a fall in output but merely a slowing down in the rate of growth. Nevertheless, the surplus produced by an expanding economy is very unevenly distributed. It does not all accrue to the capitalists, but is shared between consumers, in the form of lower prices, workers, in the form of higher wages, and shareholders in the form of distributed and undistributed profits. The nature of this distribution reflects both the operation of market forces and the relative strengths of the groups involved.

The pressures making for lower prices are felt most strongly by firms in the competitive sectors and only slightly by those in the sheltered sectors. The resistance to price reductions is weak in industries where productivity is rising rapidly — the highly mechanised industries — and strong in activities where productivity increases only slowly — the traditional illustration of this case being hair-cutting. Pressures for large wage increases are strong in conditions of full employment and slight in conditions of underemployment. Their size also depends on the organisation and relative aggressiveness of the trade unions and employers' associations.

It is worth noting in passing that while it is unreasonable and unfair to regard the pressures that make for higher wages as the sole cause of 'overheating', there is nevertheless a close link between the labour market situation and inflation. This link is due not only to the fact that wages represent the largest share of the national income, but above all to the acceptance by modern governments of the objective of full employment, a goal which tends to create a permanent manpower shortage.

The combination of these market forces exposes modern economies to two alternative but not mutually exclusive dangers. If labour shortages force wages up while prices, because of competition, lag behind, then profit margins shrink and both the incentive and ability to invest are impaired. If wages and prices rise simultaneously then, regardless of opinions as to which occurred first, the balance of foreign trade in goods and services deteriorates. In reality the situation is more complex than this because the former situation tends to prevail in the competitive sectors and the latter in the sheltered sectors, with interactions between them which make analysis and forecasting extremely difficult and hazardous.

Whether it is investment or the foreign trade balance which is affected, vigorous remedial action is essential. But such corrective action may overshoot the mark, whereupon it becomes necessary to reverse the policy, a requirement which presumably accounts for the alternation of measures to stabilise and reflate the economy, a feature of many of our economies.

It is clearly impossible to rely on the market mechanism to cope with this situation. Or rather the market mechanism could only perform this role by means of 'shakeouts' of the kind that we have known during the past twenty years, which, whilst they have not involved major slumps, have entailed recessions and regrettable losses of output. Nor is it possible to rely upon the planning machinery. Such reliance would require stringent plans that govern not only production but also consumption — and the incomes which link these two activities. In other words there would need to be an incomes, wages and prices policy of a type that runs counter to our

Western ethics, though one which might be acceptable in emergencies when the community's safety is threatened and governments are bold enough to act accordingly.

These shortcomings of the market and planning mechanisms have led to the concept of an *incomes policy*. Such a policy has two, quite distinct, elements, corresponding to two major decisions. First it is necessary to decide *what* needs to be done, and secondly, *how* to do it. The former is an intellectual task, the latter is a practical one.

Circumstances vary greatly between countries and this diversity contributes to the difficulty of the problems involved and to the value of inter-country comparisons of experience of the kind for which this Symposium affords an opportunity. For instance, we have for many years admired the logic and wisdom of the Netherlands solution, but note that a prolonged period of restraint has ended in its sudden collapse. In Great Britain, the search for a long-term policy carried out over a period of 18 months by the National Board for Prices and Incomes acting in its three-fold — educational, advisory and judicial — capacity, has been momentarily overtaken by the short-term needs of the economy, and the British Government followed measures announced on 20 July 1966 with steps for tightening the squeeze still further. Its decision should afford, as Mr. W. J. Thorne argues in a recent article,[1] 'a valuable breathing space during which employers, wage earners and politicians can if they are determined to do so learn the disciplines which limit and stimulate economic growth'.

I shall examine the case of France — with which I am more familiar and on which I may be in a position to supply some useful information — in rather more detail. The stabilisation measures taken in 1963, which were necessitated by a pronounced 'overheating' of the economy, consisted partly of traditional measures of restraint and partly of a freeze of prices. There was no wage freeze — as is sometimes mistakenly stated — but, of course, the measures that were taken, coupled with restrictions on total demand, naturally slowed down the rate of increase of wages. This combination of measures succeeded in achieving almost complete stabilisation without an undue retardation in the rate of growth (it was 3·5 per cent. in 1965), whereas without a price freeze the same result could only have been obtained by inducing a sharper recession. Of course, success had to be paid for in the form of a reduction in industry's profit margins

[1] W. J. Thorne, 'La Politique des Revenus en Grand Bretagne', *Analyse et Prévision*, SEDEIS, Paris, October 1966.

and capital investment, but even so, subsequent developments suggest that the course chosen represented the lesser evil.

At the same time the Conference on Incomes was being held and the Fifth Plan drafted. Knowing my fellow countrymen, I have never gone so far as to recommend an incomes policy. On the other hand, when major decisions concerning the Fifth Plan were being taken, I did suggest that an Incomes Study and Assessment Board should be established to pass judgment, publicly, on the behaviour of individual firms or industries. This Board would not have functioned in the same way as the traffic courts which are empowered to confiscate the licences of offending motorists ; I did not suggest that it should have the power to impose any legal or financial penalties, but merely assumed that it would have a moral influence. However, the suggestion of judicial functions and independent status contained in the words 'board' and 'assessment' was not well received and I therefore proposed to the government that an Incomes and Costs Study Centre should be established instead with its role clearly confined to research, publicity and persuasion.

In an expanding economy, activity in one year will yield a 'surplus' compared with activity in some previous year. To make this surplus as large as possible is the objective of the economic plan, to distribute it in the best way the goal of an incomes policy. At the global level, the size of this surplus is sometimes measured by the rate of growth of output. Yet this indicator does not really measure the economy's *performance*, since it signifies a different degree of efficiency according to whether it is accompanied by a constant, or increasing, active population. For this reason, the rate of growth in output per head of the active population is a better measure.

A parallel procedure is needed at the industry or firm level. For example, the rise in agricultural output has been estimated at 2·7 per cent. per annum for the period 1962–70. Yet, obviously, this figure does not reflect the 'performance' of this sector in the sense of its contribution to the whole economy, since it fails to take into account the fact that agricultural workers are being released, to the benefit of the secondary and tertiary sectors, at the rate of 3·5 per cent. per year. In the case of the coal industry, competition from alternative sources of energy means that output needs to contract by about 2 per cent. per year, but this contraction is, of course, accompanied by a fall in the number of workers, and this must be taken into account when evaluating the industry's performance.

These illustrations show that the 'surplus' concept can only be a significant one if, in its measurement, account is taken of all factors that contribute to activity in the industry or firm in question. This leads to the following definition (one which is related to the concept of total factor productivity).

The 'surplus' produced by an industry or firm between two, relatively close, points of time, is measured by the sum of the changes in the quantities of both product and factors, the latter being counted on the basis of a sign which is opposite to the direction in which they have changed,[1] each being weighted by their base year prices or returns.[2] From this an important relationship can be obtained by relating the changes which occur between the two periods to the position in the base period. More precisely it can be seen that the surplus distributed by the industry or firm is equal to the change in profits plus the sum of the changes in prices of both factors and products, the latter being counted on the basis of a sign which is opposite to the direction in which they have changed, weighted by the base period quantities. Thus, writing B for profits, capitals for quantities and the lower-case for prices, we have, in the case of one product, X, and two factors, Y and Z, the following relationship :

$$xdX + y(-dY) + z(-dZ) = dB + X(-dx) + Ydy + Zdz$$

The left-hand side of this identity shows how the 'surplus' originates from the change in outputs and inputs ; the right-hand side shows how it is apportioned among consumers and producers in the form, respectively, of lower prices and higher returns.

Thus this definition represents a synthesis of two important aspects of the problem — how the surplus is produced and how it is divided. It is also a realistic definition in the sense that it avoids arbitrary assumptions such as the specification of a particular measure of productivity. Furthermore it promises to be operationally effective, based as it is on actual accounts. Without doubt it is a heretical definition when compared with orthodox measures of productivity, but where better to be heretical than in Geneva ? It should not be confused with the Marxist concept of surplus value, since it relates essentially to a magnitude which evolves between two points of time

---

[1] So that, in effect, a rise in factor inputs is deducted from the rise in output, and a fall in factor inputs added to it.

[2] Thus, by including among the factors changes in the number of workers weighted by their base period wages, the objections examined above are taken into account.

This measurement of 'surplus' was communicated by Mr. Massé in the above form after the termination of the proceedings.

and which is not completely appropriated by only one of the socio-economic parties.

This approach, however, does raise certain difficulties. For instance, it might be criticised for the unusually large role given to prices in the definition. In fact, this feature is not, in principle, open to criticism since there can be no economic calculation without prices — a consideration which is reflected to an ever-increasing extent in planning mechanisms in both East and West Europe. Of course, the estimation of prices may pose certain practical problems. Secondly, the approach might be criticised because of the problems associated with the measurement of quality changes ; but this difficulty is in the nature of things and has nothing to do with the method employed. A third question is whether the conversion of the surplus measure into an annual percentage figure should be based on gross output or on value added. Opinions have not yet hardened about this, and the answer may well depend on the nature of the problem in hand. One conclusion, however, is obvious : that while the above approach affords a means of making approximate calculations, it could not claim any great precision.

If this definition is accepted and the necessary calculations performed, as I mentioned earlier, we can then proceed to enquire whether the surplus is large enough and to decide whether it is reasonably distributed. A review of the size of the surplus might suggest that further modernisation and reorganisation are needed. However, the calculation is of little value unless it can be compared with those for other countries and firms in the same country or in similar industries and firms in different countries. Calculations made for Electricité de France over the period 1952–62 suggest that the surplus is reasonable, but it is impossible to be more definite about this until other calculations of the same kind have been made elsewhere.

Calculations made for the Electricité de France are more informative in the case of the distribution of the surplus. They show that more than half the surplus went to consumers in the form of relatively lower prices per kWh in comparison with the trend in the average price level, while a third went to employees — representing a substantial gain — and less than a tenth was retained by the undertaking itself. Views may differ about the significance of the size of the slice taken by the employees, but it would appear to be neither unduly high nor unduly low. On the other hand, there is a sharp contrast between the share taken by consumers and that retained by the undertaking.

7

It is of course only fair and reasonable that the Electricité de France, an enterprise which is in the van of technological progress, should lower its charges in relation to the average level of prices, especially if overall stability is to be achieved by offsetting the upward movement in the prices of goods and services that benefit less from technical progress. Even so, an undertaking which, year-in year-out, must invest an amount equal to half its turnover should be able to plough back a reasonably large proportion of its earnings.

This illustration shows how it should be possible to prescribe the divergencies that are necessitated by the particular characteristics of the various industries and firms ; that is, it suggests how to solve a major problem of incomes policies, the need to allow departures from the prescribed average norm without destroying its general validity.[1]

Moving from the theoretical aspect to the practical, I would say that an ideal incomes policy should help to modify behaviour by securing 'public agreement that what it is proposing is both necessary and fair'.[2] Like any other ideal this is a very long-term objective. The more immediate question is how to deal with the existing situation. This question has been explored in that excellent report by Turner and Zoeteweij[3] and in the papers prepared for this Symposium, and therefore I will confine myself to a few introductory remarks. First, it is important to appreciate the value of international meetings such as ours. When a problem is difficult, and this one certainly is, it is an enormous advantage to be able to compare the experience of different countries and the view of their leading experts. Secondly, there is no magic formula for the solution of the problem and even the best solutions do not withstand the ravages of time. The formulae that are tried are like medicines to which germs become steadily more resistant and the nature of which therefore has to be modified at regular intervals. Thirdly, the success of an incomes policy is to some extent bound up with such political factors as a people's capacity for self-discipline, the degree of communal spirit, or the existence of a socialist or labour government which may encounter relatively less difficulty when implementing its recommendations.

The very fine paper presented by Mr. Saunders raises a fourth question which is nearer to the heart of the subject than the preceding ones — the relative effectiveness of central wage bargaining. Accord-

---

[1] OECD, *Policies for Price Stability*, Paris, 1962. [2] *Ibid.*
[3] *Op. cit.* ; see, especially, chapters vi and ix.

ing to Mr. Saunders, only a fairly small amount of cost inflation through wages can be attributed to central wage negotiations (except in the Netherlands), although he adds that the moderation observed at the centre has been effectively offset, although less in Sweden and Norway than elsewhere, by wage settlements at the periphery. There is nothing surprising about this. In a world such as ours, where interdependencies are increasing every day, wage negotiations involve more than the two parties immediately involved, the unions and management. There is a third party, which Professor Sellier has identified with the general long-term interest, and it is only natural that centralised bargaining should give greater weight to the interests of this third party than bargaining at lower levels. On the other hand, in this as in other matters, a decentralisation of decisions can be defended on human grounds, so that we return to the objective stressed in Mr. Pierre Le Brun's paper, the need to find ways of curtailing the inflationary effect of decentralised methods of wage fixing.

I should like to sum up in a few words. Experiments that have been made with wage or incomes policies in industrialised market economies since the war have met with some success and quite a few reverses. This is because it is difficult to induce men to look beyond their immediate personal goals to the long-term general interest, an interest of which, very often, they are only vaguely aware. Such an attitude, if it persists, will eventually have repercussions which will be regarded as the result of sheer inefficiency and intellectual inadequacy. These repercussions will take the form of the loss of output caused by the deliberate slowing down of the economy that follows the failure of the social partners to agree to a system of rational restraints.

I realise that the trade union movement may well be willing to pay a certain price for the benefits of remaining free and independent. It is as well, however, that it should be aware of the nature of the price to be paid, and that it should not take up a stand until it clearly appreciates both the immediate advantages of the chosen position and the dangers and drawbacks that lie ahead.

It is, I think, in this spirit that our Symposium should seek ways and means of improving wage-fixing machinery. Turner and Zoeteweij called their last chapter 'Steps towards Stability'.[1] Such steps are not yet a promise but they are already a hope.

[1] *Op. cit.*

Chapter 2

MACRO-ECONOMIC ASPECTS OF INCOMES POLICY

BY

C. T. SAUNDERS [1]

THE limited purpose of this paper is to suggest a few conclusions, and questions, arising from the fairly wide experience that we have now had in Western Europe of various kinds of incomes policies. I would like to limit the discussion mainly to incomes policies aimed directly at the development of wages and salaries (which I will call 'wages' for short) without considering in much detail policies aimed directly at the control of prices or profits. This is mainly for purposes of definition and not because the control of non-wage incomes is unimportant.

I do not wish to enter at all deeply into the problem of how we can define an incomes policy ; but for present purposes I would like to adopt a rather broad definition so as to cover any way of deliberately and directly controlling the development of wages by government, or by organised labour or management or by some form of joint control. Thus, for example, I would regard as a 'policy' any attempt to operate a co-ordinated strategy for wage claims by trade unions even if no government intervention is involved. (This allows one to include the case of Sweden, where, it is often claimed, the wage-fixing machinery has been devised by the unions and employers specifically to exclude the need for government intervention.) Such a co-ordinated strategy need not be a strategy of 'restraint' ; it might be of an aggressive or militant character. The point is that it should be a rationally worked out strategy, capable of continuous application in detail. This would exclude on the one hand a simple union 'policy' of always and everywhere demanding the maximum ; or an employers' policy of always and everywhere resisting wage claims. It would also exclude a government 'policy' of simply urging modera-

[1] The views expressed are those of the author, and not necessarily of the United Nations Secretariat. The material in this paper was collected as part of a study of 'Incomes in post-war Europe' by the Economic Commission for Europe.

tion (even if an overall figure is put on what is regarded as 'moderate') without machinery to support the urging. To urge moderation in wage claims, at least in general terms, has been accepted as a normal function of government for many generations — including some periods when it was manifestly inappropriate. I suggest that a policy must include some machinery for making it effective. Otherwise it is no more an incomes policy than a series of pronouncements advocating more frequent washing which could, by itself, be described as a public health policy.

It is thus possible for the unions, and perhaps for management, to operate an incomes policy either with or without direct co-operation with government.

INCOMES POLICIES IN OPERATION IN WESTERN EUROPE

On this broad definition, I suggest we have six countries in Western Europe which have for quite a long period been operating an incomes policy in one way or another — Austria, Denmark, Finland, Netherlands, Norway and Sweden ; [1] one country which after several experiments has embarked on a new and, I believe, more promising as well as more elaborate attempt than before — the United Kingdom ; and one country — France — where a very strong effort has been made but, notwithstanding the brilliant and devoted efforts of Mr. Massé, the necessary consensus has not yet been secured.

In the other countries of Western Europe, there is comparatively little to report. In Belgium, the government holds extensive reserve powers for price control, which have recently been brought back into use ; an attempt to reach a voluntary agreement on pay restraint a couple of years ago came to nothing. In Ireland in 1964, the main lines of the two-year wage agreements were settled by a central negotiation between the Trades Union Congress and the central employers' organisation ; but it was impossible to repeat this in 1966. In Western Germany the government has tried to influence pay negotiations both by direct intervention in specific disputes and by official guidance on what pay increases would be possible without excessive further inflation.

Four significant features are common to the six countries (Austria, Denmark, Finland, Netherlands, Norway and Sweden) in which an incomes policy, as defined above, has operated for several years.

[1] For a description see H. A. Turner and H. Zoeteweij, *op. cit.*

First, there has been a substantial co-ordination of wage-claim strategy through a relatively powerful trade union federation, and a correspondingly forceful employers' centre. (In the Netherlands, this co-ordination has doubtless been more difficult because of the division of the union movement into three political confessional centres, but co-operation between them has been perfectly possible.) Co-ordination has mostly taken the form of a periodical *central negotiation* between the central trade union and employers' organisations resulting in a general average pay increase, together with fairly narrow ranges for sectional bargaining. Yet central negotiation is not necessarily essential to the co-ordination of strategy. Thus in Norway where central negotiation has been the most usual practice for more than a decade, it has given way on several occasions to sectional bargaining. In Sweden central negotiation has been the *normal* practice only since 1956, but in Denmark during the whole post-war period. In Austria, there has never been central negotiation on the Norwegian or Swedish pattern ; but the system by which sectional negotiations can go forward only with the approval of the Joint Wage and Price Commission (on which the Trade Union Federation represents trade union interests), means that the Federation has considerable powers to select the claims which should be pressed. Moreover, the Joint Commission has also to approve settlements. What is essential is not central negotiation in itself, but that the trade union centres, and employers' centres, should be able to exercise effective control of their constituent branch organisations.

The second feature common to these six countries is that throughout most of the period the government has been in the hands of the Labour Party or Socialist Party, or in the hands of coalitions including them (except for certain periods in Finland and the Netherlands and until the recent electoral defeats of the Socialist parties in Austria and Norway).

Thirdly, in spite of important differences between the six countries in the extent to which government takes part in pay settlements, the effective operation of the system depends in all these countries on a general agreement by the unions and employers' organisations to observe the 'rules of the game'. (The extent to which wage drift should be regarded as breaking the rules, or as playing a different game, is another matter.) It is true that in the Netherlands, all agreements require government approval before they can come into effect. This is the only country in Western Europe in which government exercises this power,[1] but it is a power which can be exercised only as long as a majority would conform of their own free will. However, it does seem possible to describe the system of pay bargaining in the Netherlands, at least until recently, as almost 'tripartite'. In Norway, the government's *locus standi* is more remote ; but it can exercise an important influence, and contribute to the central pay bargain, through its influence on agricultural prices and therefore on the cost of living. The government can 'buy' moderation in the pay settlement by adjusting food subsidies. In Sweden, the government's influence is perhaps still less direct. In all six countries, the personal and political connections between the trade union leadership and the Ministers has permitted, of course, a good deal of influence to be exercised 'off-stage'.

Fourth, in all these countries there has been a certain symmetry between the co-ordination of pay and that of prices. In each country governments have certain powers to control prices. The similarity with co-ordination of pay rests in the fact that governments have exercised their powers over prices more by persuasion than by statutory powers. But there is also the important difference that only in the Netherlands has the government statutory powers over pay.

Some of these common features of the 'pay co-ordination' countries may help to explain the obstacles to the adoption of incomes policies encountered elsewhere. It is not particularly difficult to see which cap fits a given country.

COMPARATIVE TRENDS IN WAGES AND UNIT LABOUR COSTS

The first point that every sceptically-minded observer of incomes policies is apt to make is that the countries with incomes policies (however defined) have not, according to the statistical record, been any more successful in avoiding inflation than the countries which have given up, or never made, the effort. This conclusion is worth examining a little more closely if we are interested in knowing how much can be expected of an incomes policy.[2] The test is not, of course, just whether wages rose more in one country than another.

---

[1] Although the government was able to exercise it in the United Kingdom, for a limited 'emergency' period, under the Prices and Incomes Act of August 1966.

[2] This part of the discussion is concerned simply with incomes policy as an anti-inflationary weapon and we can reasonably deal in aggregative statistics.

The test must be related to productivity; one must compare rises in wages per head with rises in output per head.

An attempt to carry out this test for Western European countries, plus the United States, is made in Tables 1 and 2.[1] In these tables the effort has been made to distinguish between changes in conventional rates of wages, as established by collective agreements, and changes in actual earnings, and to show both series whenever possible. The differences between these is a simple, but not unambiguous, measure of wage 'drift'.[2]

A few points must be made about the statistics in these tables:

(*a*) As every labour statistician knows, there is, for many countries, an embarrassingly wide choice of statistical data about wages, output and employment. The problem is to get reasonable comparability in view of the multitude of concepts. I do not pretend that these problems have been solved and can only fall back on the conventional expression (or hope) that the results, if not accurate, at least reflect the right orders of magnitude. If different figures are produced from another source, I should be worried but not particularly surprised.

(*b*) The concept of 'conventional rates' — i.e. of the wage increases established by collective bargaining — is an exceedingly difficult one to apply to actual statistics. For example, how much allowance, if any, should be made for the effect of collectively agreed changes in piece-rate systems? It is impossible to go into such complications; one can only enter a general reservation. For some countries, in particular for France and the United States, no attempt is made to measure the effect of changes in conventional rates. In France, a series for wage rates exists and is entered in the table, but it is based on enquiries from employers about 'the most common wage rates' actually paid for given occupations, which is not really what is required. In the United States, because the system of union wage bargaining is much more decentralised than in most of Western Europe, the distinction between conventional rates and actual earnings has no substantial relevance.

---

[1] The help of Mr. Pohjola of the ECE Research and Planning Division is gratefully acknowledged.

[2] 'Drift' in this broad sense includes a good deal more than the results of wage settlements at the enterprise level. It includes shifts between occupations, changes in the amount of overtime, and — more important — changes in piece-rate earnings (to the extent that they are not accounted for in the index of conventional rates). Moreover, it is recognised that there are elements of decentralised collective bargaining in the drift figures thus established. The significance of the drift figure varies from country to country according to the prevalent arrangements for wage determination, as well as according to the statistical methods.

TABLE 1

PAY AND PRODUCTIVITY CHANGES IN MANUFACTURING, AND TOTAL UNEMPLOYMENT 1952–65

PERCENTAGE INCREASES OVER TWO PERIODS (ANNUAL AVERAGES)

Country	Conventional Rates (hourly)		Earnings (hourly)		Drift		Output per Manhour in Manufacturing		Unemployment (thousands)	
	1952–58	1958–65	1952–58	1958–65	1952–58	1958–65	1952–58	1958–65	1952–58	1958–65
Austria*	4·0ᵃ	6·4	5·0	8·5	1·0	2·1	4·3	5·6	137	81
Belgium	..	6·0	..	6·6	..	0·6	2·7ᵇ	6·2ᶜ	132	71
Denmark*	2·9	5·2	4·9	8·7	2·0	3·5	2·8	4·6	68	34
Finland*	5·8ᵇ	5·5ᶜ	7·7ᵇ	7·8ᶜ	1·9ᵇ	2·3ᶜ	3·3	4·6	..	37
France ᵈ	..	..	8·6	7·6	..	..	3·9	4·3	134	120
Western Germany	5·7	7·2	6·6	8·9	0·9	1·7	4·7	5·5	985	272
Ireland	3·6	6·1	4·5	6·9	0·9	0·8	2·6	4·5	64	53
Italy	4·1	8·3ᶜ	4·4	9·7ᶜ	0·3	1·4ᶜ	6·3	6·9	1541ᵈ	796
Netherlands*	6·5	5·9	8·1	8·0	1·6	2·0	3·7	6·3	63	43
Norway*	2·4	3·6	5·5	7·0	3·1	3·4	4·0	5·5	15	17
Swedeⁿᵉ*	2·8	3·3	5·8	7·2	3·0	3·9	4·1	5·1	31	26
Switzerland	2·1	4·5ᶜ	3·5	6·1ᶜ	1·4	1·6ᶜ	..	4·0	4	1
United Kingdom	5·5	4·6	6·2	6·3	0·7	1·7	2·5	3·9	366	459
United States	..	..	4·2	3·1	..	..	3·0	3·9	2960	4092

.. = not available or not pertinent. * Countries operating some form of central control.
ᵃ 1953–58. ᵇ 1954–58. ᶜ 1958–64. ᵈ 1955–58 (sample survey). ᵉ Rates and earnings in November 1952–62.
Note. Data on conventional rates and earnings cover all male and female wage-earners (for the Netherlands and Norway — male wage-earners only).

The figures of manufacturing output used to measure productivity are derived from the official indices of industrial production, except for Denmark, France and Norway ; for these three countries, the estimates of total output in manufacturing used for the national accounts are regarded as more reliable.

15

(*c*) The figures relate to manufacturing industry (sometimes to manufacturing, mining and construction); figures for the whole economy would be more relevant but are available in full only for a few countries. It must be remembered that productivity gains are generally less outside manufacturing, while there is not, as a rule, a correspondingly smaller increase in wages. That manufacturing wages rise no faster than manufacturing productivity is no guarantee of an absence of rising unit labour costs in the economy as a whole.

TABLE 2

LABOUR COSTS PER UNIT OF MANUFACTURING OUTPUT
PERCENTAGE INCREASE OVER TWO PERIODS (ANNUAL AVERAGES)

	Unit Labour Costs Based on Conventional Rates		Unit Labour Costs Based on Earnings	
	1952–58	1958–65	1952–58	1958–65
Austria*	−0·3	0·8	0·7	2·7
Belgium	..	−0·2	2·6	0·4
Denmark*	0·1	0·6	2·0	3·9
Finland*	2·4	0·9	4·3	3·1
France	..	..	4·5	3·2
Western Germany	1·0	1·6	1·8	3·2
Ireland	1·0	1·5	1·9	2·3
Italy	−2·1	1·3	−1·8	2·6
Netherlands*	2·7	−0·4	4·2	1·6
Norway*	−1·5	−1·8	1·4	1·4
Sweden*	−1·2	−1·7	1·6	2·0
Switzerland	..	0·6	..	2·4
United Kingdom	2·9	0·7	3·6	2·3
United States	..	..	1·2	−0·8

.. =not available or not pertinent.
* Countries operating some form of central control.

(*d*) Again, because of absence of information, the figures of pay are confined to wages proper, excluding salaries, and this too leads to inconsistency, since the productivity figures generally relate to change in total output divided by changes in total employment of all wage- and salary-earners. Mostly, we find that the proportion of salary-earners has been increasing, so that output per man-hour of wage-earners alone, if figures were available or had a significant meaning, would show larger increases than those in the table.[1]

[1] Also the ouput should be related not only to the number of wage- and salary-earners but to the total number engaged including 'workers on own account'.

(e) Social charges falling on employers are not generally included, and if the relative importance of these charges has changed, the figures in the table do not accurately reflect changes in total labour costs.

If we are prepared to examine the figures in spite of these qualifications, the following broad conclusions seem to emerge.

We may begin with the left-hand part of Table 2 where it is shown how far labour costs per unit of output would have risen, *if the rise in labour costs had been confined to wage increases secured by collective bargaining* (assuming that the indices of conventional rates correctly represent this purely hypothetical situation). The result is quite striking. The countries with the smallest increases or, in some, decreases in unit labour costs in 1958–65 were : five countries with a degree of formal central control (Austria, Denmark, the Netherlands, Norway, Sweden) ; and three countries without formal central control (Belgium, Switzerland, the United Kingdom). Similarly in 1952–58, the countries with the smallest increases were : four countries with central control (Austria,[1] Denmark, Norway, Sweden) ; and two countries without central control (Ireland and Italy). (Figures are not available for Belgium and Switzerland.) The Netherlands is among the countries with the biggest increase (along with, in that period, the United Kingdom).[2] On these comparisons, the performance of central control stands out quite favourably — although less so in the more recent period.

We may, however, turn now to the right-hand part of Table 2, which shows the more realistic comparison of labour costs in terms of *actual earnings*. Here the picture is much more confused. In 1958–65, the countries with the lowest increases in unit labour costs were : three countries with central control (Netherlands, Norway and Sweden) ; four European countries without central control (Belgium, Ireland, Switzerland, the United Kingdom) and also the United States. And the countries with the biggest increase included: three countries with central control (Austria, Denmark, Finland) ; and three countries without central control (France, Italy, Western Germany). In 1952–58 similarly, one cannot say that the countries with central control recorded a better performance, in terms of unit labour costs, than those without it.

---

[1] However, in Austria the present system (the Joint Commission for Prices and Wages) was not in operation in 1952–58.
[2] There are good reasons for regarding the bigger wage increases in the Netherlands in the late 1950s as a 'catching-up' after the remarkable period of restraint in the immediate post-war years.

The conclusion, so far as these admittedly crude statistics go, seems to be that efforts at the centre to achieve control of wage movements through co-ordination and central agreements have not been ineffective *at that level*. Only a relatively small part of wage-cost inflation can be attributed (except in the Netherlands in the earlier period) to bargaining at the centre. But the effects of moderation at the centre were effectively frustrated, though less so in Norway and Sweden than elsewhere, once wage settlement moved away from the centre. This brings us back to what has rightly been set as a major concern of the Symposium — how to make decentralised methods of wage determination less inflation-prone.

A test question might be : to what do you attribute the relatively small increase in unit labour costs in the United States ? Possible explanations are : high unemployment ; prevalence of decentralised trade union bargaining ; difference in 'attitudes' ; other factors.

SHORT-TERM AND LONG-TERM INCOMES POLICIES

Mostly, incomes policies have recently been regarded as a way of resisting inflation. This criterion underlies the use of the statistics just described. From this point of view, an incomes policy is concerned mainly with *aggregate* incomes. Its statistical success is not prejudiced if Peter gets more than the average, so long as Paul gets less. The only problem is the practical one of persuading Paul.

Yet an incomes policy may also be regarded in quite a different way — as a conscious policy for the distribution of income among occupations, among industries, between industry and agriculture, or between the rewards of labour and the rewards of capital. From this point of view, an incomes policy is obviously a long-term proposition, which can only gradually be expected to have an effect on the pattern of the income structure.

Existing incomes policies certainly contain long-term elements. But it is perhaps not unfair to suggest that there has so far been comparatively little explicit thinking about the desirability of any significant change in the pattern of income distribution. There has been some. Thus the Scandinavian countries, and Austria, have long pursued the principle of 'solidarity', in the sense of seeking bigger than average increases for lower-paid occupations and lower-paid industries. The principle is also described as that of 'equal pay for equal work' — meaning that the pay for a given job should not be influenced by the circumstances of the particular employer. It is thus related to the principle of the 'standard wage', a principle which goes far back into the history of trade unionism. A reduction in the sex differential, and parity of income between agricultural and industrial occupations, may be regarded in the same light.

Yet the extent to which the wage structure has been affected in practice by this principle is comparatively small ; [1] this is partly because the amounts allotted by collective agreements for above-average increases have tended to be very small, partly because the application of the principle in collective agreement has been reversed by drift at the enterprise level.

In the Netherlands, a different principle of discrimination was adopted from 1959 — that of discriminating according to relative productivity gains industry by industry. This was not a conspicuous success, partly because of the difficulties of acceptable recording of productivity changes, partly because in some branches there can be little productivity gain to record ; moreover the implied widening of inter-industry differentials was unacceptable. In the Scandinavian countries and the Netherlands, these principles have tended to be modified recently by the acceptance of rather wider inter-industry or inter-firm differences based on market conditions — in essence, the formal recognition of 'drift'.

The British incomes policy (1965 version) also allows for certain 'exceptions' (for low-paid workers, for productivity gains specifically related to increased effort, for removing obvious 'disparities'). But, again, these were intended to provide for a minority of 'hard cases' (although it may appear that the majority considered themselves in this situation).

More important, from a long-term point of view, is the establishment in 1965 of the National Board for Prices and Incomes, whose function it is to report on specific cases of wage or price increases referred to it by the government. The Board has taken a broad view of its duties, putting heavy emphasis on ways of improving the wage structure, the pricing system and the operating methods in the industries referred to it.

On the whole, however, central wage control has tended to operate by almost equal increases for all, through collective bargaining ; and, in general, the course of actual earnings, when examined industry by industry, has demonstrated a remarkable stability in the

[1] Except for the very substantial relative increase in average farm incomes in many countries, for which, however, there are other reasons.

pattern. In effect, therefore, the main principle has been the preservation of the *status quo* ; equal increases for all is the rule most likely to find general acceptance.

To find generally acceptable criteria for a distribution of incomes different from that in force, and to seek to apply them in practice, is not easy. Yet it is strange that so little thought has been given to these more fundamental problems, particularly by the trade unions ; for it is probably only from the trade union movements that a successful initiative can come.

CONCLUSIONS AND QUESTIONS

What lessons can be drawn from the operation, or attempted operation, of incomes policies in Western Europe ? I would suggest the following points — some as tentative conclusions, some as questions — for consideration :

1. I would start with the very obvious and not particularly tentative conclusion, that in the Western type of society an incomes policy, short-term or long-term, has got to depend on voluntary cooperation ; workers' and employers' organisations have got to be convinced (not necessarily all of them, but a sizeable majority) ; and not only the top level people in the organisations but a sizeable majority of the members. That pay rates (like virtue) cannot simply be enforced by statute is a platitude. However, this platitude leads on to some possibly more significant issues.

2. Is there any place, then, for *statutory control* ? Its disadvantages and difficulties are obvious. Its advantage is not that it gives the government the possibility of controlling by law the whole pay structure against the will of a majority of unions and employers ; it certainly has not been used in that way in the Netherlands. The advantage (if we wish to see an effective incomes policy) is the simple one that it gives the government the possibility of enforcing on a minority conformity with the generally agreed 'rules of the game' (a perfectly normal function of the law). From this point of view, the occasional use of statutory powers may be welcomed (perhaps not too openly) by many trade union leaders who recognise the logic of an incomes policy but, for obvious reasons, cannot apply it unless assured that everyone else will do so too. This leads to a question which may be one of strategy and administrative convenience rather than fundamental. Granted the need for statutory control, should it be *com-*

prehensive (as in the Netherlands, where every agreement requires official approval) or *selective* (as in the August 1966 British legislation, which empowers the government to declare specified agreements illegal) ?

3. Does an effective incomes policy require *central negotiation* on Nordic–Dutch lines ? It does require *some* form of control of union policy at the centre — perhaps something on the lines of the Austrian system. The innovation in Britain, by which all pay claims (by affiliated unions) are submitted for examination and comment to the Trade Union Congress before serious negotiations begin, is another alternative — and a very substantial innovation in a country where the central machinery of trade unionism has been relatively weak. This type of procedure, if taken seriously, should compel the trade union centre to establish criteria and priorities. The problems are first to establish the moral authority of the centre on the trade union side, and second to find a way by which the employers' side can be brought into the discussion. These requirements, if accepted, must bring us very near the procedure of a central negotiation.

4. Let us now touch — rather slightly — the central problem of *drift*, that is, of pay arrangements outside the framework of collective bargaining. One problem for trade unionism — if trade unions wish to operate an incomes policy — is that they must, as just suggested, strengthen authority at the centre ; but to make the policy effective, their authority at the enterprise level must also be reinforced — since it is clear that, in conditions of full employment, the intentions of collective bargaining are frustrated by drift. This is a fairly substantial programme! The same problem arises on the management side, for it is unnecessary to say here that drift is a result of competition among employers as much as of pressure by workers.

Of course, there are other ways round this problem ; for example, the emphasis put by the Swedish LO on active labour market policy to promote mobility, and on effective competition which would remove some of the profits out of which drift arises. Or systems of taxation might be evolved under which wage increases in excess of certain amounts would not qualify as costs and would have to be paid out of taxed profits. Price controls are sometimes used in this way, for example in Norway, the Netherlands and France. Are these alternative methods effective, or likely to be effective ? Could they be regarded as substitutes for strengthening the power of unions and employers' associations at the enterprise level ?

The view can also be taken that 'drift' — that is a large measure of enterprise freedom in wage determination — is valuable in itself. The questions, perhaps, are : how large a measure ? And how much do we value a system of collective bargaining which aims — unsuccessfully if drift is extensive — at a rough equality of pay for the same job ? (One is assuming that greater authority by unions or employers' organisations at the plant level would in fact result in more uniformity of pay.)

5. It was suggested earlier that incomes policies have hitherto rested basically on the preservation of existing differentials between occupations and industries and between the rewards of labour and capital. But I also suggested that a *longer-term incomes policy* could be conceived envisaging significant changes in income distribution. Do we regard such long-term changes as desirable ? My own feeling is that purely short-term, or anti-inflationary, incomes policies, conceived in macro-economic terms, have failed in part because they rest on no basic principles of income distribution beyond minor adjustments to the *status quo*.

6. This emphasis on *greater authority*, both at the centre and on lower levels, for trade unions and for employers' organisations, may well arouse misgivings. Its merits and demerits are worth discussing. All I am suggesting is that an incomes policy — short-term or long-term — is not likely to be effective in other circumstances.

There is certainly an analogy here with the problem of effective economic planning in the wider sense, in any Western society. Voluntarily accepted 'rules of the game' are still rules, setting limits on freedom of action. Of course, everyone accepts some rules. But every limitation of choice is in some sense a cost, and it is justified to ask in each case whether the gains balance the costs.

7. Finally, it is perhaps right to raise the following very broad question : if incomes policies, in the sense used here, are ineffective, too difficult to organise, and/or represent an unjustifiable loss of freedom, are there other ways of achieving the same aims (resisting inflation in the short-term context, or improving the distribution of income in the long-term context) ? Various possibilities suggest themselves. It is impossible to do more than record some of them as items for discussion :

(*a*) The obvious alternative, for countering inflation, is *demand policy*, that is fiscal and monetary policies to keep down spending.

(*b*) *Price controls* might be used more extensively — as they are used to a certain extent in France, Netherlands, Norway — to put pressure on enterprises paying wages or earning profit margins in excess of certain specified 'norms'. More generally, it is clear that the spiral of prices and wages is one that can be broken at either point. The effect on prices of a rise in wages is obvious. It is equally clear, from common observation, that price increases set off wage increases : several econometric investigations have shown how wage changes can be associated with previous price changes. Would price control (by persuasion or compulsion) represent an easier, or more effective or more desirable way of resisting inflation than direct pressure on wages ?

(*c*) Methods of '*collective profit-sharing*' by which workers would receive, in addition to wages, some proportion of profits. The kind of schemes now envisaged [1] differ from the long-standing, but never very widespread, systems under which workers share in the profits of the individual firms employing them. The proposal now is that a proportion of total profits in the economy as a whole, or in a particular industry, should be invested in some form of trust (on which trade unions would be represented) for the benefit of all the workers concerned. This proposal is relevant chiefly to the anti-inflationary aspect of incomes policy but could have other implications.

(*d*) *Redistribution* through taxation (long-term aspect). This simply implies letting the distribution of factor incomes take its course, but readjusting the results *ex post* by taxation and the provision of redistribution benefits in cash or kind. This does not, of course, directly touch the *labour costs* of enterprises.

(*e*) A more specific use of taxation has sometimes been proposed. This is that wage 'norms' should be set up with which enterprises' actual wage payments should be compared *ex post* when firms are assessed for tax. Payment in excess of the 'norms' would be heavily taxed. (This is, after all, the basis for certain systems of 'excess profit' taxes.) The tax could fall either on the employer or the worker. To state the proposal in this way reveals at once the alarming implication that some authority should determine everyone's 'correct' wage. A simpler alternative is to apply the system just to *changes* in wage payments. Increases in excess of the 'norm' would be taxed heavily. Administrative difficulties and injustices suggest themselves immediately. Are they worth facing ? Are they more serious than the administrative difficulties and injustices of other policies ?

[1] See Turner and Zoeteweij, *op. cit.*, p. 159.

Chapter 3

THE DEATH OF THE UNITED STATES
GUIDEPOSTS

BY

NAT WEINBERG[1]

THE United States price-wage guideposts are dead. They died because of the manner of their inception, grave defects in the underlying concept and the rigid and inequitable manner in which they were applied. A post-mortem examination may be useful to other countries wrestling with the problem of how, simultaneously, to achieve and maintain full employment, healthy economic growth and price stability.

IMPOSED VERSUS AGREED STANDARDS

The United States guideposts were first presented in the January 1962 Annual Report of the Council of Economic Advisers. Introducing them, the Council said that they were 'intended as a contribution to . . . a discussion' of the basis upon which the public might be able 'to judge whether a particular wage-price decision is in the national interest'. No hint was given that they would also be the basis for vigorous intervention by the government in the field of wage and price decisions. Even more serious, the promised discussion never materialised in any meaningful sense. No real effort was made to stimulate and organise participation in a responsible dialogue among the leaders in labour and industry circles who were later expected to abide voluntarily by guideposts which they had no role in formulating. There is, of course, no way of knowing whether it would have been possible to obtain the assent of both sides to any set of principles aimed at price stability. In 1962, when the guideposts were introduced, the setting probably was not ripe for agreement on

[1] The views expressed in this paper are the writer's and not necessarily those of the UAW.

stabilisation principles since there was no urgent inflationary problem at that time.[1]

Nevertheless, a carefully organised discussion, in which management and union leaders were involved, might have paved the way to agreement on stabilisation policies by 1965 when significant increases in the price level began to move from mere possibility to actuality. By that time, however, the premature attempt to impose the guideposts had seriously damaged the possibility of obtaining agreement on stabilisation principles and policies.

Given the lack of centralisation of authority in both labour and management in the United States, there is a question as to whether substantial compliance would have been obtained even if outstanding leaders on both sides had been able to reach agreement on principles. It seems reasonable, however, to suppose that agreed — as distinguished from imposed — principles would have had great moral force. Both management and unions would have been under pressure not to flout a policy developed and accepted by leading spokesmen for their respective groups. The government would have been in a position to enlist the active assistance of both management and labour formulators of the policy in persuading reluctant members of their respective groups to abide by it. Moreover, a climate of public opinion would have been created which would have inhibited those tempted to flout the policy.

The Council has now belatedly acknowledged in a back-handed way the grievous error it made in trying to impose a policy. In a statement presented to a Congressional committee on 12 September 1966, the chairman of the Council said :

> Acceptance of a wage-price policy is partly a matter of understanding — of the need for that policy, and of its logic and fairness. But it is also a matter of participation. A policy is more likely to be accepted, even if it is not thought to be completely logical or fair, if one (or one's representative) has participated in its formulation and comes to believe that it is the best of the feasible alternatives. His acceptance of something that limits his freedom is advanced if he feels that other participants whose interests are to some extent antithetical to his own have in turn sacrificed some part of what they would have preferred for the sake of an arrangement that all can accept.

[1] It is true there was a deficit in the United States balance of payments ; but the trade balance, with respect to which prices are directly relevant, was very favourable. The payments deficit throughout the 1960s can thus far be accounted for entirely by the export of American capital for investment abroad — a problem that could and should have been dealt with by direct controls.

Thus I am firmly of the belief that the current and future deliberations of the President's Labor-Management Advisory Committee can contribute to the success of a voluntary stabilisation policy because distinguished representatives of labor, management, and the public will have discussed and participated in its formulation and execution.

FORGOTTEN QUALIFICATIONS

On 18 August 1966, the President's Advisory Committee on Labor-Management Policy [1] adopted a statement which, for all practical purposes, signalled the end of the guideposts. The statement can be read, it seems to me, as an expression of the unanimous opinion of the Committee that the guideposts had broken down because they were not applied with the concern for flexibility and equity stressed by the Council when it first presented them.

Under the guideposts, the general guide for wages is that 'the rate of increase in wage rates (including fringe benefits) in each industry be equal to the trend rate of over-all productivity increase'. The general guide for prices is that 'they should fall in an industry whose rate of productivity increase exceeds the over-all rate, rise in the opposite case, and remain stable if the two rates of productivity increase are equal'. The statement of the President's Advisory Committee noted, however, that these 'general guides' were originally hedged about with numerous qualifications and exceptions. The Committee said that, in its judgment, the section of the 1962 Report of the Council relating to the guideposts 'is of particular significance'. It emphasised the following portions of the report :

1. Productivity is a *guide* rather than a *rule* for appraising wage and price behavior for several reasons. First, there are a number of problems involved in measuring productivity changes, and a number of alternative measures are available. Second, there is nothing immutable in fact or in justice about the distribution of the total product between labor and non-labor incomes. Third, the pattern of wages and prices among industries is and should be responsive to forces other than changes in productivity.

2. These are not arbitrary guides. These describe — briefly and no doubt incompletely — how price and wage rates would

[1] The Committee, created by the late President Kennedy, consists of seven executives of large corporations, an equal number of union leaders, plus five individuals appointed to represent the general public.

behave in a smoothly functioning competitive economy operating near full employment. Nor do they constitute a mechanical formula for determining whether a particular price or wage decision is inflationary. They will serve their purposes if they suggest to the interested public a useful way of approaching the appraisal of such a decision.

3. These are advanced as general guideposts. To reconcile them with objectives of equity and efficiency, specific modifications must be made to adapt them to the circumstances of particular industries. If all of these modifications are made, each in the specific circumstances to which it applies, they are consistent with stability of the general price level. Public judgements about the effects on the price level of particular wage or price decisions should take into account the modifications as well as the general guides.

The Committee declared its belief that : '. . . it is impractical if not impossible to translate the goals reflected in the guideposts into formulae for application to every particular price or wage decision'.

The statement concluded by saying : '. . . in a free society any policy to achieve price stability will be acceptable and effective only if it bears equitably on all forms of incomes'. All of the qualifications quoted by the Committee, together with many more, were brushed aside in the application of the guideposts.

Productivity

With respect to productivity, the Council had noted in 1962 that there are problems in measuring it, that a number of alternative measures are available, that there are difficulties in separating the trend from erratic short-term movements, and that the measured trend would be affected by the time period used for calculating it.[1] In the light of these problems, the Council modestly and with scholarly propriety concluded that 'the most that can be done at present is to give some indication of orders of magnitude, and of the range within which most plausible measures are likely to fall'. A table was presented showing 17 widely varying productivity figures.

In its 1963 Report, the Council mentioned no productivity figure in the context of the guideposts. By 1964, however, scholarly caution had been thrown to the winds. The Council decided that the

[1] There is also the question of whether potential productivity is not a better basis than achieved productivity. The United Kingdom appears to have chosen an estimate of potential productivity and some United States economists have urged its use.

productivity trend could be determined by simply averaging the annual percentage increases in one measure of output per man-hour in the private economy for the most recent five years. The average for the five years ending with 1963, which was 3·2 per cent., became the magic touchstone for the evaluation of all wage settlements. If a settlement was larger than 3·2 per cent. it was automatically 'in-flationary', if 3·2 per cent. or less it was 'statesmanlike'. Fortuitously the average for the five years ending with 1964 (based upon prelim-inary figures which were later revised upward) was also 3·2 per cent., which the Council's 1965 Report proclaimed as the wage guidepost for that year.

Credibility Destroyed

The average for the five years ending in 1965 proved to be 3·6 per cent. The Council's 1966 Report, however, resorted to a number of lame excuses for brushing aside that figure and for rationalising the continuance of 3·2 per cent. as the wage guidepost. By thus changing the rules in the middle of the game, the Council destroyed whatever credibility its guidepost might have had within the labour movement.

Bargaining Over Income Shares

Credibility had been damaged previously by the Council's for-getfulness about its own qualifications, and exceptions have seemed to the labour movement to be consistently biased against the worker's interests. If the length of this paper is to be kept within reasonable bounds, only a few examples can be cited.

The guideposts are aimed at achieving price stability. The be-haviour of wages is relevant to that goal only to the extent that wage increases cause price increases that otherwise would not occur, or block price reductions that otherwise would be made. The Council, therefore, was on sound ground when it repeatedly emphasised that bargaining over income shares was consistent with its guideposts. In addition to the indirect reference to such bargaining included in the Advisory Committee's quotations from the Council's 1962 Report, that same Report said:

> The proportions in which labor and non-labor incomes share the product of industry have not been immutable throughout American history, nor can they be expected to stand forever where they are today. It is desirable that labor and management should

bargain explicitly about the distribution of the income of particular firms or industries. It is, however, undesirable that they should bargain implicitly about the general price level.

Finally, it must be reiterated that collective bargaining within an industry over the division of the proceeds between labor and non-labor income is not necessarily disruptive of over-all price stability. The relative shares can change within the bounds of non-inflationary price behavior.

In its 1964 Report the Council emphasised that '. . . it is not the purpose of these advisory policies permanently to freeze the labor and non-labor shares of total industrial income, as would a rigorous, unrelieved application of the general guideposts'. In its 1966 Report, the Council reaffirmed this position.

These verbal disavowals were belied by the Council's actions. The policy followed in practice was 'rigorous, unrelieved application' of the 3·2 per cent. wage guidepost, regardless of the facts of the particular situation.

Disparate Treatment of Wages and Prices

There was no application — rigorous and unrelieved or otherwise — of that part of the price guidepost which called for price reductions. The auto industry provides a striking illustration of the Council's disparate treatment of wages and prices. Union contracts with the auto producers were due to expire in September 1964. Looking towards the negotiation of new contracts, the Council's January 1964 report recalled earlier statements affirming the propriety of bargaining over income shares, and emphasised the duty of industries with above-average productivity gains to reduce prices. It continued :

> Moreover, in industries whose trend of productivity rises faster than the national average, if wages conform more nearly to national than to industry productivity trends (as the guideposts would have them do), failure to follow the general price guide will cause profits to pile up. Such profits become highly visible to the public and constitute a lure for strongly intensified wage demands.
>
> Such circumstances pose a most unattractive dilemma from the viewpoint of the public interest. On the one hand, extra increases in wages or fringe benefits might tend to spread to other industries, creating a general cost-push from the wage side. On the other hand, *there is no justification, on either economic or equity grounds, for distributing above-average gains in productivity exclusively*

through the profits channel. The real way out of this dilemma is for the firms involved to remove its cause by reducing prices.[1]

There is reason to believe that the Council tried to persuade the auto corporations, whose profits were at clearly excessive levels, to reduce prices by at least token amounts for the purpose of creating a climate of public opinion which would make it difficult for the UAW, the union representing the auto workers, to win a settlement in excess of 3·2 per cent. These efforts by the Council were never publicised. Although the avowed purpose of the guideposts was to generate public pressure against those who used their price- and wage-making powers irresponsibly, the fact that auto prices were outrageously in conflict with the guideposts was never brought to public attention by the Council.

While ignoring the Council's private appeal for price reductions, the auto corporations sought to take full advantage of its wage guidepost. The initial offers made to the UAW by each of the three major auto corporations amounted to 3·2 per cent. When the UAW succeeded in obtaining settlements considerably in excess of that percentage, members of the Council, in contrast to their public silence concerning above-guidepost auto price increases expressed displeasure although the settlements obviously had no effect on auto prices. The auto corporations had refused to reduce their prices before the settlement when price reductions might have had some effect on their bargaining position, and they neither increased nor reduced their prices after the settlements. If there is, as the Council had said, 'no justification, on either economic or equity grounds, for distributing above-average gains in productivity exclusively through the profits channel', where was the conflict with the guideposts when the workers succeeded in diverting some of those gains to the wage channel ? What meaning does the Council's position on the legitimacy of bargaining over income shares have if it does not apply to the auto situation ? Can that position have any practical significance at all if wage gains in excess of 3·2 per cent. under such circumstances are to be blocked, if possible, for fear that they 'might tend to spread to other industries, creating a general cost-push from the wage side' ?

The Council's behaviour with respect to auto prices has been in marked contrast to its concern with auto wages. Annual model changes in the United States auto industry, followed by announcements of the prices of the new models, present the Council with a

---

[1] Emphasis not in the original.

uniquely favourable opportunity each year to call public attention to the fact that these prices are clearly in conflict with the guideposts. The Council, however, has studiously avoided public mention of that ocnflict and, at times, has come close to defending the industry's price actions.

Nominal or Real Wages

Uneven treatment of wages and prices had the most serious implications for workers — and ultimately for the guideposts. For the 3·2 per cent. wage guidepost was applied to nominal money wages while the Council was unable to block most price increases and made no serious effort to bring about the price reductions required of some industries in order to ensure that no gap would develop between real and nominal wages.

It is true, of course, that the guideposts are aimed at price stability and that nominal rather than real wages are relevant in computing the costs that — forgetting for the moment excessive profit margins — affect prices. But this truism does not negate the fact that there are two main reasons for combating inflation. One is to protect a nation's economy against balance of payments or other difficulties. The other is to avoid the inequities and hardships that rising prices inflict on some sections of the population to the advantage of others. The second goal must be pursued with no less vigour than the first — for pragmatic as well as moral reasons. For if equity is neglected, anti-inflationary policy in a free society will sooner or later break down.

The Council's reports and statements on the guideposts are replete with references to equity. Indeed, its statements of the premise upon which the guideposts rest take specific note of the essential condition that must be met if equity is to be preserved in the face of the application of a productivity standard to increases in nominal wages. In its 1962 report the Council said, '*if all prices remain stable*, all hourly labor costs may increase as fast as economy-wide productivity without, for that reason alone, changing the relative share of labor and non-labor incomes in total output'; and in its 1964 report, the Council pointed out that 'it is a matter of arithmetic that labor's share in total income will remain unchanged if total hourly labor compensation rises in the same proportion as labor productivity *when prices are constant*'.[1] It follows that labour's share in

---

[1] Emphasis not in the original.

total income will fall if hourly labour compensation rises parallel with productivity while prices increase. If the rise in prices is rapid, real wages could fall despite rising productivity.

In the period 1960–65, output per man-hour in the private economy increased 20·4 per cent. but total real hourly compensation of employees rose less than two-thirds as fast, by 12·8 per cent. The lag of real compensation behind productivity is accounted for almost entirely by price increases since nominal compensation rose 20·2 per cent.

Confronted with these facts, members of the Council and its staff have hitherto relied on two defences. The first is that price indices, by failing to adjust for quality improvements, overstate the extent of price increases.[1] But price deflators are also used when computing productivity. If the price indices should be adjusted downward, the productivity index should be adjusted upward. The gap between the increases in real employee compensation and in productivity would remain. The second defence is that the guideposts are applied to nominal rather than real compensation on the assumption that adherence to the guideposts would mean price stability, in which case labour's share would not suffer. But the assumption has been demonstrated to be without basis in fact. The cause, as is well known to the Council, lies to a major extent in unjustifiable price increases and in the refusal to follow the guidepost advice that prices be reduced in industries with above-average productivity gains. The Council acknowledged in its 1964 report, in an obvious understatement, that 'it is fair to say that large industrial enterprises thus far have not widely heeded this advice'.

Equity would require that, if the government fails to achieve the goal of price stability, it should accept a moral obligation to protect those who would otherwise suffer from its failure. One way to do this would be to give active encouragement to the negotiation of cost-of-living escalator provisions in wage agreements and to provide for similar escalation of statutory transfer payments. The escalators, of course, would remain inoperative if the government were successful in converting price stability from an unreal assumption to a practical fact.

The guideposts do, in fact, provide escalation for industry. According to the Council's 1966 Report, for example, '. . . increases in price above the general guidepost standard may occasionally be

---

[1] Quality adjustments *are* made in the price index and there is reason to believe that at least some of them are excessive. Product changes that are not taken into account could as well reflect deterioration in, as improvements of, quality.

appropriate — to reflect increases in unit material costs, to the extent that such increases are not offset by decreases in other costs and significantly impair gross profit margins . . .'. Certainly, the impairment of workers' living standards or their share in the nation's product is no less serious than the impairment of profit margins.

The Council took note, in its 12 September 1966 statement, of the fact that 'so far this year the annual rate of increase in consumer prices has been 3·6 per cent.'. This means decreases in real compensation, in the face of rising national productivity, for workers whose compensation follows the 3·2 per cent. guideposts. Yet the Council to date has done nothing more about this development than to hint that there might be a 'temporary departure from the pure productivity standard for wage increases'. It seems entirely safe to predict that a 'temporary departure' — and one, according to some indications, that will offer only partial compensation to workers for price increases — will not serve to rehabilitate the guideposts in the eyes of the labour movement.

The 'Low-Wage Exception'

Among the least understandable of the Council's many rigidities with respect to workers' interests is its attitude toward increases in the statutory minimum wage. The Council had played a major role in launching the so-called 'war against poverty' and its members are known to be wholeheartedly in support of full equality for Negroes, whose present inequality is in substantial part a result of low incomes. There are two million families (disproportionately Negro) who remain in poverty even though the family head works full time; a half-million single individuals suffer the same plight. An adequate minimum wage is an obvious answer to their problem, since nearly four-fifths of them are employees.

From the beginning, the guideposts have provided a 'low-wage exception'. The Council's 1966 Report, for example, said that 'wage increases above the general guideposts may be desirable . . . where wages are particularly low, that is, near the bottom of the economy's wage scales'. Nevertheless the Council sought to limit proposed increases in the statutory minimum wage to amounts that could be rationalised on the basis of the 3·2 per cent. wage guidepost. In addition, while the legislation was under consideration by Congress, the Council reportedly sought to postpone the effective date of the second step in a two-stage increase in the minimum wage.

INCOMES POLICY VERSUS GUIDEPOSTS

Aside from mistakes made in introducing them and the one-sided rigidities and inequities in their application, the guideposts suffer from a fatal defect in concept. Knowledgeable Americans are under no illusions regarding the equity and effectiveness of European 'incomes policies' as opposed to the United States guideposts. Nevertheless, there is a fundamental difference which becomes clearly apparent when the guideposts are contrasted, for example, with the British 'Joint Statement of Intent'.

The relationship central to the guideposts is that between increases in wage rates and in productivity. In contrast, the corresponding relationship in the 'Joint Statement' is that between changes in 'total money incomes' and in 'real national output'. Although the end result sought in both cases is the same, the difference is by no means purely semantic. There are practical consequences which are reflected under the guidepost approach in the divergent treatment of incomes arising from different sources — mainly, although not entirely, as between income from work and income from property. An incomes policy, at the very least, involves a moral commitment to deal even-handedly with all forms of income. It is also relevant that the Joint Statement is based, in part, on the United Kingdom Government's pledge that its '. . . social objective is to ensure that the benefits of faster growth are distributed in a way that satisfies the claims of social need and justice'.

Property Income versus Employment Income

No labour movement in any country can acquiesce for very long to a policy which applies as disparately to different forms of income as do the guideposts. Only one form of income — wages — is affected directly, and then only when determined through collective bargaining. Wage and salary increases put into effect unilaterally by non-union employers are not covered. Certain other forms of income — for example interest, professional income, executives' salaries and bonuses and capital gains — are completely untouched. The attempt to restrain still others — profits and dividends — is indirect, based on vague productivity criteria concerning prices.

But, in contrast to the widely publicised 3·2 per cent. wage guidepost, the individual industry productivity figures that are supposed

34

to guide price decisions are non-existent for many important industries and are known only to the experts where they do exist. Thus the public, which is supposed 'to judge whether a particular wage-price decision is in the national interest', has been told all too explicitly — and in grossly over-simplified terms — when it should frown upon a wage settlement, but is left almost completely at sea with respect to the posture it is expected to assume concerning specific price increases or failures to reduce excessive prices. The Council has not attempted to right this imbalance.

In concept and application alike the guidepost approach is in direct conflict with what seems to me the central thesis contained in a report of the OECD Working Party on Costs of Production and Prices.[1] As that report states, 'experience shows that whatever may be the mechanism of cost inflation, wage-earners will ask for some *quid pro quo* in return for any agreement to accept a more moderate increase in wages. As the Trade Union Advisory Committee has put it :

> An argument can be made out for planning or guiding incomes : an argument can also be made out for leaving them unplanned and unguided : but there is nothing at all to be said for planning or guiding half the incomes and leaving the other half unguided and unplanned and subject to market forces or varying degrees of monopoly control.

The existence of a policy for wages clearly gives this argument considerable weight. Those whose incomes are subject to restraint will naturally demand the establishment of criteria by which the inflationary or non-inflationary behaviour of other incomes can be clearly established, and the assurance that action will be taken if the assumption that — discounting short period fluctuations — other incomes will follow the development of wages, turns out to be wrong. In other words, it is not enough for justice to be done — it must be seen to be done ; and it must be seen that the government has the ability to intervene effectively in cases where intervention would be justified.

The Source of Inflation

Paradoxically, the main cause of recent price increases in the United States has turned out to be not undue increases in wages — the only form of income with which the guideposts are directly concerned — but successful efforts to enlarge other forms of income to

[1] OECD, *Policies for Prices, Profits and Other Non-Wage Incomes.*

which the guideposts apply, if at all, only indirectly.[1] There is an abundance of statistical evidence available to document this point, some of which is presented in the accompanying table.

Since concern about the balance of payments was probably the main motivation for the promulgation of the guideposts, and since the trade component of the payments balance is heavily affected by prices of manufactured goods,[2] it seems appropriate to focus first on manufacturing industry. In this context the table is very revealing.

The table shows that unit labour costs have remained remarkably stable. In fact, they decreased significantly from 1960 to late 1965 and, although they have since risen, they are still below the 1960 level. Wholesale prices, however, did not reflect the decrease in labour costs between 1960 and 1965; prices began to rise in the third quarter of 1964 and the rate of increase has tended to accelerate. Clearly, the increase in prices was without justification in terms of changes in labour costs. Changes in the profit to sales ratios [3] show that the price rise also was not based upon increases in non-labour costs. Even though profits were not unduly low at the beginning of the period — the figure for the second quarter of 1960 is included in the table because that was the peak quarter of the last business cycle prior to the 1960–61 recession — the rate of profits on sales was 18 per cent. higher in the second quarter of 1966 than in the second quarter of 1960; the rate of profit on net worth increased by 36·0 per cent.

Moreover, except in a few industries, primarily those making capital equipment, there was no excessive pressure of demand upon capacity. The over-all rate of utilisation of manufacturing capacity, including the capital goods industries, was 90 per cent. in December 1965 (the latest available data) compared with an optimum rate reported by the manufacturing corporations of 93 per cent. Only one conclusion is possible. Prices were not raised because of any necessity to do so, they were raised to increase profits.

The index of the ratio of prices to unit labour costs in manufacturing industry rose to 106·9 in July 1966 — higher than at any time since the 1950–51 speculative boom set off by the outbreak of the Korean War. The annual rate of profits on net worth of manu-

---

[1] Another factor in recent months has been a shortage of some agricultural products.

[2] The guideposts, of course, do not apply to prices of agricultural products.

[3] These figures would show an even greater increase if their comparability had not been affected by changes in rules governing depreciation charges. Note that the ratios are not seasonally adjusted.

UNIT LABOUR COSTS, PRICES AND PROFITS IN UNITED STATES
MANUFACTURING INDUSTRIES 1960–66

	Index of Unit Labour Costs* 1957/59 = 100	Index of Wholesale Prices, Manufactured Goods† 1957/59 = 100	Changes in the Ratio of Wholesale Prices to Unit Labour Costs* 1957/59 = 100	Profits Before Taxes‡ As a Per-centage of Sales	Profits Before Taxes‡ As a Per-centage of Net Worth
Annual					
Averages					
1960	100·7	101·1	100·4	8·0	16·7
1961	100·4	100·7	100·3	7·7	15·9
1962	100·4	100·8	100·4	8·2	17·6
1963	99·7	100·6	100·9	8·5	18·4
1964	99·6	101·1	101·5	8·9	19·8
1965	98·8	102·8	104·0	9·4	21·9
Quarterly					
Data					
1960—II	101·2	101·1	99·9	8·4	18·0
1964—I	99·4	101·1	101·6	8·6	18·5
II	99·5	100·8	101·5	9·5	21·4
III	99·8	101·1	101·2	8·7	19·0
IV	99·5	101·4	101·7	8·8	20·2
1965—I	98·8	101·8	102·9	9·3	20·8
II	99·2	102·5	103·4	9·9	23·4
III	98·8	103·2	104·3	9·1	20·6
IV	98·3	103·7	105·4	9·5	22·9
1966—I	98·7	104·8	106·1	9·5	22·2
II	99·5	105·4	106·1	9·9	24·5
Percentage					
Change					
1960—II to					
1966—II	− 1·7 %	+ 4·3 %	+ 6·2 %		

* U.S. Commerce Department 'Business Cycle Developments'.
† U.S. Bureau of Labor Statistics.
‡ U.S. Federal Trade Commission and Securities and Exchange Commission; not adjusted for seasonal variations.

facturing corporations in the second quarter of 1966 was 24·5 per cent. before taxes and 14·7 per cent. after taxes — higher, respectively, than at any time since 1955 and 1950, both years of extraordinarily high profits.

The ratio of profits to net worth, that is income per unit of capital, may be appropriately compared with employee compensation per man-hour, income per unit of labour. Taking both on a before-tax basis, the profit ratio in manufacturing increased at an annual rate of 8 per cent.[1] between 1960 and 1965 while hourly employee compensation in manufacturing increased at an annual rate of 3·6 per cent.[2]

The 3·6 per cent. annual rate of increase in hourly compensation of employees refers to compensation measured in nominal terms. It was less than the increase in productivity in the total private economy during the same period, which averaged 3·8 per cent. ; it fell even further short of the rate of productivity increase in manufacturing, 4·2 per cent. Thus, under the guideposts, manufacturing prices should have been cut rather than increased. Living costs were rising throughout this period with the result that real hourly compensation of manufacturing employees rose at an annual rate of only 2·3 per cent., about three-fifths as fast as productivity in the total private economy and little more than half as fast as productivity in manufacturing.

Despite these facts, the Council found it possible, in its statement of 12 September 1966, to say : 'the import of all this [3] for the strongly organised workers in manufacturing is clear : *if workers in manufacturing attempt to catch up with the past rise in consumer prices in order to achieve real wage gains equal to the trend in over-all productivity, a sharp rise in manufacturing prices can be avoided only by an appreciable squeeze of manufacturing profits, especially now that the cushion of extra productivity gains can no longer be assumed.'* [4]

This raises three questions : does the Council accept the industri-

---

[1] On economic grounds it is questionable, however, whether there should have been any increase at all in rates of profit — as distinguished from aggregate profits which, of course, will tend to grow as the amount of capital in use increases.

[2] This comparison is on an annual basis because reliable quarterly data on hourly employee compensation are not available.

[3] By implication, the Council's statement made it appear that the real income position of manufacturing workers had been undermined primarily as the result of gains by farmers, by low-wage workers in the service industries, and the exercise of 'market power' by the building trade unions. Despite the evidence to the contrary, the impression was created that manufacturing corporations' price increases and refusals to reduce excessive prices played a relatively minor role.

[4] Emphasis in the original.

alists' one-way ratchet view of profits — that no matter how excessive they are, any reduction is a 'profit squeeze'; with investment in new, and often revolutionary, equipment running at such extraordinarily high levels that the Administration, with the support of the Council, has proposed legislation designed to reduce it, is it reasonable to assume that productivity gains will diminish; and what price equity as between workers and corporations? The excessive profits which must not be 'squeezed' clearly reflect gains obtained by violating the guideposts. Those gains were at the expense of the workers (among others) in terms of their real wage position. Why should those victimised by violation of the guideposts not attempt to recover what has been improperly taken from them?

Suppose, however, that the Council were to recognise that an inequity had developed and that workers were entitled to gain wage increases to offset the increase in living costs that occurred between the second quarters of 1960 and 1966. How badly would profits have been 'squeezed' in the extremely unlikely event that all manufacturing workers had been able to obtain increases of that magnitude? The increase in living costs during the period was 9·4 per cent. Compensation of employees in the second quarter of 1966, at an annual rate, was $143 billion. Thus, an adjustment for increased living costs would have cost $13·4 billion. Manufacturing profits before taxes in that same quarter were $14,014 million, equal to an annual rate of $56·1 billion. The assumed cost-of-living wage increase would have reduced such before tax profits to $42·7 billion. Based upon the 40·2 per cent. effective tax rate implicit in the FTC–SEC data, profits after taxes would have been $25·5 billion, 56·4 per cent. higher than in the second quarter of 1960. Profits of that amount would have represented a rate of return on net worth (as of the beginning of 1966) of 11·7 per cent. compared with the actual rate of 10·2 per cent. in the second quarter of 1960.

These figures, it must be emphasised, assume that *all* wage and salary workers would have been able to obtain increases in pay and fringe benefits sufficient to compensate them in full for the rise in consumer prices subsequent to the second quarter of 1960 and that such increases would have been in addition to the increases actually gained. Even on that assumption, which is far outside the realm of probability, profits would have been substantially higher than in the peak quarter of the last business cycle. As a practical matter, the assumed change in the Council's policy would inevitably have had far less effect on profits than the figures suggest. Non-union manufacturing workers would not get such wage increases except in cases where the employers, possibly under labour market pressure, chose to grant them. A very large proportion of union members would not be able to obtain such wage increases immediately because their contracts are not open for negotiations. Other unions would not be strong enough to negotiate the full amount required — or in some cases any amount — to compensate for the cost of living increase. (Many unions have been compelled to accept settlements below the 3·2 per cent. wage guidepost.)

Thus, even if the Council were to give the green light to wage settlements providing full catch-up for all cost of living increases since 1960, the increases would be put into effect only gradually and partially, and profits would remain high even if prices were not increased. That the corporations would try to increase their prices under such circumstances is no reason for depriving workers of their real wage share of productivity gains. It is rather a reason why the government should find a more effective way to prevent unjustifiable price increases. If it be said that some firms would have no choice but to raise prices if they paid the wage increases assumed above, it can also be argued that the profits of other firms would still be excessive after payment of such wage increases, enabling them to make offsetting price reductions.

The Distortion of Income Distribution

Inevitably, as the following figures show, the lag of real employee compensation behind productivity distorted the distribution of income to the disadvantage of wage- and salary-earners and in favour of property holders.[1]

	Per cent. Increases, Second Quarter 1960 to Second Quarter 1966
Employee compensation	45·0
Profits before taxes	60·0
Profits after taxes	75·2
Dividends	56·6
Personal interest income	81·5

[1] These figures take no account of capital gains (except, indirectly, retained profits which represent capital gains for stockholders) which, of course, went disproportionately to those individuals who benefited from the great increases in profits and interest.

The rise in interest income is attributable in major part to increases in interest rates. Higher carrying charges added to costs of production and to mortgage payments which are reflected in the Consumer Price Index. Thus, increased interest rates, inappropriately chosen as a weapon to combat what is largely an administered price inflation, have instead given another twist to the inflationary spiral and aggravated the distortions of the income distribution that stabilisation policies should seek to avoid. The guideposts, as noted, ignore interest income.

The facts and figures cited tell an ironic tale. Wages, the only form of income which the guideposts take directly into account as a potential source of inflation, have presented no problem. Even in nominal terms they increased less than productivity, and they would have increased even more slowly but for the pressures generated by rising prices and profits.[1] The real source of such inflation as has occurred is to be found in those forms of income with which the guideposts are concerned only indirectly or not at all.

It is reasonable to ask whether the distortion of the income distribution is a result of the guideposts — which is another way of asking whether the guideposts have been effective with respect to wages. It is impossible to measure exactly how effective they have been ; but beyond question they were, until recently, a major restraining influence on the size of many wage settlements. A wage guidepost is much more effective than a price guidepost for the simple reason that wage-setting through collective bargaining is a bilateral process while price-setting is unilateral. The 3·2 per cent. wage guidepost was a useful bargaining weapon for every employer facing a strong union and inevitably influenced arbitrators. It would be difficult to explain on grounds other than the effectiveness of the guideposts the sizable lag of real wages behind productivity in a period when unemployment was declining.

However, the situation has changed drastically in recent months. As the rise in consumer prices accelerated, the wage guidepost inevitably lost its effectiveness. It is significant that an agreement negotiated in the White House to settle the airlines strike, with the prestige of the President behind it, was rejected by the workers because it did not include a cost-of-living escalator provision. When the government is unable to prove to workers that it can restrain

---

[1] Some workers, including the great majority of UAW members, have their wages adjusted automatically to price changes under cost-of-living escalator changes. The wage increases obtained under such clauses obviously would not have been paid if there had been no increases in prices.

increases in prices, the workers see no reason to exercise restraint in their wage demands. In fact, they feel compelled to enlarge their demands to protect their families' living standards. Published reports of profits rising to ever-higher levels also contribute, of course, to insistence by workers on substantial fringe benefit gains.

WHERE DO WE GO FROM HERE?

As this is written, there is utter confusion in high government circles regarding the status of the guideposts. On 12 September the Council would go no further than to suggest the possibility of a 'temporary departure' from its 3·2 per cent. wage guide to take account of increases in living costs. On that same day, in the same hearing, the Secretary of Labor said :

> If the wage-price guideposts are to be more than statements of an ideal — and therefore unreal — set of facts, they have to include provisions for adjustment when the facts get out of kilter.
> There is the problem right now of what to do when prices for food and services (and for goods in general) go up by more than the over-all increase in productivity. For the guideposts assume that *real* wages will increase as productivity does — and this would require significantly more than 3·2 per cent. wage increases today.
> What account is to be taken of the fact that wages have been traditionally — but irrationally — lower in agriculture and food processing and in a good many service trades than in most durable manufacturing industries ? If these wages are to go up, by more than the productivity 'par' for the economy as a whole, is this to mean lower increases for manufacturing workers — whose cost of living increases as a result of higher prices for food and services ?

On 25 September the Chairman of the Council, appearing on television, was asked, 'how long can you follow a guidepost policy where the cost of living exceeds the recommended increase in wages ?' He replied that 'the guidepost arithmetic doesn't change simply because prices have been going up'. When questioned further, however, he refused to say whether the Council would 'stick with' its 3·2 per cent. figure. On another broadcast the same day, the Secretary of Commerce, while stating that he thought the guideposts concept 'is still an important concept', continued, 'I think it is questionable that we will have specific figures that become a sort of symbol of everything that happens in the economy'. Asked whether he 'would do away with the 3·2 per cent. figure and have no figure at all', he replied, 'I would, personally, yes, because I think that the use of a specific figure like this tends to mislead rather than guide'. Regarding the cost of living and the guideposts he recognised that '. . . it is important for unions in specific situations to talk about [cost of living increases] and to make them a part of the whole consideration before a wage settlement is reached' ; but he 'strongly opposed' attaching a cost-of-living escalator to the wage guidepost.

Such discordance among the heads of the government agencies most intimately concerned with the guideposts clearly points to the need for a new stabilisation policy. Despite gestures in the direction of permitting the President's Advisory Committee to participate in formulating a new policy, the indications are that the Council will try to resuscitate its guideposts. In my opinion, they are too battered and discredited for that effort to succeed. The only sensible choice, it seems to me, is to provide for the genuine participation of labour and industry in the formulation of a new policy.

It will not be easy to win agreement on a new policy. The difficulties are compounded by the inequities that have developed under the guideposts. Very likely, labour spokesmen insist that these be taken into account in order to arrive at an equitable starting point for the application of a new stabilisation policy, and such a demand would be certain to meet with strong resistance from the industry side. The danger that both sides may be faced with controls if they are unable to develop alternatives might be conducive to agreement. But controls, in my judgment, are not imminent. As a result, it may be some time before the opposing sides feel under pressure to move towards agreement, and the effort may be suspended if the occurrence of a recession relieves inflationary pressures. Sooner or later, however, the United States, like other industrialised countries, will have to find an answer.

Ultimately, that answer must be some form of broad incomes policy founded on the premise that equity and social justice cannot be subordinated to the goal of price stability but, rather, are essential to its achievement. It therefore seems to me that the next moves in the United States will have to be in the direction of an incomes policy. There are useful and intriguing suggestions for implementing an incomes policy in several recent OECD and ILO publications, but the determination of which of these, or of others still to be proposed, are suitable for application in the United States will require intensive study and discussion. In all probability, we are faced with a long evolutionary process from which a rounded stabilisation policy will emerge only gradually.

Immediately, however, the search in the United States, as it is already in a number of other countries, will have to be directed toward more effective means to deal with prices and non-wage incomes. Since price stability is the goal, it seems inevitable that attention will be focused sharply on mechanisms to assure a greater degree of responsibility in price decisions. For nearly ten years, the UAW has been urging the adoption in the United States of a notification-and-hearing procedure much like that in the prices and incomes legislation recently enacted in the United Kingdom. The UAW proposal, however, would rely entirely on informed public opinion, educated through public hearings, as the restraining influence on price abuses rather than on direct government control over price and wage increases. The proposal envisages a Review Board for conducting the necessary hearings and a Consumer Counsel representing the public interest. Advance notice would have to be given of any price increase proposed by the corporation that functions as the 'price leader' in any major industry ; [1] probably not more than a hundred corporations would need to be covered by the procedure. However, it would seem advisable to empower the President to extend the application of the procedure to other companies on a case-by-case basis, when he believes that a serious threat to price stability is involved.

The Consumer Counsel would be able to initiate hearings in cases where he believed prices should be reduced. Subpoena power would be available to ensure the attendance of necessary witnesses and production of all pertinent data. Unions would be required to participate in the hearings and to justify their demands in cases where the corporation involved claimed that granting those demands would necessitate the proposed price increase or would prevent a decrease. While all American unions do not subscribe to the UAW proposal, it seems evident that no new stabilisation policy will be acceptable to the labour movement unless it provides more effective means than the guideposts for dealing with prices.

The need to place much more emphasis than hitherto on prices and profits is receiving increasingly widespread recognition. The

[1] The recent partial 'roll-back' of price increases by Ford and Chrysler, to bring their prices nearer to those later announced by General Motors, is evidence that subjecting only the price leader in an oligopolistic industry to the procedure would be sufficient to influence the entire industry.

Chairman of the OECD Working Party on Costs of Production and Prices recently wrote :

> During the preparation of its second report, the Working Party had several discussions on the role of profits in the process of cost inflation. It concluded that 'While it is difficult to disentangle the role of different elements in total costs, it seems probable that the failure of cost reductions to be reflected fully or immediately in prices is an important feature of the process by which costs and prices are levered up under conditions of cost inflation.' *As a result of the work of the Experts, the Working Party feels that it should have been rather more positive about the role of profits.* In this connection, the evidence presented in Chapter VI of the Report suggesting a quite strong relationship between profits and changes in profits, and wage movements, is both interesting and significant. While this evidence is open to alternative interpretations, it seems to provide further support for the view that a successful incomes policy must cover prices, profits and other non-wage incomes as well as income from employment.[1]

The profits problem presents at least the same urgency in the United States.

Prices and profits, of course, have an important bearing on dividend income. But the evolution of stabilisation policy cannot stop there. Means will have to be found to ensure a degree of stabilisation in other non-wage incomes at least reasonably comparable to that in employment income. Capital gains, for example, although difficult to deal with, can certainly not be ignored.

In so far as implementation of any new United States policy is concerned, it would appear advisable to remove the Council from the picture and, in so far as possible, the White House as well. The manner in which the Council has applied the guideposts has eroded labour's confidence in its impartiality. The President should be kept as remote as possible from the stabilisation process in order to prevent his prestige from being dissipated by too frequent involvement and to conserve his effectiveness for the most important situations.

Whatever the details of the policies and the method of their implementation, they will have to be inspired by two principles already noted. Firstly '. . . in a free society any policy to achieve price

---

[1] OECD, *Wages and Labour Mobility*, Paris, 1965, Foreword by P. de Wolff, pp. 13 and 14, emphasis added.

stability will be acceptable and effective only if it bears equitably on all forms of incomes'. Secondly '. . . it is not enough for justice to be done — it must be seen to be done ; and it must be seen that the Government has the ability to intervene effectively in cases where intervention would be justified'.

Chapter 4

BUYING OFF WAGE INFLATION

BY

J. PEN

I. THE PROBLEM

THIS paper is concerned with the question of what benefits might be offered to wage-earners in exchange for a moderation of inflationary wage demands. We start, therefore, from the assumption that such an exchange is not only desirable but possible. This, in fact, is not obviously the case. For if wage rates and wage increases are completely determined by purely 'economic' factors, there can be no such exchange. For this reason, we set out, in Section II, the assumptions concerning the factors that determine wage increases.

Depending on the objectives of wage policy, even the desirability of the suggested exchange might be questioned. This paper is mainly concerned with one objective, the avoidance of wage inflation, which means limiting wage increases to the rate of increase of the productivity of labour.[1] However, it is difficult, if not impossible, to attain this objective, especially when prices are rising. Therefore the policy objective may have to be modified according to circumstances, and a measure of wage inflation may sometimes be acceptable or even desirable. This question is discussed in Section III.

We are not concerned in this paper with the role of demand factors in the inflationary process. While the moderation of wage increases may make an important contribution towards limiting inflation by retarding the rise in total expenditure, our attention is focused on cost inflation, so that it is assumed that inflation attributable to excess demand is handled with other instruments — fiscal policies, for example. Therefore, such devices as the 'investment wages', currently being recommended in Germany and Holland,

---

[1] In the terminology employed in this paper every increase in wage earnings in excess of improvements in labour productivity — that is, every increase in unit labour costs — is defined as wage inflation, no matter whether it is caused by cost push or demand pull, by the union or by competitive bidding for scarce labour resources.

47

prove not to be very helpful for solving the problem examined in this paper because they may limit consumption but do not reduce increases in wage costs ; we return to this question in Section VI.

The arrangements we propose to discuss are long-term wage contracts, profit-sharing, investment wages and capital sharing. However, since none of these have yet been applied on any scale it is as yet impossible to make a final appraisal of their effects. Furthermore, our views are determined in part by our socio-economic *Weltanschauung*, which is examined in the next two sections. Briefly, I believe that inflation is partly caused by social tensions, and that a satisfactory rate of economic growth can be made compatible with full employment and the absence of substantial price increases only when more harmonious social patterns are established. In my view, it is of little use to remedy wage inflation in the short term while tolerating the long-term causes of conflict and tension. This is why a wage policy should be part and parcel of an incomes policy and, more generally, be accompanied by the pursuit of a more harmonious social atmosphere. Only in this context do anti-inflationary policies have a promising future — though this opinion may not be shared by all.

II. ELEMENTS OF WAGE INCREASES

The present discussion is meaningless to those who believe in economic determinism as expressed, for instance, in the theory of the Phillips curve : a unique relationship between the unemployment percentage and the rate of increase in the wage level. Certainly the level of unemployment influences the rate of wage increase, but the author believes that wage determination also depends, in part, on voluntary factors. The following paragraphs identify the factors bearing on the wage-determination process, which need to be taken into account when evaluating the merits of long-term contracts, profit-sharing schemes, etc.

The trade union movement is concerned about labour's share of the national income, which is determined by the ratio between the real wage rate and labour productivity. In order to keep this share constant, the percentage increases in the wage level must equal the sum of the percentage increase in labour productivity and the rise in the price level.

In fact, trade unions may seek an increase in labour's share. This is made possible because the elasticity of substitution between labour and capital is less than unity, so that upward pressure on money wages (as well as increases in the amount of capital per worker) will raise labour's share.   The force of this additional pressure for wage increases depends, *inter alia*, on the unemployment percentage (the Phillips curve relationship) and on a complex of other factors that may be collectively described as 'tensions'.   These tensions include socio-psychological reactions to various social conflicts, frustrations, fears and anxieties.   It is useful to view these conflicts as broadly as possible ; none should be excluded on the ground that its relationship to wage questions is too remote.   For instance, workers may feel frustrated by the existing income distribution and social stratification, in which case an appeal for moderation in wage demands will have little chance of success.   Circumstances at the place of work may incorporate elements which stimulate inflationary behaviour and conspicuous consumption by the well-to-do can have the same effect. These cases are obvious.   But it is also possible that price fixing in the pharmaceutical industry, or the workers' political judgment of the tax system, may have similar impacts.   Especially important is the way in which the government treats non-wage incomes.   When a government tries to moderate wage increases but leaves profits, land prices and other incomes undisturbed, the importance of 'tension' from this source will probably increase.[1]

Apart from the various factors that determine the contract wage, wage drift also influences the level of actual earnings.   We can summarise these relationships in the following formula :

$$w = h + p - \phi(U) + c + d$$

where w represents wage increases, h the rise in labour productivity, p price increases, U unemployment, c wage increases due to tensions and d wage drift.

It is neither possible nor desirable for w to be smaller than h ; this is the very minimum.[2]   The rise in price, p, must be kept as small as possible by means of both an incomes policy and the avoidance of excess demand.   The function ϕ is influenced by the degree of labour mobility, which can be raised by an active manpower

---

[1] For an elaboration of the proposition that all social conflicts and all elements of social harmony should be regarded as an interdependent system, see the author's *Harmony and Conflict in Modern Society*, McGraw-Hill Publishing Company, Maidenhead and New York, 1966.

[2] At least, if p is smaller than h.   If prices increase more than labour productivity, the political *minimum minimoram* for w is p.

policy. An optimal value exists for U (though opinions differ as to whether it should be, say, 2 per cent. or 4 per cent.) and this can be attained by Keynesian policies affecting aggregate expenditure, changes in government expenditure and taxation being the principal instruments. However, this paper is not concerned with these matters, nor with the wage drift d. The central theme of this paper is the reduction of factor c.

III. GOALS

In the present context, the strictest policy objective is $w = h$, which yields a constant wage cost per unit of product and no wage inflation. This rule is simple and has the practical advantage that, with a certain degree of optimism, the long-term value of h can be estimated for most European countries at about 4 per cent. (More precise calculations might put it at 3·8 per cent., but such refinements cannot be reflected in the actual process of wage determination.) However, this limitation of wage increases is acceptable to the trade unions only if $p = O$; this is a minimum condition. But contrary to the widespread belief among the employers, $w = h$ by no means guarantees that $p = O$; to suggest that it does blames all price increases on wages. Conditions for $p = O$ include : constant import prices, profit margins, interest rates, rents of dwellings and land — and, sometimes, a constant capital-output ratio.

An incomes policy can try to control profit margins and rents. The results of such a policy are uncertain, but it will certainly be impossible to attain its objectives when w substantially and continually exceeds h. Unfortunately incomes policies have not been extended to the interest rate, a limitation that has recently created difficulties in some countries. At the same time w cannot be limited to h when prices rise. In other words, the wage-price spiral cannot be controlled by attempts to control only wages.

Yet a wage policy based on $w = h + p$ would be a step forward. This seems to be a reasonable objective since it assures that the share of labour is maintained — the least which the unions would accept. But in a number of countries in recent years the effect of $\phi(U) + c$ has been substantial. Price increases have been of the order of 2 per cent. or 3 per cent., so that if $w = h + p$, w amounts to, say, 6 per cent. or 7 per cent. In a number of countries (Austria, Denmark, Western Germany, Italy, the Netherlands), and especially during the last seven years, wage earnings per hour have increased more than this. This excess of w over $h + p$ provokes a desire for unemployment in some circles. Opinions differ about the optimal value of U. Some economists consider that a level of unemployment below 3 per cent. is the source of much modern evil, and there is no doubt that over-full employment is a headache for many employers. I should like to draw attention, however, to the strong stimulating effect which low levels of unemployment have on investment in labour-saving machinery and to the possibility that this may be favourable to growth. We might try to combine the advantages of over-employment and capital intensification with some limitation of c. That is the problem discussed in this paper.

It must be acknowledged that a wage policy based on $w = h + p$, implying a constant wage share, is unacceptable to some trade unions which seek an increase in labour's share of the national income. Therefore, a bargain might be struck which, in return for their acceptance of a constant wages share, would offer the trade unions certain benefits including progressive government policies with respect to employment, social security, minimum wages, the fiscal system and, especially (to ensure equal opportunities for all), education. The employers, for their part, should provide every incentive that does not imply higher costs or smaller profits. These would be the essential features of the bargain.

Insistence on the adoption of a constant wages share as the objective of wage policy neither rests on metaphysical considerations nor on some image of the just society. To my mind, it merely affords a means of helping to control wage inflation. If this principle were completely abandoned, a government trying to shape an incomes policy would be entirely at sea. But it should be realised that this target is a conservative one, since it freezes a relationship inherited from the past. In exceptional situations, for example when extensive minimum wage legislation is introduced, deviations from $h + p$ might be acceptable, but these deviations should be explicitly recognised. The norm itself might also be abandoned in times of prolonged deflation, but that is not the situation we have in mind at this Symposium.

Some economists object on quite different grounds to a policy that aims at a constant share of wages. They observe that the share going to wages is subject to laws of its own. In most countries the share has risen considerably over the long-term and, in some countries, even in the short-term (in the Netherlands it was 55 per cent.

in 1955 and 68 per cent. in 1965, an increase of almost one-quarter during a decade). This is not the place for a discussion of the theory of the share of wages. However, I do not believe that it is determined entirely by factors other than wage policy. The view that the share is fixed by the elasticity of a production function of the Cobb-Douglas type is belied by the fact that the elasticity of substitution between labour and capital is smaller than unity. Furthermore, neo-classical reasoning cannot account for profits — an important weakness in a theory of distribution ! According to another, non-classical theory (Kaldor's), the distribution of income is independent of the wage level, being determined by the proportions saved out of wage and non-wage incomes ; curiously, this theory assumes that the average propensity to save is fixed — which makes nonsense of it. In my opinion, any theory of the share of labour should include the wage level as an explanatory variable. The gradual or abrupt rise in the wages share that has occurred in various countries cannot be properly understood unless the sharp increases in money wages are taken into account. Of course, wage increases have not been the only explanation ; other causes include increases in the capital-labour ratio and shifts in the production function.

As has been said, certain modifications might be made to a wage policy based on the principle of $w = h + p$ though it is not necessary to examine them in detail here. There has been much discussion of the international harmonisation of economic and social standards and it has been argued that countries with relatively low levels of money wages should adjust them to the international level (whatever that may mean). In Holland this has been used as an excuse for a wage inflation that could not be controlled ; in France the harmonisation issue has been raised by people whose real aim was to lessen foreign competition in French markets.

A more attractive way of qualifying the basic principle might be to raise wages in sectors like agriculture where they have seriously lagged behind general wage movements. It may be thought that the burden of such adjustments should not be borne entirely by other workers, though it should not be forgotten that these lags occur because other wages rise too quickly. I believe it is desirable to avoid such rapid wage increases in expanding industries, for they distort the wage structure, lead to tensions and are eventually matched by wage increases in the low-paid sectors. I shall return to this point in the discussion of long-term contracts and profit-sharing schemes. Wage and price inflation is a game in which some are always running ahead and others catching up — and those running ahead should pay part of the price of anti-inflationary policies by moderating their claims.

Thus, we do not exclude the possibility that the objective $w = h + p$ will occasionally be deliberately violated ; but this means that some additional inflation is knowingly accepted. In addition, however, the rule will often be violated unintentionally ; this causes the wage inflation that we all recognise and which everyone claims to be against.

IV. LONG-TERM CONTRACTS

In most countries a tendency towards the negotiation of longer wage contracts can be observed. If the above objectives of wage policy are accepted it will be clear that such contracts should provide (at least from the macro-economic point of view) for annual wage increases of about 4 per cent. plus the guarantee of additional annual wage increases in accordance with rises in the cost of living.[1]

The obvious objection is that this is inflationary. This is true, but in a country where there is a strong trade union movement and full employment it is usually impossible to get away with less. Even an effort to do so gives rise to distrust, tensions and an increase in factor c. Only in exceptional circumstances can trade unions be called upon to accept a deliberate reduction in the share of wages, and then only temporarily. And such acceptance is forthcoming only if employers and the government explicitly accept the principle of a constant wages share.

Escalator clauses are regarded with disfavour not only by economists, but also by employers. The latter fear that the acceptance of such clauses imposes obligations which they may be unable to honour because profits may not permit. This attitude ignores two considerations. First, the relationship between profits and the cost of living is such that as a rule, the two move in the same direction —

---

[1] More accurately, the adjustment should be not to the cost of living increases but to changes in the price deflator of the national product. Whilst changes in the cost of living can be measured by more or less generally accepted means, changes in the price deflator of the national product are more difficult to quantify. Nevertheless perhaps it would be possible to agree, in principle, that price increases which result from a rise in import prices or from tax increases should not be compensated by wage increases. Of course, the enforcement of such an agreement would be likely to give rise to disputes about the statistics but this source of conflict might be accepted.

just as aggregate wages and profit margins tend to rise together. Secondly a refusal to include escalator clauses in long-term contracts does not protect employers from additional wage claims during the life of the contract. It is not possible to control a trade union by purely legal manœuvres, and it may react by raising a 'living document' issue, in which the special nature of labour relations is contrasted with legal obligations and advanced as a reason for waiving these obligations.[1] In that event long-term contracts will not be viable. If it is desired to eliminate the factors $\phi(U)$ and c, then a clear legalisation of the $h + p$ principle is necessary.

A thorny problem is posed by the translation of a macro-economic figure of, say, 4, 3·8 or 3·1 per cent. into a rate of productivity increase for individual industries. The national average is constructed from sectoral figures that range from 0 to 10 per cent. or more, and whilst it is relatively stable and predictable, productivity developments in individual industries are not.

One result of this is that each industry, in order to err on the safe side, will tend to under-estimate h when negotiating collective agreements. Therefore, if the intention is to guarantee that $w = h + p$, there should be an opportunity of correcting such estimates *ex post*. Such corrections might take the form of a lump sum wage payment (calculated not on the basis of profits — for this would give another twist to the wage-price spiral — but on the actual growth of productivity).

A second and more serious complication is that it is difficult to measure productivity trends in individual industries, even 'ex post'. Indeed, the margin of error in the available data may be wider than the margin within which the results of traditional wage negotiation can be arrived at. Furthermore, in these circumstances wage negotiations may assume a strange and somewhat surrealistic character, becoming pseudo-scientific discussions of the measurement of productivity.

In Holland, experience with these problems in the period 1959–63 has led to a fairly general repudiation of the productivity criterion. The objections to the method are real, and they crop up whenever too much weight is given to the increase of productivity in individual industries. Yet given a sense of humour these complications could be managed; unfortunately a sense of humour is not usually a

---

[1] The expression 'living document' was used in the dispute over the General Motors Contract in 1963. That contract included a cost-of-living clause, but the UAW thought it inadequate.

characteristic of these negotiations. Measuring productivity is difficult and the result subject to uncertainty, but it is not complete nonsense.

The above complications are avoided to some extent by the fact that productivity changes in individual industries should not be adopted as the criterion for wage increases. Wage determination should also be based on the growth of macro-economic productivity. Otherwise substantial inter-industry wage differentials would develop and be regarded as unfair in the industries where wages lag behind, leading to claims for wage adjustment. In other words, wage determination on the basis of individual industry productivity performances is inflationary because wages in the industries where productivity is lagging will be adjusted to the higher productivity increases of the other industries. This can only be avoided if the industries in which productivity grows fast limit their wage increases and translate part of their productivity improvements into falling prices. Without this rule no effective wage policy can be pursued. For industries where productivity grows slowly will have to concede wage increases that exceed the productivity improvement and, in certain cases, this will lead to price increases.

Theoretically it is possible to base all long-term wage contracts on the rate of growth of macro-economic productivity and to ignore completely productivity increases in individual industries. Such an extreme application of the principle would accord with concepts of equal pay for equal work. Yet it would not work in practice, for it demands too much centralisation, too much restraint and too much solidarity. Some average of productivity increases in the individual industry and in the economy at large will need to be accepted. A rough and ready recipe may be devised for the calculation of such an average. And, indeed, a warning against refinement is not superfluous. At one time formulae were proposed in Holland for a weighted average between changes in sector-productivity and in national productivity, of a rather ridiculous precision, which contributed to the abandonment of the productivity criterion. In practice it will be necessary to make a rough estimate of productivity growth in the individual industry and then to take the simple average of this estimate and 4 per cent. If this procedure still makes too high demands on the ingenuity of the calculators, it should be possible to state simply that industries where productivity grows rapidly may grant wage increases as high as 6 per cent., while the others would be limited to a maximum of 2 per cent. (plus the amount of any price increase).

With this method, inter-industry wage differentials and, as a result, tensions and wage inflation may again become excessive. If so, still greater weight should be given to the macro-productivity figure.

This approach leaves considerable scope for policy-making, since the general rule can be applied in many different ways. It is important, however, that the rationale of this policy, that is the objective of the protection of the worker's share *and* the share of profits, should be explained to all concerned. Unless this is done the arithmetic will look appallingly artificial and will fail to provide an adequate basis for negotiation and for the avoidance of wage inflation.

V. PROFIT-SHARING

Profit-sharing has been advocated for more than a century. The arguments in favour of it are well known — a reduction in income inequalities, the strengthening of the labour-management partnership, an increase in the sense of responsibility among the workers, a sharpening of production incentives, the encouragement of a feeling of solidarity and a recognition of the worker's dignity. In the previous section it was proposed that wage increases be linked to productivity growth and to price increases but not to profits. Indeed, linking wage rates to profits would be an undesirable element of anti-inflationary policies. Though many employers stubbornly deny it, a rising wage level leads to rising profits ; this is evident both from econometric investigations as well as from casual observation of the inflationary processes. If, in these circumstances, rising profits are allowed to lead to higher contractual wages a new spiral is created. Tying wages to both productivity and price increases is already inflationary ; no further inflationary link should be added.

Nevertheless, it is quite reasonable that workers' earnings should benefit from higher profits, provided that this does not take the form of higher contractual wages. Therefore, profit-sharing is a handy device for making corrections to a wage policy of the type advocated in the previous section ; it adds flexibility to workers' remuneration without necessarily increasing costs.

Yet the non-inflationary nature of profit-sharing schemes can easily be exaggerated. Some economic text-books are misleading in this respect. The economist is inclined to observe that profit-sharing does not effect the intersection of marginal cost and marginal revenue curves and, therefore, that it cannot lead to price increases.

But this is too simple a view. In the first place, marginal analysis pays inadequate attention to the most important market form, oligopoly. Sweezy's kinked demand curve saves the marginal theory formally but not in substance, and when prices are determined by oligopologists' anticipation of each other's reactions a broadly conceived system of profit-sharing may very well raise prices. General, compulsory systems of the kind found especially in South American countries almost certainly have this effect.

There are other reasons why profit-sharing may lead to higher prices. When wage-earners are entitled to a part of profits the cost of new capital increases, for the introduction of such a scheme means that whilst old shareholders must acquiesce to a fall in dividends new shareholders will be tempted to provide more capital only if new shares are issued at appropriately lower prices. In the long run, this increase in capital costs will be reflected in higher prices.

Also, profit-sharing may create differences in remuneration that are resented by those groups of wage-earners whose share in profits is low or nil. These groups may seek compensation in the form of higher wages, so that profit-sharing, instead of reducing inflationary pressures, may in fact strengthen them.

It must be concluded, therefore, that profit-sharing can make but a limited contribution to the elimination of wage inflation. It can be adopted only in enterprises where conditions are favourable, that is where labour-management relations are sound. When tensions prevail within the enterprise, profit-sharing is unlikely to yield any results. Schemes intended for widespread application and, especially, those that are legally compulsory, may have a certain ideological appeal, but they are ineffective in mitigating inflationary pressure since there is a considerable likelihood that their cost will be reflected in higher prices.

The potential contribution of profit-sharing schemes is also limited in a quantitative sense. In most countries the share of wages in the national income is about 70 per cent. The share of profits is of the order of 20 per cent., but this includes a large element of 'implicit wages' in the income of small businessmen, farmers and self-employed professionals, so that profits available for sharing are unlikely to be much in excess of 10 per cent. of the national income. If, after taxes, about half of this amount were reserved for wage-earners, not much more than about 3 per cent. of the national income would be available for distribution, that is about 5 per cent. of the total wage bill. Thus, the introduction in a given year of a radical and generally applied system of profit-sharing could result in a rise in wage-earners' income equivalent to about one year's wage increase. As a result, in the year in question, there might be no *wage* inflation (although the scheme would tend to raise prices, not to mention other effects). However, workers would gradually come to regard this additional source of income as normal. Profits and wages might continue to rise, but the annual increment of profits would not be larger than 5 per cent. of the annual increase in wages — hence, if the annual wage increase were 7 per cent., the rise in wage-earners' income due to profit-sharing would be of the order of 4 per thousand. Thus, when looking at the matter in terms of increases, which is the view normally taken of growth processes, the amounts involved become infinitesimal.

However, the impact of profit-sharing schemes is mainly a psychological one. If the profit share is paid once a year (the freezing of these sums is considered below) the feeling may be engendered that a true extra bonus is received.

Thus by its psychological effect profit-sharing may facilitate wage control. However, experience has also shown that profit-sharing can have certain negative psychological effects. Many schemes, introduced with the best of intentions, were eventually abandoned after a few years' operation, usually because profits proved to be disappointing. It is, however, difficult to generalise. In the long run profit-sharing may be a feature of a more peaceful society. At present it is certainly not a simple recipe for minimising factor c. At best, when circumstances are favourable, it may supplement a policy linking w with $h + p$; but it is not a general panacea.

VI. INVESTMENT WAGES

Many schemes have been proposed for reducing inequalities in the distribution of wealth. Those considered here have in common the fact that part of the earnings are frozen in an account and not paid as cash. Their object is capital formation by the worker ; the means is forced saving. A considerable amount of attention has been given to such schemes, during the last fifteen years, especially in Germany, and a number of plans, all requiring that part of the workers' wages should not be paid immediately as cash, have been proposed.

According to the well-known principles of O. von Nell-Breuning,[1] the average worker should save enough, during his active life, to finance the average investment cost of a job. This notion has been elaborated by E. Häussler,[2] who proposed that the level of the 'investment wage' be fixed by a collective wage agreement. The resulting financial resources would be paid into a fund that would help to finance the industry concerned. Workers would receive certificates from this fund, and after a certain period would be allowed to sell them. Häussler believes that this system would foster growth and reduce inflation, but apparently he has in mind demand, and not wage, inflation.

A similar proposal that has attracted much attention is the Leber Plan of 1964, named after the chairman of the West German Trade Union of Construction Workers.[3] Under this scheme, the investment wage would be fixed at 1·5 per cent. of the normal wage, and be paid by employers into a new investment fund, either in the form of cash, or shares, or bond equivalents. The fund would give priority to investment in the construction industry. The plan was rejected by the employers, but a savings scheme emerged from the negotiations. By this scheme workers who voluntarily saved a certain annual sum would receive a supplement from the employers and the total be invested by the workers themselves. The investments must conform to the regulations in the Federal Republic that exempt such schemes from income tax and social insurance premiums, which in practice means that the investments are frozen for a period of five years.

Our comment on these plans can be brief. Whatever advantages they do possess, reducing inflationary wage increases is not one of them since investment wages are costs. Indeed, freezing a part of remuneration may give an additional stimulus to wage inflation because total wage claims (the normal increase plus the frozen element) may easily be larger than would otherwise have been the case. Something is added to $h + p$. The scheme could help to mitigate demand inflation and this may not be unimportant, but it is of no avail against cost inflation. In the short run it might even foster psychological tensions, because whilst employers must pay more, workers receive no immediate cash benefit.

It is not impossible that, eventually, plans of this type might lead to a moderation of wage claims, but this would be very much a

---

[1] *Eigentumsbildung in Arbeiterhand*, 1955.
[2] *Der Arbeitnehmer von Morgen. Mit-Eigner und Mit-Träger in der Wirtschaftsgesellschaft*, 1956.
[3] *Vermögensbildung in Arbeitnehmerhand ; ein Programm und sein Echo*, 1964.

long-term effect when workers have accumulated so much capital that, as small capitalists, they limit their own wage claims. From this point of view such schemes fit well with the image of a better society. But in the short-term they cannot help to fight wage inflation.

VII. CAPITAL-SHARING

Capital-sharing too is an old idea (for instance, it was advocated in 1847 by P. F. Reichenspergen) that has recently become fashionable again. It differs from both profit-sharing and investment wages. In the case of profit-sharing schemes a portion of profits is paid to the workers; in the case of investment wages nothing is paid to workers, but the employers contribute to the investment fund a sum which they regard as wages and therefore costs; in the case of capital-sharing schemes nothing is paid to workers, nor is the employer's contribution in the nature of a wage cost. Capital-sharing means that the workers become owners of part of the undistributed profits. As a rule no cash payment is made but part of the profits ploughed back into the enterprise change ownership.

The origin of capital-sharing schemes is to be found in the recognition that it is difficult to transfer part of the economic surplus to the workers without causing all sorts of complications. The object is to promote a greater equality in the distribution of wealth without obliging workers to save. The proponents of the idea (especially B. Gleitze [1]) have pointed out that in modern society wealth tends to concentrate particularly in large enterprises, but that to hamper this concentration would be harmful to growth and productivity. Nor can the workers' aspirations be met by excessive wage increases since this would cause inflation. Gleitze and others believe that increases in capital should remain primarily the property of the enterprise. However, he thinks that the secondary ownership should be changed since it would be wrong to let the yields of such an increase in capital accrue only to shareholders given that the increase originated in the enterprise community which includes the workers too. At present it is customary for shareholders to receive first a dividend and then, in addition, a claim on ploughed-back profits. The proposals for capital-sharing would leave untouched their claim to dividends, but would reduce their claim to the secondary ownership of undistributed profits — it might, for instance, be halved. The

[1] 'Lohnpolitik und Vermögensverteilung', in *Sozialer Fortschritt*, 1957.

remainder would be allocated to a fund, established industry by industry, or for the country as a whole, in which the workers would share.

A similar plan to Gleitze's has been proposed in Germany by H. W. Büttner.[1] The Sozialdemokratische Partei Deutschland have also discussed capital-sharing at a party congress in 1960. It was proposed that a 'Deutsche Nationalstiftung' be established and receive, for investment purposes, the revenues from several capital taxes, death duties, taxes on wealth and a levy on the reserves of large concerns, which might be paid either in the form of cash or in securities. All Germans, not only the workers, would be able to participate in this foundation by acquiring 'Deutsche Volksaktien'. The SPD has, however, dropped this proposal, there being no reference to it in the 1964 publication *Eigentum für Alle : Aufgabe unseres Jahrzehntes* — though this contains much about the stimulation of workers' savings. The DGB has not supported capital-sharing proposals.

The three main Dutch trade union federations issued, in 1964, a report entitled *Bezitsvorming door vermogensaanwasdeling*,[2] the proposals in which conform more or less with Gleitze's. This report is 'under consideration', though the plan has not been strongly advocated by the trade unions. From time to time it has been discussed during negotiations about the future legal arrangements for a Dutch wage policy, but without attracting much attention. This lack of attention is understandable. It is partly due to the fact that these negotiations have moved from one crisis to another and partly because the trade unions themselves are finding it difficult to make up their minds about the plan and have not pushed it very hard.

The essence of capital-sharing is the transfer of property rights. At first sight this would appear to be a fairly quiet operation, with no monetary or costs aspects and, therefore, a very suitable way of reducing wage claims. Closer scrutiny, however, suggests that this is doubtful, especially in the case of small firms. Capital-sharing plans evidently find their inspiration in the financial arrangements of joint-stock companies which can transfer bonus shares to their new owners. A non-corporate enterprise cannot do this. In this case the proposals provide for payments in cash or for the firm simply to owe a debt to the investment fund on which interest would have to

[1] 'Eigentumsstreuung über Sozialkapital', in *Sozialer Fortschritt*, 1958.
[2] 'Formation of private property through the distribution of increases in enterprise capital' — a rather long and unimaginative title, unattractive even to a Dutchman.

be paid. But either a cash payment or the creation of a debtor-creditor relationship is a burden on the firm, which it will pass on as a price increase, especially in an oligopolistic market situation.

In fact, further reflection shows that the same reaction is likely to be found in the large corporations. It would be naïve to believe that a part of ploughed-back profits can be transferred to the workers without consequences. Shareholders do not view the increase in their capital which results from the ploughing back of profits as an agreeable but unexpected windfall. On the contrary, when buying shares they anticipate such capital gains, and if they have to share them with others, shares will be valued less and their prices fall. This amounts to a higher rate of interest for new issues, which, no doubt, will lead to a rise in prices in the long run.

In my opinion there is a clear analogy between capital-sharing and a corporation tax. At any rate, employers will certainly feel that there is such an analogy. The difference is that a tax will impair the firm's liquidity more quickly than a capital-sharing scheme though even this contrast hardly applies in the case of non-incorporated firms. Advocates of capital-sharing schemes must realise that they would reduce the Treasury's revenue. And, because of this, followers of J. K. Galbraith should be sceptical about the merits of capital-sharing schemes.

In the context of a discussion of cost inflation a crucial question is the extent to which the burden of a corporation tax, and therefore of a capital-sharing scheme, can be shifted to the consumer. We know far less about this question than is desirable but it is certain that the traditional view, endorsed in old-fashioned text-books, that the incidence of a profit tax cannot be shifted, is much too optimistic. Most probably such taxes are partly passed on as price increases, although we do not know to what extent. There are still other ways in which capital-sharing may lead to price increases. If capital-sharing schemes are introduced in some industries but not in others there will be claims for compensatory wage increases — the very result to be avoided.

As a means of fighting cost inflation, the prospect for capital-sharing schemes does not seem altogether favourable. It would appear that, in this case too, voluntary and limited schemes are better than elaborate and compulsory arrangements covering entire industries but which are not suitable for checking wage inflation.

There remains the question of the extent to which capital-sharing may be desirable for other purposes. My view is that levying an extra tax on the profits of corporations to finance collective consumption and capital-sharing schemes are competing measures and that therefore the priority between these two approaches should be established. The criterion for determining this should be which of the two methods will make society more harmonious in the long run, and thereby reduce the risk of cost inflation. The answer to this question depends to a great extent on one's *Welstanschauung*.

VIII. CONCLUSION

Investment wages are a completely unsuitable means of buying off wage inflation. Nor are capital-sharing schemes very helpful in the short run, and they conflict with Galbraithian proposals. Profit-sharing, provided it is introduced in a limited way and implemented in favourable conditions, may lead to some moderation in wage claims. Long-term contracts, provided they clearly specify that wage increases should correspond to productivity increases (some average of the increase of productivity in the industry in question and in macro-economic productivity) in addition to price increases, can help to moderate the wage-price spiral.

However, such arrangements can be effective only if they are incorporated within the framework of an incomes, and a Keynesian, policy, and, more generally, in the context of endeavours to promote a more harmonious society. All social conflicts are inter-related. There are no simple recipes for suppressing the 'pushfulness' of the unions. A specific bargain which aims at checking wage increases may evoke distrust and do more harm than good. The fight against inflation requires a comprehensive approach.

Chapter 5

INCOMES POLICIES AND THE EUROPEAN ECONOMIC COMMUNITY

BY

L. H. J. CRIJNS

THE encyclical 'Mater et Magistra' of Pope John XXIII declares 'socialisation' to be one of the most characteristic developments of our time. Modern life endows human relationships with increasing and complex diversity, and in many instances this complexity entails action at the policy level and the establishment of new institutions.

Policy action, indeed, is increasing all the time, as can be seen from the European policy, the Atlantic policy and even the space policy which is now evolving. Moreover, policy action extends increasingly to various aspects of community life — for instance, to the demographic, economic, social and cultural fields. It is also designed as never before to embrace whole aspects of life ; witness the policies for youth, the family, old age, health, etc. Even within the confines of a single major policy, such as economic or social policy, there are signs that it influences people's spontaneous activities to an ever-increasing degree. For proof of this we need to look only at the policy of economic expansion, employment and vocational training policy, competitive policy, scientific and technical research policy, amalgamation policy, regional policy, sectoral structure policy (e.g. agricultural, industrial, energy, transport, distribution and tourist policies), monetary policy, public finance policy, budgetary policy, fiscal policy, credit policy, capital market policy, trade policy and so on.

Some years ago, a new policy was added to this list — incomes policy. This subject is increasingly debated by all circles — governments, employers' and employees' organisations — whose interest is apparent from the documents, reports and resolutions that they publish. It is a subject that is thought about in all countries, in the members of the European Economic Community, in Great Britain, Austria, the Nordic countries, and even in the United States, where the President's Council of Economic Advisers has proclaimed guidelines for wages and prices.

What lies behind this phenomenon ? Two major common socio-economic factors can be identified in all the highly industrialised free democracies of the Western hemisphere. The first is the governments' responsibility for the simultaneous and co-ordinated achievement, in optimum balance, of five objectives : rapid and continuous economic growth ; full employment, or at least a very high level of employment ; internal monetary balance, that is price stability ; external monetary balance, that is equilibrium in the balance of payments ; and an equitable distribution of greater prosperity. The second is the independence of labour and management and their freedom to fix wages and other conditions of work by means of collective bargaining.

Now it is well known that labour and management may on occasion fix wages at a level which seriously hinders the simultaneous achievement of the economic and social objectives for which the government is responsible. For instance, should labour and management raise wages so much that the increase in unit labour costs could not be offset by a reduction in other production costs or smaller profits, this would cause, firstly, an increase in prices and thereby weakened competitiveness relative to other countries, and secondly a deficit in the current balance of payments, a retardation of productive investment, a threat to future employment, and a deceleration of economic growth. Inflation also gives rise to speculation and causes injustices to fixed-income receivers, and, in extreme cases, it may proceed to the point where the official exchange rate must be revised or the free movement of goods and services restricted, perhaps severely. In other words, it can cause an abrupt halt to economic progress.

But it is well known that the reverse can also occur, that the authorities may directly or indirectly implement an economic and social policy that prevents labour and management from fixing wages or working conditions that are regarded as reasonable. For instance, it is perfectly possible to have a price increase that is not caused by an undue increase in unit labour costs but by such other factors as : too soft a monetary policy — for example, a huge credit expansion leading to too high a liquidity ratio in relation to the increase in national output ; a public finance policy entailing enormous public expenditures without any offsetting limitation on private consumption or on productive investment in the private sector ; a lack of self-discipline in income categories other than wages (prices, profits, distribution margins, agricultural and other rents, charges for public or private services, etc.). When such factors operate demand ceases to be related to the supply of goods and services ; and inflation is born not of an increase in cost-push but of too high over-all demand. In these circumstances, self-discipline is not required from management or labour — especially the trade unions — but from the public authorities, monetary institutions and entrepreneurs.

In short, therefore, labour and management have a certain moral responsibility for the simultaneous achievement of a balanced set of economic and social objectives ; governments, by the same token, must implement an economic and social policy (monetary, budgetary, price, distribution and competitive policies, etc.) which will enable labour and management to fix reasonable wages and other conditions of work.

In order that these two requirements may be combined, there must be periodic meetings between the groups in question, for the exchange of information and mutual consultation. Indeed, only thus can governments and labour and management achieve the conditions in which they can best carry out their specific duties. Each of the parties retains its own responsibilities, but close co-operation is essential if these are to be met in the most suitable and fruitful way.

In particular, although we have drawn a theoretical distinction between inflation caused by labour costs and inflation caused by demand, in practice both elements are almost always present, though in different degrees of intensity. In these circumstances a remedy requires that both the public authorities and labour and management must consent to the necessary discipline, consent which can only be achieved in a climate of consultation and close co-operation. If this is absent, nothing can be achieved and each group is dissatisfied. For whilst a high rate of investment, substantial wage increases and large public expenditures are each individually very desirable in so far as they all help to raise the standard of living, the pressure of all these factors together may threaten the economy, with all the consequences that this implies. In short : 'you can't do everything at once'.

On the other hand, those objectives which can be achieved must be jointly discussed and implemented. Therefore, it occasions no surprise that more and more countries have established or are establishing institutions for promoting this sort of consultative co-operation. Whilst some countries may not yet have progressed as far as this, the evidence suggests that this is certainly not because they have felt no need for it. This is made clear by Professor de Broeck [1] in a

---

[1] Secretary-General to the Belgian National Labour Council and Professor at Louvain University.

recent survey based on reports on six countries dealing with collaboration in the socio-economic field, between governments, labour and management, and which is to be discussed by the central labour and management group at the Community level.

It is most important that neither direct nor indirect negotiations between governments, labour and management should be restricted to the question of wage incomes. In principle all incomes should be treated in the same manner, not only for economic reasons but also on social and, above all, psychological grounds. Otherwise, close co-operation between governments, labour and management will be impossible. The aim should not be a wages policy, but an incomes policy in the widest sense. Moreover, wages and other incomes cannot be considered in isolation, but must be examined in the context of all economic and social phenomena, since it is impossible to assess the formation, distribution and use of income other than against the background of the whole spectrum of economic and social policy. In other words, all the economic and social data which are meaningful in this context, whether they stem from actual experience or arise out of forecasts and projections for the short, medium or long term, should be put on the table.

This leads me to discuss the various concepts of incomes policy currently held. There are some who would limit the field of an incomes policy to the formation of primary incomes, that is to the proportion of income provided by total gross wages and the proportion provided by capital and ownership. There are those who would expand this concept to include the distribution of primary income, for example, the distribution of total gross wages between agriculture, industry and the tertiary sector, between expanding branches and branches in recession, between developed and under-developed regions and between the various occupational categories (unskilled labour, specialised and skilled workers, medium- and high-grade officials, and so on). There are others who would also include the distribution of secondary income, that is the transfer of income with particular reference to social welfare.

Finally, some would prefer incomes policy to be accompanied by measures concerned with savings and ownership, for example, policies relating to profit-sharing by workers, productive investment, self-financing and the appreciation of assets in the firm. In this category fall such schemes as the *Investivlohn* in Germany, the *Vermogensaanwasdeling* in the Netherlands and contractual savings in Italy.

My feeling is that all these concepts should be integrated into a *systematic* incomes policy, which in its turn should constitute an integral and essential part of any political or social economy. This raises a complex and delicate problem, associated with certain political, economic, social and psychological difficulties. These difficulties include : the exact delimitation of an incomes policy ; the criteria to be used when applying it ; the lack of exact and incontrovertible data about certain relevant variables, notably non-wage incomes (for example, the complexity of the taxation system in the matter of income assessment) ; the sharply contrasting methods of organisation that exist in various countries (especially in France and Italy) ; and, of course, the conditions and opportunities for applying such a policy.

However, these difficulties do not justify a failure to take any action. Governments must contact the representatives of the main economic and social groups, particularly labour and management, in order to agree on a common approach and at the same time to safeguard the independence and specific responsibility of all arbitration machinery in this sphere. Obviously, there is no question of trying to abolish the independence of any part of this machinery, but there is a need to establish a procedure by which mutual persuasion can succeed, firstly, in relating total distributed income to the size of output, and secondly, in ensuring a more equitable distribution of income amongst all sections of the community, while achieving a relationship between consumption and investment that avoids any threat to the future development of the economy.

But it is not enough for efforts in this field to be restricted to the national level, and the Commission feels that given the degree of interdependence that exists between the six EEC countries, a simultaneous and co-ordinated approach should be evolved at the Community level. Close co-operation between Community institutions, governments, management and labour is indispensable if price stability is to be achieved over as wide a field as possible and if there is to be an equitable distribution of the fruits of such stability, both in the short and longer terms. Such co-operation has already occurred on two occasions, once in the framework of an *ad hoc* policy statement and once in connection with the formulation of medium-term economic policy.

On 15 April 1964 the Council of Ministers, at the proposal of the Commission, approved a Recommendation to member States concerning measures to be taken for re-establishing the Community's internal and external economic balance. Incomes policies are directly referred to in Point 8 of that Recommendation.

The Community's medium-term economic policy is also dealt with in the Commission's 25 July 1963 Recommendation approved by the Council on 15 April 1964. The need for an incomes policy emerged clearly not only at the meetings of the group of independent experts concerned with medium-term projections for the period 1966 to 1970, but also at the meetings of the Committee for Medium-Term Economic Policy. The draft project for the first programme for medium-term economic policy was completed in March 1966, and was submitted to the Commission, which in turn formulated the projected First Programme for subsequent formal presentation to the Council. Chapter III, which comprises the main statement of the general guidelines for medium-term economic policy in the next few years, contains a section of major importance for incomes policies.

Its general tenor is to require a moderation in rises in incomes, so as to contain nominal increases within limits that are compatible with the rise in the volume of production. It is clearly stated that such a policy must relate to all incomes. That is, it must extend both to distributed and undistributed profits (the project stresses the need for more information in this sphere), as well as to direct or indirect wages, and must take into account not only all primary income but also secondary income, i.e. transfers. It is also stated that incomes policies, in addition to their economic objectives, have a social purpose, which is to adjust the distribution of aggregate income for the benefit of the less favoured categories.

In connection with trends in wage incomes, governments are advised to make every effort to enlist the support of labour and management for the principles and procedures of an over-all incomes policy, to take account of the right of these parties to free collective bargaining, and, in particular, to provide for a regular exchange of views with the parties in question. Weight must be attached to the provision of appropriate price policies, since labour and management cannot be expected to accept a wages policy unless price trends can be directly contained within a comparable discipline ; and this implies that there is a special need for close contact between governments and firms. Finally, it is proposed that the incomes policy should be accompanied by measures relating to the distribution of capital, designed to reconcile the investment requirements with the workers' desire for a share of profits.

Chapter 6

COLLECTIVE WAGE BARGAINING AND THE CONDITIONS FOR ACTIVE MEDIATION

BY

F. SELLIER

Attempts by the State to influence wage-fixing procedures on the basis of certain guiding principles have more in common with its essentially economic role in former times, the fixation of the gold value of the monetary unit, than with its new activities in the social field. Whether the economy is operated on a 'gold standard' or a 'labour standard', or a mixture of the two, State mediation in these matters means that the authorities behave more like a monetary or banking institution than like a social institution. Control of wages can be viewed as the best way of regulating the economy in the same way that influencing the rate of interest was fifty years ago. Controlling the rate of wage increases, rather than manipulating the rate of interest, enables the State to enjoy the low and stable rates of interest that it prefers, and might allow everyone to reap the benefits of an elastic credit system and flexible exchange rates. Yet such control is a rather complicated way of managing the economy, and involves a rise in the degree of State intervention since it has a direct impact upon both public and private employers and wage- and salary-earners and changes the role of their representatives in collective bargaining procedures at all levels.

THE ECONOMIC CONTEXT

Actual earnings are determined at the plant level from a base of collectively bargained rates and their level is influenced, to a greater or lesser degree, by the strength of the trade unions and conditions in the labour market. Where there is an excess of over-all demand and credit is plentiful, the incentive for employers not to accede to too high wage claims may be weak ; it is even weaker when they have an oligopolistic position in the market. Only if a balance of payments problem arises will the State tighten credit and restrain demand. Thus, to the State, intervention in wage-fixing procedures appears to be closely related to the problem of monetary management.

This is not, however, how it appears to wage-earners or even to employers. And in fact, it is not solely a monetary problem. More precisely, intervention in wage determination procedures cannot avoid such equity problems as the following : the development of wage inequalities as a consequence of the fact that firms are not equally endowed with resources for paying wages ; and the fact that producers of goods for which the income elasticity of demand is low, and people in receipt of transfer or fixed incomes, do not benefit to the same extent from the growth of money incomes.

The State already participates to some degree in wage determination procedures since it commonly provides mediation services for the bargaining parties. In the following paragraphs the nature and implications of the use of State mediation as a means of influencing collectively bargained rates are examined.

We can define mediation, in the widest sense but excluding the question of compulsion, in terms of three factors : the provision of relevant information ; the acceleration or retardation of the decision process ; and the influence exerted on the decision other than by the provision of information. The importance of these factors differs according to the level at which mediation takes place and according to whether the mediation is 'passive' or 'active' in nature. In principle, mediation is passive when it seeks to promote a settlement simply on the basis of the best interests of the parties immediately concerned. A mediator is active when he takes account of information relating to the economy as a whole which the parties themselves have not requested and may wish to leave out of the picture.

The choice of a particular piece of information presupposes that a certain relationship exists between the nature of this information and the decision to be taken. Consequently, mediation in general, but especially active mediation, cannot be considered as a neutral process, since the active mediator can select the additional information to be used. In France, for instance, the mediator has the right to ask for information about the economic position of the industry or firm ; employers are frequently, but not always, opposed to the use of such information by the mediator. Also, it has been decided in France that information relating to past changes in earnings in the public and nationalised sector should be collected and used by the new wage determination institutions for evaluating the cost of wage increases. Information introduced by the mediator has a differential effect on the relative bargaining power of the parties concerned, according to the level at which the mediation takes place and according to the source of the information. As pointed out, employers tend to object to the use of specific information relating directly to a given industry or firm. In contrast, employers are less opposed than the trade unions to the introduction of general economic information pertaining to the economy as a whole. For whilst in principle such information should not affect the relative bargaining positions of the parties, the establishment of a guiding light, for example, based on a specific national economic requirement (such as the need for the Netherlands to be internationally competitive) and supported by union leaders, can restrain wage demands by marshalling public opinion against strike action. Employer representatives at the French 'Incomes Conference' (October 1963 to January 1964) maintained that, in respect of wages and salaries, 'it was essential to act at the central level', while the unions thought that attention should also be paid to conditions at the industry level. Neither unions nor employers wished to negotiate in this field at the firm level.

An attempt has been made in France since 1965 to formulate indicative plans in terms of current values as well as in constant prices — the only form in which the 4th Plan was presented. Data in current values are more comprehensive and lend themselves more easily to analysis than simple guidelines since they are founded on a balanced framework for development. They are devised to provide criteria for an incomes policy and are more suitable for this purpose than pure productivity criteria. The more aggregated this type of information is, the more reliable and useful it will be in this role, since adherence to firm and industry productivity criteria gives rise to irrelevant and unjustifiable wage differentials. Unfortunately the introduction of such global information has little impact on the behaviour of the parties in plant level bargaining.

Both active and passive mediation can have important impacts on wage negotiations, varying according to whether the firm or industry is expanding or stagnating, by accelerating or delaying the wage negotiation procedures. During the transition from a recession to prosperity, when the labour market tightens, mediation may be useful to employers by slowing down or diminishing wage increases. During the transition from prosperity to recession, mediation may be useful to unions — at least if there is no danger of unemployment and given the tendency of mediators to compromise half-way between the wage claim and the employer's offer. Examples of both situations can be found, particularly among firms where economic conditions differ from those at the national level and which would be unduly willing to grant wage increases in the very early stages of an upswing or sufficiently strong to resist high wage claims in a downswing. The government might use mediation procedures to co-ordinate the timing of wage discussions so that individual firms or industries are prevented from granting wage increases at times when it suits them but not the economy as a whole.

Although he cannot make the necessary decision himself, the active mediator must seek to influence the wage determination procedure in such a way that, on average, increases conform with a guideline that is compatible with the ultimate achievement of equilibrium growth. Obviously the task is more difficult than that of passive mediation since its objective is not merely to promote agreement but to ensure that the final outcome lies between certain limits. The active mediator must try to show each party that a failure to reach a decision within his prescribed limits can be injurious to their long-term interests, to convince them of the accuracy of his economic reasoning and then to help them reach agreement within these limits. In a weakly competitive economy the active mediator when defining the limits within which the parties must seek agreement, should try to impose those limits that would be typical of a similar situation in a strongly competitive economy. This he cannot do unless the economic milieu is changed to some extent.

It has been suggested that when, in the process of negotiations, the attitudes of the parties immediately involved are incompatible with national economic objectives, the structure and power of their organisations should be modified.[1] Perhaps it is the case that, as Chamberlain has suggested,[2] there is an optimum structure for trade unions in the context of collective bargaining for wages. But what structure is optimum from the point of view of the desirability of restraining wage claims is not easy to see. Certainly it does not seem to be the case that the strongest centralised trade union movement uses its powers to demand the largest wage increases. Such a union organisation in Sweden has not yielded the worst results in this sense, whilst in France — where effective wage increases are negotiated at

[1] OECD, *The Problem of Rising Prices*, Paris, 1961. See the statement of F. Lutz and W. Fellner, p. 64.
[2] E. H. Chamberlain, *The Economic Analysis of Labor Union Power*, American Enterprise Association, 1958.

73

the firm level [1] or are the result of unilateral action by employers — wages have risen considerably. Moreover, whilst collective bargaining in the United States is mainly conducted at the level of the firm, the unions involved are often very large indeed.

The degree of homogeneity in a union, that is the extent to which common goals exist at each of its various levels of activity, is probably more important than its size or structure in determining its strength, and a more important factor in the establishment of an incomes policy. Four possible levels of negotiation can be identified : national, industry, branch and enterprise ; to these might be added the regional level. Thus employers in the French metal industry have always favoured bargaining at the level of the whole industry rather than for individual branches (such as automobiles) ; however, they have preferred such bargaining to be at the regional level.

The functions of the different levels of a trade union sometimes give rise to a degree of competition between these levels, especially in the case of wage bargaining. The extent to which wages are determined at one level deprives another of part of this role ; and it is as important in this connection that union activities at the level of the firm should not be completely deprived of a given role as it is to leave the whole of one function to its competence. The presence of militancy in certain types of unions is a major reason why a considerable amount of wage bargaining is left to officials at the firm level. Yet such a practice is sometimes considered as a danger to the achievement of the union's wage policy and then the competence of the union at the firm level is strictly limited, as it is for instance in Germany. No doubt the best solution to this problem is to be found in some systematic division of wage bargaining functions between the various levels. Although the systems differ between countries and industries, an approach along these lines has been tried in the British textile industry and is being tried in other countries.[2] In Italy, the Netherlands and Sweden a systematic allocation of negotiating responsibilities is being tried between the industry, branch and enterprise levels. Such improvements in the system of industrial relations imply more formalisation of methods of payment, job classification and evaluation, both at the industry and firm levels. The introduction of such methods is viewed with caution ; by employers because they fear they will cause a general rise in wages, and by workers

---

[1] Industrial unions such as those in the metal and building industries negotiate only minimum rates that are far from actual earnings.
[2] See Turner and Zoeteweij, *op. cit.*, p. 164.

because they fear that the opposite will occur.

Since a wage policy is, in effect, intended to be a form of monetary policy, new measures must be taken in order to change the environment in which the active mediation takes place. If the system of wage determination by collective bargaining is to be retained in circumstances where price competition is too weak to limit employers' wage concessions, then non-market forces need to be used to change the attitudes and actions of the parties immediately involved in the required direction. In particular, measures should be taken so that wage increases above a stipulated guidepost should attract some kind of tax or other monetary penalty. M. D. Steuer has proposed a double scheme. First, excessive wage increases should accrue in a special fund and eventually be paid to workers only if prices do not rise. Secondly, in order to prevent a redistribution in favour of non-wage incomes if price increases prove excessive, profits should be taxed at higher rates when prices have to be raised.[1]

It would seem that such a system would allow the State to perform its role in an appropriate fashion : it would permit it to influence attitudes and actions in the required direction without actually controlling them. Moreover, this system would have an anti-cyclical effect : the eventual repayment of the frozen wages and the reduction of the profits tax at times when prices fall would tend to coincide with a rise in unemployment and thereby have the effect of correcting the mistakes of the economic planners as well as compensating the victims of these mistakes.

A possible objection to the Steuer proposal is that the profits tax fails to ensure that prices will be reduced in industries where productivity improvements should permit this. For if oligopolistic market situations do prevent such price reductions, then the general price level will continue to rise given that more and more goods and services are being produced in tertiary industries where opportunities for productivity increases are fewer. Yet any attempt to take account of the conditions which exist in particular industries by the establishment of different price norms, would contradict the simplicity essential to Steuer's scheme.

Nevertheless, some scheme, comparable in its effects to that proposed by Steuer, seems to be necessary if current systems of collective bargaining are to be preserved in conjunction with a form of active mediation that is not tantamount to the state control of wages. The

[1] M. D. Steuer, 'Economic Policy and Union Activity', in *Industrial Relations*, ed. B. C. Roberts, London, 1962, pp. 250–3.

effect of such a system would be, in effect, to introduce new checks on the issue of 'wage-money'. Since in conditions of oligopoly and flexible credit, wage rates can be fixed within very wide margins, there is certainly a need to have new instruments for limiting the issue of 'wage-money' — a need which is all the more pronounced when, as now, the large amount of self-financed investment has severely impaired the traditional and not unimportant regulatory role of the rate of interest.

THE SOCIOLOGICAL CONTEXT [1]

In industrial societies, incomes policies constitute a method of persuading the community to subscribe more wholeheartedly to certain goals which they have set themselves and to support the measures considered necessary for their attainment. In fact, the principal objective is to combine the greatest possible degree of individual freedom with the highest possible level of efficiency, rather than to regard these two ends as essentially incompatible and to stress one at the expense of the other. Those formulating the wage policy will therefore need to invoke the principle of the good of society as a whole, and point to the uselessness of wage rises that are swallowed up by inflation and the common perils which they can cause — a slowing of economic growth and social injustice. Whilst unemployment and the evils it entails were once regarded as inevitable, this is no longer the case and in return for this improvement in the management of the economy and the avoidance of unemployment crises, workers must moderate their wage claims. We must try to explain why this has failed to come about.

An arbitrator can be said to intervene actively when he bases his aims on the welfare of society as a whole and endeavours to obtain support for these aims from both sides to a dispute. He is not concerned with explaining to one side the views of the other, but rather with revealing to both parties how their dispute affects the whole community. He must try to lower the heat of the discussions, make the parties understand the effects on the community of the positions they take up and persuade them that they too have a stake in the collective welfare.

By inducing the negotiating parties *at whatever level* (national, sectoral, firm) to be mindful of the national interest, a conflict of

---

[1] This section was communicated after the termination of the proceedings.

interest may be introduced since individuals and the community do not necessarily have the same immediate aspirations. What is implied is that there must be compromise rather than conflict — whence stems the need for mediation, an activity which promises to constitute a new form of industrial relations.

At the firm level, the foreman, the personnel officer and the works council are institutions through which the objectives of the employer and of the employee can be harmonised, whilst incentive systems of remuneration and profit-sharing schemes constitute devices which make workers feel that their immediate interests coincide with those of their employers. Nevertheless, a conflict of interest is still revealed in appeals for 'restraint' and the integration of bonuses in workers' wages. Similarly, works councils are not sufficiently powerful to change a clash of interests into fruitful co-operation ; at this level, organs dedicated to compromise too often become instruments of deception, or merely constitute a forum in which both parties reveal their mutual incomprehension. Thus organs established to promote co-operation are deflected in their aims and fail to eliminate the traditional conflicts of interest.

At the national level, the position is rather different since the mediator can take a more disinterested view ; whilst not closing his eyes to the clash of the individual objectives, he tries to surmount this difficulty by making an appeal to the prior claim of higher goals. What are these higher goals ? In France, the mediator has emphasised two principal objectives : the need for more collective consumption and for the economy to become more internationally competitive. Although essentially economic in nature, these two objectives are based on the collective welfare. Yet the promotion of the collective welfare has implications for individual interests : collective consumption can only be promoted at the expense of private consumption ; and improved international competitiveness requires a rise in the self-financing of firms' investment.

How can the interdependence of these various interests be made clear and explicit ? This is the task of national accounting and economic planning. What is sought is no longer the maximum immediate advantage for the individual firm, but an optimum, the medium- or long-term national economic equilibrium, to which all groups in society can aspire.

Thus, instead of striking a balance between the interests of two parties, the active mediator is concerned with three, the third one being the community at large. Hence, his success will depend on

D

the extent to which the other two parties can identify their own interests with those of society as a whole and, thereby, participate in their achievement. At this juncture some pertinent questions can be posed : to what extent are the interests of the parties identifiable with those of society as a whole ; how persuasive is the mediator ; and what are the obstacles to a compromise solution ? We shall examine these questions in turn.

The first question raises the problem of comparing — on the basis of some common yardstick — immediate individual benefits and collective benefits, the enjoyment of which is delayed for some time. This is, in fact, the old dilemma between saving and consumption. Scitovski emphasises the contrasting rationales, in this context, of the decision-making units. Society has always sought to impose its own scale of preferences, which attaches more weight to the future, on that of individuals, which favours immediate consumption. In a developing society the cost of growth to the individual can only result in an attitude of mind that eschews long-term aims.

There is one way of encouraging the longer view, the manipulation of the rate of interest. It might be thought that there is always a certain minimum real rate of interest which suffices to produce a certain volume of voluntary savings. But when growth is proceeding very fast and obsolescence is rapid, such a rate would doubtless be too low. Moreover, the real rate of interest (as opposed to the monetary rate) offered to individuals as an inducement to saving, is strikingly low, about 3 per cent. Despite the inflation of commercial interest rates, society continues to favour immediate consumption as much by the low interest rates offered on savings, as by the tenor of its publicity. If we are to manage without the bait of attractive rates of interest, we shall have to use constraints, or have recourse to appropriate propaganda — in the best sense of the term — as a means of changing individuals' scales of values. This, in fact, is the change which the active mediator is called upon to bring about. If his message is to carry weight, it must be convincing. What are his chances of being believed ?

If the picture which the mediator draws of the future path of development is to be credible — that is to say if it is to be a future which is not to be immediately dismissed as utopian — it must be based on, and related to, the actual current situation. It follows that the mediator must not only insist on certain sacrifices, but must also relate his actions to current developments. There is always the likelihood that economic success, as it gains momentum, will make people less sceptical of the future. On the other hand, if the current situation is unduly bleak, it will be correspondingly difficult for individuals to listen to the mediator when he preaches immediate sacrifice in favour of some hypothetical improvement in their lot.

A small country which is very dependent on external developments will have rather obvious collective economic interests and objectives. If growth proves to be not too unbalanced, people will be fairly ready to subordinate individual to collective interests. But if, despite sacrifices — even those voluntarily accepted — people look abroad and feel themselves much less well off than they might be, they will lose their loyalty to the collective goal. In an affluent society the active mediator is, strictly speaking, superfluous. On the other hand, passive mediation, the catalyst by which the parties reach the agreement already latent in the situation, will always have a role to play.

The higher a community sets its sights, the more it is neceessary to provide it with some compelling reason for striving towards these objectives — and the harder it becomes to do so. If recourse to rigorous constraints and controls is to be avoided, effective propaganda enlisting the energies of the whole community in a common effort will be necessary. To arouse sufficient concern in the community, advocacy of a desirable objective (for example an increase in collective consumption) must be accompanied by arguments based on stark necessity, such as a reference to the threat of international competition.

In France, for example, much emphasis has been placed on the irreversibility of trade liberalisation and on international competition within the Common Market and in the world at large. Such arguments, based on economic realism, are used to moderate individual aspirations. Stress is laid not on a concept of 'solidarity' in the attainment of collective benefits — an approach that has a high moral appeal but is a little remote in impact — but on the urgent need to defend existing living standards, an argument that carries immediate weight.

The active mediator can support his proposals by explaining, with all the clarity that quantitative economic techniques permit, the importance of the balance that is being sought. But in a country that is largely sheltered from foreign competition, where the agricultural sector is important, and visible unemployment is small, the community may fail to appreciate the exigencies of the current situation or to understand any diagnosis of it.

Of course, negotiations have an intrinsic attraction, in so far as they bestow prestige on the negotiators. But if the structure of the unions is such that much weight is attached to militant behaviour, such prestige becomes superfluous, and there is a danger that negotiations will be used to enhance the position of the more belligerent rank and file *vis-à-vis* their leaders.

However, there is another obstacle in the way of compromise, the fact that the union leaders themselves may be less advanced in their thinking than the mediator, especially if the objectives he sets before them are lofty ones. International competition may be a factor which a union leader can readily grasp, whereas the need for a rise in collective consumption may be beyond his comprehension.

But the gravest difficulty lies in the fact that employers are not as nearly concerned as they might be with the implications and realities of international competition. If all employers were highly efficient and directed their energies with equal enthusiasm towards export markets, any scheme proposed by a mediator would command their common consent, a fact which in itself would tend to make the trade unions more co-operative. But if there are contrasts in the technical ability, in the energy and in the concern for export markets, of different entrepreneurs, then the proposals of the mediator will be far removed from the goals of many firms, and it will be correspondingly difficult to make the union rank and file believe in the practicability of the future which the mediator holds out. In this way, the sociological conditions for effective active mediation are related to the structure of the economy. The active mediator may find that the collective objective which he proposes is received with disbelief, or indeed is rejected.

International competition can require far-reaching structural economic changes and thereby gives rise to such serious social problems as redundancy and downgrading. As a result, there is a clash between individual and collective interests which can be avoided only by dint of a social welfare programme that requires efforts which society is usually unwilling to make. If, in these circumstances, the collective interest is to prevail, society must make efforts, based on the concept of 'solidarity', which convince the community of their effectiveness by the immediate fruits which they bear : these efforts include a rise in the lowest wages and the elimination of poverty by social welfare schemes. Thus, action by the active mediator to raise the lowest wages would be regarded as some proof of the credibility of the collective goal.

But if such action merely has the effect of losing the sympathy and support of the employers, or has disastrous economic consequences, its advantages would be lost.

In a situation where international competition is becoming fiercer, it may prove the case that a rise in the lowest wages, by helping to eliminate the marginal firms, would be well received by the relevant national employers' association. The French textile industry affords an example of the unions and employers raising wages in this fashion in order to eliminate those firms which had based their competitiveness on low wages.[1] In such cases measures must be taken to deal with the ensuing unemployment ; in France, a National Employment Fund has been established to meet the social costs of policies for raising national productivity by rationalisation. If such an increase in the lowest wages is not to raise the general level of wages, it must be implemented within the framework of a national solidarity campaign, so that these increases are offset elsewhere in the economy.

Apprehension about the purely economic impact of action such as this may mean that it is avoided. In this case attempts to obtain voluntary support will be doomed, and recourse to compulsion and controls will be needed, and conflict ensue. The combination of active mediation with compulsion gives, of course, 'compulsory arbitration', a form of interference which neither side, employers or workers, will normally accept voluntarily unless it feels that the government favours its case. Compulsory arbitration may be accepted in special circumstances. Thus, in France in the period 1937–1938, the arbitrators adopted the rather original approach of, on the one hand, urging a moderation in wage claims whilst, on the other, differentiating between the wage increases granted, on the basis of the extent of family responsibilities. And it is significant that certain commentators, looking to the period that will follow the current wage freeze in the United Kingdom, have emphasised the need for raising family allowances and the lowest wages.

The final obstacle to the acceptance of a compromise solution is distrust. In particular, there is suspicion that the application of the compromise agreement will not have the anticipated results : wage increases for the lowest paid workers *may* raise the general wage level, or an agreement to limit wage increases may *not* prove sufficient to prevent prices rising. That mistrust should exist is hardly surprising. All employers will not be equally enthusiastic about the mediator's proposals, and he cannot guarantee that his forecasts will be

---

[1] F. Sellier, *Stratégie de la lutte sociale : France 1936–60*, Les Éditions Ouvrières, Paris, 1961.

borne out. The uncertainties which attend international competition also make it more difficult to reach an acceptable compromise. It is not a normal business practice to conclude a contract of sale without guaranteeing delivery; and workers cannot be expected to rally to a proposal which asks them to step (perhaps irreversibly) into the unknown — except when higher considerations, such as those which are present during war-time, are involved.

There are not only external uncertainties, but also those which attach to the bargain itself. Thus, national accounts, on the basis of which the economic balance is prescribed, are subject to a degree of uncertainty : data may not be available for individual firms, and the calculation of economic growth is based on criteria which, to some extent, can be considered arbitrary. There is, in fact, an element of uncertainty in the concept of technical progress. And unless we have blind faith in technical progress as an end in itself, we cannot claim that the submission of society to the forces of technical progress with all the transient but costly readjustments which it entails, is in itself a rational objective. Man is liberating himself from servitude to nature, but if one master is merely being exchanged for another the process can hardly be considered as worthy of society's acceptance.

Such an attitude may, in so far as it questions the law of progress, be considered unrealistic. But collective enthusiasm cannot be aroused for a law which is blind. If we believe in this law, but if our faith is not transmitted to others, we shall be obliged to use compulsion.

Members of society cannot be expected to favour investment over consumption unless there is some prospect that by so doing they will change not only their economic situation but also their position in society. A call for investment will never be enthusiastically received unless it provides the occasion for a redistribution of power.

Chapter 7

TRADE UNION ACTION AND THE LEVEL OF COLLECTIVE WAGE BARGAINING

BY

PIERRE LE BRUN

It is intended that the Symposium should examine methods of reducing inflationary wage pressure in conditions of full employment and economic growth, with special emphasis being placed on possible ways of making existing decentralised methods of wage determination less inflation-prone. In this context it has been alleged that in Western Europe and Britain a major difficulty in implementing principles of wage policy would consist of applying at the plant level any agreements reached at the industry or economy level, on account of the weak influence of national trade union (and employers') organisations in the enterprise.

It is on this latter point that I have been asked to contribute to the Symposium, making special reference to the absence or insufficiency, particularly in France, of collective bargaining at the plant level, the lack of assurance that agreements concluded at the national or industry level will in fact be applied in all undertakings, and the problem of giving the unions more say in wage determination at the plant level. As a former Secretary of the General Confederation of Labour (CGT) responsible for handling economic affairs for the Confederation for twenty years, I shall concentrate on the economic aspects of these questions.

Collective bargaining at the plant level does occur in France, but not to a sufficient extent. Its inadequacy is illustrated by the following data which the General Department of Labour and Employment at the Ministry of Social Affairs has kindly supplied to me. Since the Act of 11 February 1950, which ended state control of wages and reintroduced legislation covering collective agreements, the competent Ministry has been informed of the conclusion of only 526 agreements at the plant level and 2,170 partial agreements or supplementary clauses to plant-level agreements (after deduction of the number of agreements whose termination has been notified to the

83

Ministry) ; all these instruments do not necessarily contain provisions relating to wages. Between 1962 and 1965 (inclusive) only 262 of the notified annual average number of independent wage changes registered in undertakings were the result of plant-level collective agreements. A further 86 stemmed from special wage agreements. To these must be added 529 increases resulting from unilateral 'decisions' by individual employers.

Such a poor performace by collective bargaining at the plant level is itself the outcome of the inadequacy of collective negotiations held and agreements concluded for an industry at the national, regional or local levels. Since the 1950 legislation, 204 collective agreements and 2,351 additional clauses at the national level have been notified, 155 and 1,786 at the regional level and 407 and 4,690 at the local level. Between 1962 and 1965, there was a yearly average of 112 wage changes under agreements and settlements at the national level, 133 at the regional level and 529 at the local level ; there was also an annual average of 143 collective recommendations and decisions by employers.

This same inadequacy is also, and perhaps even more closely, linked with the limited foothold of trade unions within undertakings, the insufficient union membership and, last but not least, divisions within the trade union movement itself.

In principle the agreements concluded for an industry at the national, regional or local level are applicable to the undertakings covered by the signatories to the agreement, and are even legally binding on all undertakings in the industry throughout the country, region or locality if an order has been made for the extension of the agreement in question. Since 1950 the coverage of 55 of the agreements and 687 of the additional clauses (referred to above) at the national level, 25 of the agreements and 88 of the additional clauses at the regional level, and 22 of the agreements and 157 of the additional clauses at the local level, has been extended in this way. All instruments, the effect of which is extended by this means, must contain clauses dealing with wage rates.[1] It is important for the unions to be sufficiently strong within the undertaking to enforce the implementation of these provisions, calling on the competent services of the Ministry of Labour for help where necessary.

By and large, the wage rates stipulated in these agreements are

---

[1] Thus, the remuneration of about 50 per cent. of wage- and salary-earners in industry and services, about 75 per cent. in agriculture, but almost *none* in the public sector, are prescribed contractually.

much below the actual wage rates paid in the large, and in many of the medium-sized, French firms. It has recently been observed that in two important metal trades these divergencies were of the order of 20 to 35 per cent., according to occupation, at the time when negotiated rates were reviewed, and as much as 40 to 60 per cent. two and a half years later. To these differences must also be added a further margin of about 20 per cent. between actual hourly rates and actual hourly earnings as a result of overtime work and miscellaneous bonuses.

To a certain extent the existence of such differences is quite natural. Firstly, there are some elements of remuneration that can only practically be determined at the plant level. Secondly, wage rates negotiated at the industry level are applicable — within the limits and subject to the conditions described above — to all undertakings in the industry, including the smaller, less efficient enterprises, and therefore they tend to be relatively low in order to be within these firms' capacity to pay. It is undeniable, however, that wages negotiated at the industry level in France are excessively below those paid in a great many firms. This is due not only to rather natural and understandable employer attitudes, which can be easily explained on a number of grounds, but also to a factor that is rather particular to the French scene — the lack of unity in the trade union movement.

The 1950 legislation also introduced a guaranteed minimum inter-occupational wage (SMIG) with the objective of ensuring the protection of the earnings of the least privileged wage-earners — those employed in the less efficient firms where frequently union influence is weakest — against rises in the cost of living and against a fall in their living standards relative to other groups of workers. For the past ten years or so successive governments have done everything in their power to prevent the SMIG rising, with the result that it has lagged further and further behind average real wages. At the same time changes in the SMIG have ceased to exert a healthy pressure on trends in guaranteed wages or to act as a spur to the conclusion or revision of arrangements or agreements at all levels. A radically different policy in this respect is advocated by the trade union movement.

Like practically all trade unionists in France, I do not consider that wages and the unions are responsible for inflation; it is not necessary to invoke the Marxist theory of value [1] to make several observations about this question. First of all, it is not correct to say

---

[1] From which, incidentally, no valid theory of inflation can be derived.

that an inflationary rise in prices can result from relative changes in primary incomes in the production sphere. Furthermore, one cannot deny that the theory — until recently in favour — of the inflationary gap, with its three elements, the budget deficit, the foreign surplus and the inflation of credit — is well founded. Thirdly, it can be recalled that total savings can be divided into enterprise savings, household savings and government savings, each combination of which requires an adequate and appropriate economic, financial and social policy. Finally, it is not difficult to detect, in certain theories currently in vogue, and under pressure from a resurgence of economic liberalism that is not confined to international trade, a traditional and deeply rooted predilection for a distribution of value added to the national income that is unfavourable to wage-earners, even at the price of some unemployment. Yet it does not follow that a wages policy is unnecessary — 'wages policy' and not 'incomes policy', since wages are determined more or less in advance whilst other forms of income cannot be so effectively controlled except under a regimen of strict 'administrative' planning.

It is within the framework, and by means, of the planning — but 'democratic' planning, decentralised and socially acceptable — of the national economy or even the whole European economy that the above objections may be overcome by enabling trade unions to play an active part in framing and implementing a wages policy.

Even within such a framework as this, however, the unions — or at least those in France — would fight to preserve their freedom to discuss wage questions, their internal democracy and their independence of the State. How can state control of wages be justified when all developments in planning techniques, both in the East and in the West, are towards a decentralisation of the decision-making processes and the maximum possible autonomy for individual economic institutions ? Conscious of the solidarity which unites all workers, what incentive would the trade union movement have in challenging a plan, a *programmation en valeur*, in the framing of which it had been closely associated, the social aspects of which it found satisfactory, to which it had given its approval and support and in the implementation of which it was also associated ? With these thoughts in mind I cannot but approve some of the suggestions made in *Prices, Wages and Incomes Policies in Industrialised Market Economies*.[1]

[1] The more so since the most urgent claim of French workers is a demand for more security of earnings ; Turner and Zoeteweij, *op. cit.*, chapter ix.

But, in the situation I have portrayed, might not the difficulties stem from the other party, in the form of a failure to observe the social standards prescribed in the Plan ? In conclusion I would suggest therefore that it is advisable to develop immediately a system of contracts or quasi-contracts between the State and groups of firms, under which the various forms of public aid to these firms could be reorganised and made conditional upon the existence of collective agreements or wage settlements the terms of which, subject to differences in micro-productivity rates, would conform with the social and wages objectives prescribed in the Plan.

Chapter 8

EMPLOYERS' AND WORKERS' WAGE POLICIES AND THEIR EFFECT ON INFLATION

BY

HEINZ MARKMANN

IN view of the fact that wages and salaries at one and the same time represent the major factor cost and strongly influence the largest expenditure category, consumers' expenditure, and because of the permanent threat to the economy's stability from the steady rise in the price level, the extent to which the wage policies of employers' and workers' organisations contribute to inflationary tendencies is a matter of considerable importance. Since wage-fixing operations are the concern of various socio-economic groups, any discussion of the establishment of wage policies for price stability is coloured by the contrasting views of these various sectional interests. The purpose of this paper is to help dispose of sterile polemics about the wage policies that are conducive to stability. I shall attempt to do this by presenting, as soberly and objectively as possible, the relevant facts and observations about the methods used by the parties to wage-fixing operations in the Federal Republic of Germany. I believe that West German experience in this field can yield valuable pointers for wage policies in other market economies.

A number of sound enquiries — such as the two annual reports of the Federal Republic's Council of Economic Experts on Over-all Economic Development — have demonstrated that existing statistical methods cannot really determine whether the cause of inflation lies in cost-push or in demand-pull factors. It is often suggested that the supposed price-increasing effect of wage rises should be remedied by tying changes in wages to improvements in productivity; but this is impracticable in a market economy where wage agreements are negotiated freely. In the Federal Republic, at least, an objective discussion of this question is coloured by the various attitudes of the different groups, since the achievement of economic growth, full

88

employment and price stability are dependent on the flexibility of the economic and social structure.

In a market economy — characterised by the entrepreneur's freedom to determine prices — logic demands that wage-fixing too should not be bound by regulations. No policy that ties wages unilaterally to economic performance can be regarded as compatible with the system of a market economy. If the aim is to establish an incomes policy that will harmonise the distribution of the national product and the general goals of economic policy, it is widely agreed that the policy must be comprehensive and apply to all types of income, not just to wages.

The functional and personal distribution of income is determined essentially by the politically conceived regulations of parliaments and governments, so that market forces are not really relevant to the discussion. The insistent demands for an equitable distribution of the fruits of economic activity among the various socio-economic groups are more easily met if the process of income distribution is conducted at a point where it is readily visible ; this point is the firm or its various establishments.

However carefully wage guidelines may be discussed and drafted, and even if the representatives of employers and workers participate in their formulation, the meticulous adjustment of earnings right down to wage fixing at the level of the undertaking, remains essential. Otherwise tensions and structural distortions would result, inevitably impeding growth — an outcome that can be more perilous to the economy than temporary and limited price increases.

Individual and isolated indices do not provide an adequate basis for economic or wage policies because each figure is affected by a variety of shortcomings in methods and techniques. The framework for a rational wage and incomes policy can only be constructed from the kind of comprehensive data that is provided by global economic accounting.

For human, social, economic and political reasons the achievement and maintenance of full employment is a central objective of government policy in all democratic countries. One might even say that any conflict between the requirements of price stability and of full employment will always be resolved in favour of the latter. Naturally enough, this basic factor, the pursuit of full employment, places the wage policies of employers and workers in a light that is quite different from that of a few decades ago. This is particularly true in the Federal Republic of Germany where the swing to full employment towards the middle of the 1950s has meant that traditional views about influencing the labour market by means of economic conflict have been replaced by the concepts of 'tending the labour market' and 'promoting labour-management collaboration'. Considerable importance is therefore attached to a clearer delineation of the labour market, to the promotion of manpower mobility and to vocational guidance and training. Participation by the State and its agencies in these endeavours is unchallenged by both the trade unions and the employers' organisations, for in no way does it impair their autonomy with regard to wage policies in the broadest meaning of the term.

These general introductory comments should not be allowed to obscure the fact that the negotiation and conclusion of collective agreements constitutes the only real means by which trade unions can exert a direct influence on a country's economic and social policy. In turn, economic and social policy has no small effect on wage policy.

It should be noted that even in centrally planned economies — in the Soviet system for example — certain price increases occur which are not ordained by the planning authorities. Similarly, wage patterns are geared to a considerable extent to factors that cause them to follow courses that are not necessarily parallel to the provisions of the global economic plan. The occurrence of wage drift indicates labour shortages in the East no less than in the West. Whatever the economic system, undertakings are compelled to adopt similar practices in order to cope with labour shortages.

TRADE UNION WAGE POLICY

In a democratic market economy, where the parties to wage negotiations enjoy the fullest possible autonomy, a trade union wage policy is based on the following general premises : the national product, the result of the joint efforts of all social and economic groups, should be fairly distributed ; the share of wages and salaries in the national income should be raised ; full employment should be achieved and maintained ; the living standards of workers should be improved by the provision of more leisure time, by making work less strenuous and by affording protection against avoidable risks ; a balanced wage structure should be created ; the earning capacity of undertakings should be maintained, but not to the point where marginal firms are feather-bedded ; and continued optimum economic growth, combined with the maximum stability of the price level, should be ensured, but without the prescription of individual prices. Workers and their trade unions are aware of the economic factors that are amenable to empirical observation at the actual workplace, namely : costs and prices, earnings and profits ; the relationship between capital and labour ; and the difference between nominal and real incomes. In accordance with their democratic structure and decision-making procedures, experience acquired at the level of the undertaking is incorporated in the wage strategy of trade union wage committees. This experience is examined in the light of the trade unions' principles, leading to the formulation of the wage policy guidelines that are to be adopted.

The central trade union authorities are in a position to supervise the wage-determination procedures by virtue of the fact that the wage committees, responsible for conducting negotiations with the employers, include central or regional trade union executives as well as the representatives of the work force immediately involved — elected members of joint works councils or shop stewards. It is the latter who subsequently are primarily responsible for negotiating the works agreements that prescribe the actual wage and piece rates, supplements, bonuses, etc.

The trade union structure has important implications for wage policy. The system of industrial union federations in the Federal Republic makes for centralised agreements, but, at the same time, leaves the representatives of the work force considerable latitude in the final determination of wage levels, and as a result tends to increase wage drift. Organisation by occupational group, such as is dominant among British and American trade unions, tends to restrict wage drift. However, it is an obstacle to the implementation of centralised wage guidelines and hinders the intervention of trade union federations, thereby favouring local and works organisations.

There are two fundamental questions which constantly recur in discussions of employers' and workers' wage strategy : do the wage policies of trade unions and employers consist purely of noting decisions that have already been dictated by market forces ; or do wage-policy decisions result in the conscious and deliberate change of economic and social situations ? Experience shows that, in varying degrees, a wage policy can have both these effects — effects which are in fact interdependent. The balance between them varies at any time in accordance with, first, the extent of the influence of external structural considerations — that is factors that are more or less independent of the particular wage policy that is chosen — and, secondly, the nature of the measures that flow from trade union policy and distribution policy.

Examples of the second group of factors can be found in the termination of the wage freeze that had existed in Germany between 1936 and 1948 as a result of the trade union wage policy of the early 1950s, in the application of the principle of equal remuneration for men and women and the gradual abolition of differentiation according to local categories in collective agreements.

For some years the German trade unions have been exploring new paths along which their wage policies might develop. They were compelled to do so because traditional methods of wage-fixing have proved wanting and inflexible in the face of the changes — many of them very far-reaching — occurring in the world of labour. These efforts of the German trade unions are, however, consistently frustrated by the employers' associations whose wage policy is largely restricted to repeating the need for wage increases to be geared to productivity improvements. This over-simplified approach implies that every wage rise will lead to a price increase if it is in excess of improvements in national productivity, defined as the change in output per employed person or per hour worked. The trade unions, with the support of leading economists, have always rejected this. However, a more complete review of the controversy would go beyond the terms of this paper.

The equally negative attitude of employers and their organisations to the concept of a 'plant-level wage policy' is more relevant in the present context. Plant-level wage policy was at the centre of discussions in the trade union federations some years ago when they were becoming increasingly disturbed about the development of autonomous wage policies at the plant level. Their misgivings related primarily to organisational questions and later gave rise to the view that it is impossible to achieve the optimum increase in the incomes of the workers by means of centralised wage negotiations. As a result an attempt was made to conclude general wage agreements by means of centralised bargains for the individual organisational sections of the trade unions — which largely coincide with the various economic or industrial sectors — while at the same time supplementing these general provisions by plant-level wage negotiations.

The aim was to ensure that wage levels, and changes in them, would correspond as closely as possible to the circumstances in the individual undertaking. This approach, first advocated by the powerful Metal Workers' Union, eventually fell foul of the employers' refusal to depart from their strategy of centralised wage negotiations for the largest possible sectors. Nevertheless, there are a number of sectors such as food, drink and tobacco, the textile and clothing industries and commerce, banking and insurance, in which plant-level wage bargaining is conducted. The employers also oppose the introduction of modern wage-fixing methods although — partly as a result of rapid changes in the methods and organisation of work — traditional wage-fixing techniques no longer meet the bill. Here again there are obvious exceptions ; new methods have been intro-duced in a large number of undertakings on the basis of plant-level agreements.

The deliberate aggravation of the political and psychological climate in which wage negotiations are conducted greatly hampers efforts to direct wage policies along new paths. Trade unions' wage claims are turned down with much display of the type of propaganda which creates the impression among the public that the whole well-being of the economy is at stake in the negotiations. Attitudes to the role of wage policy in economic development vary with the situation : in times of healthy development all the credit is claimed for government and management policies, whereas if conditions take a turn for the worse the responsibility is ascribed to autonomous associations and especially to the trade unions. It is then often sug-gested in public debate that imposing restrictions on the bargaining freedom of trade unions and employers' associations is the only effective means of regulating economic and social policy.

As a result of general political considerations, the attainment and maintenance of full employment is the declared aim of every national system of economic and social policy, and this now applies to supra-national systems also. Where there is a situation of lasting full employment, such as has now existed in the Federal Republic for more than ten years, the balance of power in the labour market naturally shifts in favour of the trade unions. Full employment frequently means that there exists excess demand, in other words that rising wage costs can more easily be passed on to the consumer. In such circumstances, therefore, the trade unions' wage policy can have particularly important repercussions. An examination of actual economic developments shows quite clearly that the German trade unions have recognised their responsibilities in this matter and have framed their policies accordingly. The trade unions have clearly understood the requirements and potential effects of wage-fixing operations in the various sectors covered by collective agreements, and have proved largely immune to the temptation to misuse their power. Their executives have managed to demonstrate the limits of trade union power to the officials and members, thereby protecting the economy from damage.

In a situation of full employment the interdependencies that exist between wages in the various sectors make a completely independent wage policy for, and adapted to the potential of, a particular undertaking largely illusory. Competition among employers on the labour market inevitably results in the payment of wage rates in excess of contractual levels so that the present labour force can be retained or new workers attracted. This helps to offset the restricting influence of the existence of marginal firms on the wage increases provided in regional collective agreements. German employers regard the 'market wage' as a function of, on the one hand, the economic situation and the state of the markets facing individual firms and branches, and on the other, of the general labour market situation, but it is the influence of the latter which normally predominates.

Germany is generally regarded as a country in which wage policies are largely centralised. A few figures may be quoted to show that this view is subject to important reservations. Even before formal legislation bearing on collective agreements was introduced there existed in the German Reich in 1907 more than 5,300 collective agreements covering some 110,000 undertakings. Even at that early date it was scarcely possible to speak of a centralised wage-bargaining structure. At the end of 1929, before the world economic crisis developed and before the advent of national socialism, barely 1 per cent. of all collective agreements (including those not concerned with wage contracts) concluded within the sphere of competence of the Socialist General German Trade Union Confederation, covering some 20 per cent. of the labour force, applied to the whole country. Whereas more than 40 per cent. of all collective agreements, covering 4 per cent. of the labour force, applied only to single firms and some 35 per cent. of all collective agreements, covering about 15 per cent. of the labour force, applied to individual localities. The main effect of wage policies, particularly in terms of workers covered, was felt at the district level. In the case of agreements relating only to wages and salaries, at the end of 1929 more than 4,200 were in force in the German Reich, applying to some 8 million employees in 430,000 undertakings. Of these wage agreements some 38 per cent. were with individual firms and some 62 per cent. with employers' associations.

As for the current situation, an incomplete compilation made by the collective agreement archive section of the Trade Union Institute of Economics lists 3,780 regional agreements ; 167 cover the whole of the country and 2,490 are concluded with individual firms. These figures include both wage and salary agreements and agreements dealing with general conditions of work.

This review of the structure of the system of collective agreements suggests that the system is very flexible and highly adaptable to economic conditions at various levels.

WAGE POLICY AT THE PLANT LEVEL AND WAGE DRIFT

As in many other countries where wages are fixed by autonomous associations the phenomenon of wage drift constitutes an important problem in the Federal Republic of Germany. Generally, contractual wage increases are fully reflected in changes in actual earnings — which, in the industrial sector at least, are usually higher than the contractual wage rates — and firms do not normally make use of the theoretical opportunity to offset contractual wage increases against actual wage levels. This may be explained by three factors. First, workers generally regard contractual wage increases as a *fait accompli*, and expect general wage agreements, whether or not they are negotiated centrally, to be put into effect. Secondly, attempts to offset contractual wage increases against actual wage levels are regarded as an assault on acquired social rights, particularly where wages in excess of the contractual level were offered to attract labour. Thirdly, management must allow for the reactions of workers' representatives even where they are not associated with the establishment of rates in excess of contractual levels. The workers' representative on the works council is regarded as the exponent of trade union wage policy in the undertaking and does all he can to retain this function. Therefore he tries to prevent any discrepancy arising between the wage pattern preferred by the trade union and actual rates paid in the firm in question.

Employers use these arguments to justify their implementation of an independent wage policy at the plant level, partly to counter criticisms from their own central organisations. German employers admit that wage rates above contractual levels are unavoidable when there is full employment, particularly where a wage agreement covers many heterogeneous firms so that the contractual wage rates merely represent the minimum rates binding the firms. It is virtually certain that the payment of wage rates above those negotiated in the contract will become increasingly common. The payment of these higher rates over a number of years is undoubtedly regarded by the trade unions as a reflection of inadequacies in the collective negotiations which they seek to remedy.

The employers' natural resistance to increases in contractual wage rates is reinforced by the consideration that they cannot be absorbed without any rise in actual earnings. Certainly, employers try to keep the wages they actually pay within the limits dictated by the labour market. But it is not easy to determine these limits, and some latitude should therefore be allowed to wage policy at the plant level. It is relatively rare for plant-level wages to rise out of all proportion to the basic contractual wages, and where this occurs it is mainly due to an acute shortage of manpower.

During the currency of a collective agreement, wage drift may occur when actual wage earnings rise without any corresponding increase in contractual wage rates — the latter having taken place when the agreement was signed. Increases in actual earnings stem largely from competition for manpower, although the contents of collective agreements are also a factor to the extent that they change the wage structure and give rise to wage increases in related branches or undertakings even before their contractual commitments expire.

In recent years payments in excess of contractual rates as a proportion of contractual wage rates have remained constant in many industries, but in absolute terms they have increased with the rise in contractual rates. Thus in the chemical industry where the relative value of additional earnings remained constant between 1960 and 1965, in absolute figures there was an increase of 22 Pfg. — from 37 to 59 Pfg.[1]

Several considerations need to be borne in mind when considering this trend. First, only in a minority of cases is there a percentage relationship between additional earnings and the contractual wage, though not only the absolute level of additional earnings but also their proportion to the contractual wage is the subject of plant level wage determination. Secondly the situation of the labour market has a marked influence on the margin. Thirdly, insistence on the payment of additional earnings increases with every year that they are paid.

Even though wage drift is very common, there are some important

---

[1] These figures are averages of wage groups and contract areas concerned with work other than that rated as simple.

sectors where contractual rates and effective wages are more or less identical. This is particularly true in the public services, where some two million persons are employed in the Federal Republic of Germany. The margin between actual earnings and contractual wage rates is also fairly slight among salaried employees in the tertiary sector, for many women workers in industries where female employees predominate, and for employees in structurally stagnating or declining industries.

Methods of wage payment also have a substantial influence on the margin between contractual and effective wage rates. The introduction of new piece rates yields earnings above those of time rates since they are calculated on the basis of a higher basic wage with the result that firms are then obliged to raise the time rates in order to prevent the differential between the two forms of wages from becoming excessive. Realistic piece rates are frequently unattainable with modern conditions of work, because new demands on the worker can no longer be adequately measured by traditional methods. Firms avoid the predicament which this causes by returning to a system that combines time rates with bonuses, particularly where production is highly mechanised or automated.

Changes in the number and definitions of wage groups also causes wage drift. In order to make levels of remuneration fairer, the former 3 to 5 contractual wage groups were subdivided in the postwar period in the Federal Republic into 8, 11 or as many as 30 new categories. Equal remuneration for men and women, which in all sectors has been achieved or formally established as a desirable objective, also contributes to this trend. The statistical measurement of general wage trends is complicated by the existence of such wage differentials, but at the same time rational systems of wage-fixing and the adjustment of wage changes to conditions both in the individual firm and in the economy as a whole is made much easier. Indeed, the greater the degree of differentiation within the wage structure, the less is the likelihood that wage changes will have inflationary effects — provided that the wage groups are clearly defined and workers are grouped accordingly. Quite apart from the schedules prescribed in collective agreements, wage groups are often further differentiated at the plant level in order to allow for the particular conditions, a factor that also tends to moderate cost inflation in the firm.

The size of the firm also influences wage levels; in general the larger the firm the higher the wage. There are certain notable exceptions,

however, such as highly specialised and efficient small-scale undertakings, where, for given occupations, incentive wages may be somewhat higher than earnings in larger undertakings. The clear
tendency towards industrial concentration and a rise in the average
size of firm is likely to lead to higher wage levels. But whilst large-
scale undertakings are naturally in a better position to offer incentives
in excess of contractual rates, labour shortages force small-scale
undertakings to raise their wages. Indeed this can lead to a narrowing
of wage differentials between large- and small-scale undertakings;
extensive investigations have shown that the wage differential between large- and small-scale undertakings in the West German metal
trades fell from 16 per cent. to roughly 8 per cent. between 1951 and
1962.

Statistical shortcomings make it extremely difficult to calculate
wage drift with any degree of accuracy in the Federal Republic of
Germany. In particular, the information available about contractual
wages is such that a measure of the contractual hourly wage cannot
be derived. Nevertheless, details of certain elements of the wage
are presented in the statistics of actual earnings that are contained in
firms' records. In some branches of industry — in steel and coal-
mining for instance — there are comprehensive systems of payments,
in addition to the minimum laid down in collective agreements, that
are normally provided for in works agreements negotiated by management and the works council.

Owing to the statistical shortcomings — which can hardly be
remedied given the present nature of the available information and
which can, at best, be empirically mitigated only by means of case
studies — it cannot be shown to what extent payments in excess of
contractual rates are provided in the form of regular wage elements.
The extent of this 'hard core' wage drift is therefore a subject of
controversy. Estimates of it fluctuate between one-third and one-
half of the total wage drift that can be identified by statistical means,
and between 10 and 15 per cent. of the total wage bill, a proportion
that remains constant irrespective of any economic fluctuation. This
hard core includes undertakings' margin for manœuvring, a margin
that must be retained in order to preserve the flexibility of the internal wage structure as well as the allocative function of wages.

There is a clear functional relationship between total wage drift
and economic fluctuations. Lagged effects — resulting from the
fact that the provisions of a collective agreement are valid for a
certain length of time during which the economic situation can change

— merely slow down or accelerate the particular conjunctual trend, and are of little consequence when the full course of an economic cycle is considered. In the past fifteen years economic cycles in Germany have followed the same basic pattern : each has been led by a rise in exports ; this was followed by an investment boom and a sharp rise in profits ; and at the peak of the cycle, wages have followed the rising trend, but in the first instance the rise has generally been limited to actual earnings.

Only during the downswing in the cycle has the effect of the wage increases been fully felt, so that by the end of the cycle consumers' expenditure, bolstered by the increase in mass incomes, has provided the spring-board for the next upswing. This cycle has generally taken about five years. Therefore it is desirable for any discussion of the possible inflationary effect of wage trends to focus on changes in wage, price and output levels over the course of a complete economic cycle, or even over a 15-year period, rather than on short term or annual changes in these variables. There can be no doubt that wage payments in excess of contractual rates react comparatively quickly and sharply to economic fluctuations. It would be useful to examine this functional relationship in greater detail on some occasion.[1]

Leaving aside the effects of fluctuations in the economy, it can be seen that the gap between contractual and effective wage rates is constantly expanding ; in the West German metal trades the margin lay between 17 and 25 per cent. in October 1962, compared with an average of 30 per cent. for 1965. This fact is of equal concern to the trade unions and the employers, even if for different reasons. For the trade unions it represents a slackening of control over wage trends ; for employers it signifies increasing cost-pressures in marginal undertakings and an obstacle to the chances of offsetting contractual wage increases against actual levels of remuneration.

In a market economy, any attempt to regulate wage-fixing accentuates wage drift. And where there is full employment and intersectoral differences in rates of growth, wage drift is inevitable, even when no attempt is made to regulate wages. This is why both employers and trade unions in the Federal Republic of Germany are opposed to any measures that impinge on their autonomy.

In their policies the German trade unions draw no distinction of principle between wages and salaries, although these two forms of

[1] The sharp decline in economic growth towards the end of 1966 has almost eliminated wage drift in the last few months.

remuneration behave differently with regard to wage drift. Wages of industrial production workers are generally more flexible owing to the opportunities for working overtime, for obtaining supplements in respect of more strenuous working conditions and for variations in contractual rates. It is true that incentive bonuses also exist for salaried employees in industry, but these are essentially tied to material output — that is, they depend on the performance of the production workers. Moreover, socio-psychological motives play a greater role in determining the attitude of salaried employees to their earnings. Some salaried employees who may have poor earning prospects feel this is compensated by a higher social status and prestige consumption, their proximity to management and their genuine or imagined promotion prospects.

It is occasionally debated within the trade union movement, and also by the public at large, whether contractual wages and salaries should not be linked to the cost-of-living index in such a manner that they would be automatically raised when prices increase. Hitherto the German trade unions have not been in favour of such experiments and there is no intention of including such index clauses in wage policies. The trade unions fear that such a provision may spark off price increases or give rise to an acceptance of constant price increases. They have also noted that, in certain countries where it is customary to tie wages to the cost-of-living index, there is a permanent danger that the price index might be manipulated for political reasons. Nevertheless, this attitude of the trade unions in no way excludes a demand that wage negotiations should make good losses in purchasing power already sustained by workers' incomes.

In recent years proposals concerned with workers' property ownership have been brought into discussions about wages and prices. The idea of setting aside a portion of income, on a long-term basis, for the purpose of property formation, is viewed as a possible stabilising factor. Such proposals have a dual aim : the redistribution of property with a view to greater social justice ; and the diversion of purchasing power in an attempt to curb rising prices. However, this latter, anti-inflationary, aim of promoting workers' savings can only be attained if the additional sums paid by firms into the saving fund are not regarded as a cost and reflected in price increases. This new element in wage policy, aimed at stimulating property formation by the workers, has now progressed beyond the experimental stage and theoretical discussion, but it cannot yet be determined to what extent it will affect price trends.

The trade unions in the Federal Republic of Germany have recently had to consider the problems posed by a comprehensive incomes policy. Other countries' experience of such policies is not calculated to convince the German trade unions of their value. With full employment and constant growth of the national product, market forces — particularly in the labour market — have regularly proved stronger than any device designed to influence wage trends in accordance with the over-all economic situation for any considerable period of time. The greater the flexibility that can be achieved in the implementation of wage policies, and the more effectively such policies can mould conditions in individual economic systems, the better the prospect of preventing wage trends from having inflationary effects. This raises the question of the extent to which trade union confederations can control wage-fixing operations at the level of the undertaking. As I have already pointed out, however, the trade union organisations in the Federal Republic of Germany certainly do not lack the means for supervising the wage negotiating activities of their officials and members, without the trade union representative in an individual firm being prevented from making appropriate use of the particular conditions obtaining there. Fundamental revision of methods of wage-fixing at the plant level will be of decisive importance in the future. A start has already been made, but the tasks facing the trade unions and the employers are so complex that rapid results cannot be expected.

Chapter 9

WAGE DRIFT AND INFLATION

BY

S. ESKILSSON

BY far the larger part of the continued decline in the value of money in Western Europe since the Second World War has been a consequence of an imbalance between supply and demand. Wage increases above the rate of growth of productivity have been part of this inflationary process. In recent years, however, the impact of wage increases on costs and on the international competitiveness of firms has been attracting special interest. Arguments for a government incomes policy have only rarely been based on estimates of the size of a cost-push effect. Rather, as a rule, many voices in the political debate seem to have been content to conclude that 'wage increases are too big' and there has been a search for means of restraining them. Even though this is a theoretically unsatisfactory approach to the matter, it can be justified on the grounds that idealistic attempts to distinguish and quantify the various causes of inflation cannot be realised, because of shortcomings in the statistical material. In this field we have progressed no further in Sweden than proving that fluctuations in the wage trend reflect rather closely the business cycle fluctuations and the labour market situation.

Statistical deficiences have frustrated attempts to show, for example, that in recent years wages have risen faster than they formerly did in a comparable labour-market situation. Nevertheless, in Sweden as in several other countries, the discussion of wage-determination procedures has become increasingly prominent when the problem of inflation is examined — and for very sound reasons.

Although it may be difficult to apportion in retrospect blame between demand-pull and cost-push causes, situations can arise in which the evolution of incomes in the economy has been preconditioned from the outset by the fact that an inflationary trend has been taken for granted and will be stimulated irrespective of the development of demand. We have such a situation at present in Sweden, where a three-year collective contract has been concluded for the period

1966–68 that provides for wage increases of more than 20 per cent. for these three years. Perhaps it was regarded as a foregone conclusion that during the first contractual year the economic situation would be characterised by continued price rises resulting from excess demand, but this can scarcely have applied to the two succeeding years.

For these two years the total rise in labour costs is forecast at about 14 per cent. or about twice the likely size of a favourable productivity trend. However, less than one-third of this 14 per cent. will be due to contractual cash increases of the traditional kind. The balance is attributable on the one hand to certain government measures with respect to social-security contributions and the reduction of working hours, and, on the other, to the anticipated wage drift.

To limit the rise in total labour costs to the level of the productivity trend would require actual reductions in contractual cash wages. It is hardly reasonable to expect such a result from negotiations between more or less evenly matched bargaining parties in a country where there is full employment ; the trade union movement must be able to justify its existence to its members and present a not wholly insignificant wage increase as a result of its endeavours. This means that if the total wage increase is to be kept within the limits of productivity growth then, firstly, we must try to prevent the authorities from mortgaging the available margin to an excessive degree, and, secondly, we must seek to curb the extent of wage drift.

To a large extent the phenomenon of wage drift is inherent in the system of free price determination by the market. But to take action against wage drift does not necessarily mean that the free evolution of wages as determined by the forces of the market will be suppressed. The extent of wage drift is conditioned by demand, but a given labour-market situation does not lead with the inevitability of a natural law to a wage drift of a certain definite size. The extent of wage drift also depends on institutional factors that can be influenced by employers and by the contracting parties. This can be expressed by saying that wage systems of various kinds differ in their tendency to produce wage drift or in the degree of demand elasticity associated with them.

This paper gives an account of various ways in which the scope for wage drift might be reduced — while retaining full employment — that have emerged from discussions of the subject in Sweden. Since the concept of wage drift varies between countries and since purely descriptive accounts of wage drift occur only infrequently in international literature, we begin with a brief review of wage drift in Sweden, based mainly on a study carried out by the Swedish Employers' Confederation.

THE DEFINITION AND SCOPE OF WAGE DRIFT IN SWEDEN

In Sweden, wage drift is taken to mean that proportion of the total annual growth in earnings that cannot be ascribed to contractual increases. It is measured by calculating the difference between the observed growth in earnings and the contractual increase during the period under review as estimated by a special mathematical procedure. Certain difficulties are associated with the estimation of the contractual increase, and the final result is subject to some degree of uncertainty. On various grounds — which it would take too long to elucidate in this paper — there is reason to believe that the contractual increases are systematically underestimated, which means that the wage drift set out in the table below is somewhat overestimated.

CHANGES IN HOURLY EARNINGS OF ADULT MALES IN MINING AND
MANUFACTURING, 1956–65
(Percentages)

	1956	1957	1958	1959	1960	1961	1962	1963	1964	1965*
Actual increase in hourly earnings	8·5	5·7	6·0	4·3	6·9	8·1	8·1	6·8	6·8	9·2
Contractual increase per calendar year	4·1	2·5	2·7	1·7	3·6	3·4	4·0	2·7	1·6	3·6
Wage drift	4·4	3·2	3·3	2·6	3·3	4·7	4·1	4·1	5·2	5·6

* Second quarter 1964 to second quarter 1965.

Wage drift, in the sense of rises in earnings during the period between successive contractual reviews, is found in all industrial countries with a prosperous business climate and full employment. In Sweden, however, it has come to occupy the centre of the stage in the debate on wage policy to a greater degree than in any other country. This is not only due to many years of thriving business and a tight labour market but also to the special institutional features of the Swedish labour market.

A point of decisive importance in this connection is that contractual increases in Sweden are calculated not on wage rates but on the basis of current earnings. In this way there is no automatic inclusion of the wage drift of the preceding period in the contractual increases such as is found in countries where the increase is primarily in the wage rates prescribed by the collective contracts. Wage-drift calculations of the Swedish type moreover presuppose a fairly high degree of centralisation and co-ordination of contract negotiations if they are to be feasible in practice. In a country which has a very large number of collective contracts, many of them covering only a single company and terminating at different times, any calculation of the average annual contractual increase over the whole industrial sphere is a matter of great difficulty.

For these reasons there are, so far as is known, no wage-drift calculations outside Scandinavia of the same kind as the Swedish. The term 'wage drift' as used in Great Britain, for example, usually refers to the difference in the changes of two indices, one relating to total earnings, the other to contractual wage rates. Wage drift computed in this fashion cannot be related directly to the Swedish definition, but the British technique generally yields a lower figure since the contractual increases will successively include the increases of the preceding period along with those provided for by contract.

THE DISTRIBUTION OF WAGE DRIFT

Wage drift is unevenly distributed among different groups of workers. Men have a higher wage drift than women, and those who work on piece rates have a higher wage drift than those paid by time rates. The impact of wage drift on the total earnings of different groups has tended to be countered by contractual provisions. That is, to a large extent there has been a refusal to accept changes in the wage differentials caused by wage drift, and when contracts have fallen due for renewal there have been special increases for groups having a wage-drift rate that is below the average. The result is that the wage trends for various groups have been rather uniform and changes in the wage structure have been relatively small.

However, if we look at wage drift in the context of any individual industry we find that in recent years there has been a tendency that gives food for thought. Since the middle of the 1950s there has been a higher than average wage drift for certain highly paid groups of workers. This is particularly true in the building industry, and contractual provisions have not been such as to prevent the over-all wage trend in the building industry from rising rather more quickly than in other trades. As a result, the gap between the average wage in industry as a whole and in the building industry, already considerable, has grown from 30 to 40 per cent. during the last ten years.

It is very tempting to regard this change in the wage structure as a result of domestic inflation and of the varying degree to which different trades are able to adjust to it. Export industries and those industries that are exposed to foreign competition on the domestic market cannot allow the prices of their products to be decided by domestic developments. Their pricing policy is dictated by world-market prices, which by and large have remained stable since the middle of the 1950s. Since total wage costs have risen by about 8 per cent. per annum, considerably more than the growth of productivity achieved during the same period, this has resulted in an unfavourable trend in profits for many companies in these sectors, particularly during the first half of the 1960s. In contrast, firms in industries facing only domestic competition have been able to relate their price changes to the general domestic inflation. It would be quite natural if this fundamental difference in the economic climate in which these two groups of firms operate were to find expression in the relative strength of their resistance to wage drift, industries exposed to foreign competition displaying less wage drift than those that are sheltered. In the table below, wage drift is shown separately for these two groups.

WAGE DRIFT 1960–65 IN EXPOSED AND SHELTERED INDUSTRIES
(Percentage increases)

	1960	1961	1962	1963	1964	1965	1960–65
Industry exposed to foreign competition	3·1	4·4	4·7	3·3	5·3	5·7	4·4
Industry sheltered from foreign competition	4·7	5·7	5·0	3·3	6·0	5·6	5·1
Of which the Building and Construction Industry	5·4	6·3	5·7	3·5	7·0	5·6	5·6

Note : Calculated from the Swedish Employers' Confederation's earnings statistics for the second quarter of each year.

The various contractual spheres have been allocated between the two groups according to the orientation of their main activity. It is obvious from this that there can be no sharp dividing line. The whole of the metalworking industry, for example, has been bracketed with the sector exposed to foreign competition, even though it would no doubt be possible to find numerous products made by this industry which are sold only on the home market and are free from foreign competition.

On the face of it, the table suggests that the hypothesis is correct ; in recent years the rate of wage drift in exposed industries has been less than in sheltered industries. But, in fact, within the latter group, trends in different sectors have shown little uniformity. Above all, wage drift in the building industry and allied trades has been very high, and if this industry is left out of account, the sheltered sector has actually experienced a wage trend that is more restrained than in the export industries.

The probable explanation of this is that most sheltered industries use, to a relatively large extent, fixed wage forms : time rates and piece rates with a time-rate base. This is true, for example, of the brewery trade, the foodstuffs sector and road haulage. The contrasting wage trend in the building industry can be attributed to the particular working conditions that characterise this industry. But even if the major explanation is to be found in the market situation and production characteristics of this industry as they are shaped by government controls, shortcomings in its wage system have also contributed to the size of the wage drift.

LINES OF ATTACK

Traditionally, wage determination and its influence on the over-all stability of the economy become a matter for discussion only when the collective contracts are due for renewal. An additional reason for this periodicity was that wage drift was regarded as a temporary boom phenomenon which could not be included in calculations for the coming contractual period. The negotiators therefore concentrated on reaching agreement about the contractual increases and the expected growth of productivity, leaving wage drift out of account. However, in the contract negotiations of recent years the employers have asserted that wage drift must be taken into account when determining the scope for contractual increases. In effect, it has been assumed that full employment will persist throughout the period of the contract under discussion and that wage drift would therefore continue at approximately the same rate as in earlier years. Not until the negotiations in 1966 can this approach be said to have been accepted by the trade union movement.

However, as shown by the data pertaining to the recently concluded three-year contract and cited earlier, this by no means signifies that the negotiators have succeeded in bringing the rise in total labour costs down to a reasonable level. Given the institutional framework of the Swedish labour market, and particularly the strong trade union movement, the total increases in wage costs can be limited to the rate of productivity growth only if the rate of wage drift is substantially reduced.

Since the extent of wage drift is influenced by the size of demand, it can of course be said that the natural solution lies in improving the over-all balance of the labour market, and indeed, if an anti-inflationary wage policy is to be successfully pursued it is necessary to achieve a better over-all economic balance than we had, for example, in Sweden during 1964–65. But it would be wrong to expect that wage drift could be altogether reduced by this means. Experiences in previous years show that there is considerable wage drift even when the labour market as a whole cannot be described as overheated. A further tightening would mean abandoning the full-employment policy, a step no government is willing to take.

Accordingly, the objective is to reduce the rate of wage drift while maintaining full employment. This can be effected by changing those institutional conditions that are dominated by the employers and by the contracting parties. In reality, of course, there will be fluctuations in the level of 'balanced full employment', so that in practice the objective will be to achieve a slower rate of wage drift in any given labour-market situation. That it is possible to make progress in this way is illustrated, among other things, by the variations in the size of wage drift that are encountered among branches that have different wage systems. One conclusion to be drawn from such variations is that it is possible to limit the scope of wage drift by adopting forms of payment that are less liable to promote it.

WAGE DRIFT ASSOCIATED WITH PIECE-RATES

Piece-rate systems are the main form of wage remuneration for Swedish industrial workers. Of the total number of hours worked in Swedish industry about two-thirds are paid at piece rates. The commonest forms are straight piece-rate systems which are used for about 45 per cent. of the total number of working hours. It is in the nature of piece rates that the resulting earnings trends will show variations, since their basis is that improved performance be rewarded by higher earnings. The problem is to isolate the influence on production of the worker's performance from other factors. In the last resort much wage drift can be traced to deficiencies in techniques for accomplishing this.

A certain degree of wage drift results when piece rates are recalculated. Deficiencies in the bases of these calculations, combined with the ever-present vigilance of the workers and their desire that the rates are not set too low, result in there being greater scope for exceeding the norm than was intended, but even where piece rates remain unchanged there is usually a considerable degree of wage drift, particularly over longer periods of time. This is associated with the fact that the nature and content of a given job seldom remain unchanged for long. There are continual improvements in methods, and unless they are accompanied by changes in the piece rates, either wage drift or restrictions in performance result. In fact studies have revealed that the latter two factors are commonly found together and successive reductions in performance occur in order that wage drift can be limited to a reasonable rate. From the economic point of view, idle production capacity resulting from performance restrictions can be just as significant a problem as the more easily detectable wage drift.

Changes in method that are unaccompanied by changes in piece rates are sometimes of a wholly tangible character, such as those associated with the alteration of the speed of a machine or the replacement of certain tools or materials by others. More difficult to identify are the improvements in methods that occur without any obvious outward signs. Such improvements may be brought about by, for example, minor alterations to the workplace that render the movements of the worker more economical, and the better administration of tool and material issues.

The technical difficulties of control sketched out here will result in an over-all wage drift only in the setting of a 'seller's labour market'. If unemployment were endemic, enabling the employer to formulate his wage policy without regard to the risk of losing personnel or finding himself faced by recruiting difficulties, the situation would be quite different. In these circumstances, irrespective of the technique being employed, he can always set the piece rate so that it results in a number of negative wage drift elements large enough to ensure that the effect of positive wage drift is offset. If the management of a company is to control the rate of increase of piece-rate earnings, a well-developed and sophisticated piece-rate measurement technique is essential. In the majority of cases this technique must be based on work studies and should comprise a careful method description of the work, a continuous check on its development and an efficient reporting system within the firm. At present these prerequisites are found only rarely in Swedish industry. True, work studies are used on a fairly large scale, with some 70 per cent. of piece rates now paid being based on work studies — but in many cases there is reason to believe that they are not sufficiently accurate. Above all, however, a continuous review of the methods, a condition which is so essential for effective wage control, is found only in exceptional cases.

In the foreseeable future, piece rates will remain a predominant wage form in Swedish industry and therefore it will be a primary objective of wage policy (for the employers) to promote the spread of efficient work study techniques. This will bring piece-rate wages, as well as time-rate wages, more fully under the control of management than they are at present. Greater efficiency in the application of work studies can be brought about by the increased use of standard data and predetermined time systems. In Sweden methods of time measurement are employed on a relatively large scale by the bigger firms. Yet over all, only about 2 per cent. of the total number of piece-work hours are rated by this means. One factor preventing a large expansion in the use of methods of time measurement for piece-rate setting is that the great accuracy of the technique is very costly. By making the elements in the system larger, the costs can be greatly reduced without an undue sacrifice of accuracy; large-scale investigations of such systems are at present in progress in Sweden.

Alongside their efforts to improve piece-rate techniques the labour-market organisations might well seek to promote the adoption of wage forms that are less prone to wage drift, that is, mixed incentive systems and time rates. For employers the avoidance of wage drift would be one of the main motives for this; for workers these forms of payment carry greater security in terms of earnings growth and better prospects of pursuing a wage policy based on the principle of 'solidarity'.

The main reason why it is not possible to win general support for a rapid switch to incentive systems with a large fixed proportion and to time rates is the fear that the incentive effect of the pay system will be lost. Of course, such a failing would have a great deal of significance for the inflationary process, since a production increase that fails to materialise will have basically the same negative effects as an excessive wage rise. On this question of the incentive effect of wages, and particularly of piece rates, practical men often hold firm but conflicting opinions, which can be neither confirmed nor refuted by scientific argument. There are good reasons — though there is no space to enlarge upon them here — for believing that the widespread adoption of piece work in Swedish industry has played a role in the rapid growth of productivity in recent decades, but that its impact is now declining in importance. This decline is associated especially with the influence of technical progress on the nature of workers' jobs, though another factor may be the greater insight being obtained into the complex factors that govern the behaviour of human beings in their work lives. Nevertheless, the opinion that still predominates, even in more sophisticated circles, is that wages can and should be utilised as a means of stimulating the workers to greater effort.

I shall conclude this paper with an account of the major principles, relating to wage differentiation, that are now fairly widely accepted in Sweden. Wage differentiation should take account of three criteria, so that wages rise with : the difficulty of the job ; the performance of the worker ; and the capability of the worker.

The first criterion relates to the work, not to the worker. A systematic rating on this basis is usually referred to as 'job evaluation'. All the job-evaluation systems currently used in Sweden are 'point' systems. These systems are based on the principle that every kind of job requirement, such as theoretical knowledge or economic responsibility, is measured against an individual scale. The final evaluation is obtained by adding the individual results. The various systems (which as a rule are formulated to suit the particular needs of a given industry) take account of some ten to twenty different factors, which can be classified into the following groups ; skill requirements (acquired by training, for example) ; responsibility and mental effort requirements ; physical effort requirements ; and requirements associated with the place of work. There is an evaluation scale for each of the evaluation factors. Each scale is divided into a number of point stages known as evaluation grades. The magnitude of these stages need not be common to all factors, nor need it be the same within one and the same factor. There need not be an equal number of stages in each factor. In one of the Swedish systems there is a factor known as 'physical demand', divided into the following grades : light work ; light to medium-heavy work ; medium-heavy work ; heavy work ; and very heavy work. Each of these grades has a definition : for example, light work is defined as : work with light workpieces, tools or controls ; posture not fatiguing, muscle load not concentrated ; machine-tending job, writing job. In Sweden it is usual for both the construction of the systems and the classification to be carried out jointly by the employer and employee, the classification being based on the job descriptions.

The performance of the worker can be measured by various work-study techniques which will not be examined here. The capability of the worker can be measured by merit rating, and since this is a more controversial technique, systems that are in use in Sweden will be briefly described. Merit rating refers to the degree of capability of the individual worker. The rating is always made in relation to the requirements of the job and the extent to which the worker exceeds or falls below these requirements. This means that the rating is dependent on both the worker and the work.

The merit-rating systems used in Sweden are point systems. With such systems, different aspects of capability are measured on special scales and the final result is obtained by adding the component results together. The structure of a merit-rating system is thus very similar to a job-evaluation point system. The essential difference is that the systems are used to measure different things — the capability of the worker and the difficulty of the job. Every aspect of capability for which there is a special scale is called a rating factor and, as in the case of job evaluation, each is defined in words. One Swedish system uses the following factors : quality of work, quantity of work, care of tools and machinery, attendance, length of service, education.

A wage system based on the three types of differentiation referred to above may be constructed so that a worker's pay is composed of : a minimum hourly wage that is the same for all wage-earners ; a job-evaluated bonus ; a merit-rated bonus ; and a flexible component varying with production. As long as the flexible component is not unduly large, say, 25 per cent. of the total, a wage system constructed in this way will be relatively resistant to wage drift when productivity improvements occur. Moreover, it should have a good chance of being regarded as fair and of stimulating the individual

wage-earner to work harder. It goes without saying that job-evaluation and merit-rating systems can never claim to be scientifically
objective, since they rest essentially on subjective evaluations. But
this does not prevent them from serving as useful instruments for
establishing a more systematic form of wage-setting.

SUMMARY AND CONCLUDING REMARKS

The steady progress of inflation in post-war Europe has been
largely governed by demand. However, this does not rule out the
existence of cost-push influences, and institutional contrasts in wage-
setting systems yield different rates of cost increase in any given
labour-market situation. Therefore, while we cannot attribute a
specific portion of inflation to the cost factor, we can regard the wage
system as a parameter of action for limiting the inflationary effects of
full or overfull employment.

Demand and supply conditions in the labour market do not determine the wage for a worker or for a particular job with any precision.
As a result of the operation of other factors, the scale of pay can vary
within certain limits without jeopardising the equilibrium of the
market. Correspondingly, a given labour-market situation does not
mean that wages will increase at some predetermined rate ; the rate
of wage increase can vary within certain limits without harming the
market.

The unduly large wage increases that have occurred in Sweden
during recent years have been composed of three elements : contractual increases, government impositions and wage drift — with
the latter accounting for more than half the total increase. All
three elements must be attacked if we are to achieve the desired result, a wage increase within the limits of the growth in
productivity.

Wage drift can be reduced by switching to a wage system which
will react more slowly to the pressure of demand. As far as Sweden
is concerned this means changing from straight piece rates to mixed
incentive rates and time rates. The technique of piece-rating can be
improved by the wider use of work study. Job-evaluation and merit-
rating schemes are instruments which can be used to create pay
systems that are less likely to promote wage drift, yet which exert a
stimulating effect in the sense of encouraging greater effort on the
job. Examples have been given of how these techniques can be

formulated and put into practice. Some other possible approaches have not been touched upon.

Finally, it should be emphasised that an improved wage policy, including measures for combating an unduly large degree of wage drift, can usefully supplement a restraining economic policy; but it can never replace it.

Chapter 10

WAGE RELATIVITIES

BY

AUBREY JONES

A POLICY that has as its objective the achievement of stable prices by equating on a national scale increases in incomes to increases in productivity, seeks to modify the operation of factors which have previously determined the price of labour. Against a background of full employment the exertion of trade union power through collective bargaining normally raises wages faster than productivity, and market forces too act as an autonomous factor helping to raise the average price of labour faster than productivity, thus raising unit costs and prices. An incomes policy has to devise methods of holding these factors sufficiently in check for the movement of incomes to be kept in line with productivity growth.

But there is a third factor governing pay increases which has to be brought under control if the objectives of the incomes policy are to be achieved and that is 'comparability'; it is this factor which is closely connected with wage relativities. It takes the form, at its most general, of the argument that 'if they have had a pay increase of x%, we must have a pay increase of x%'. On the trade union side comparability is regarded as ensuring fair treatment, so that everyone keeps up with everyone else, and on the employers' side it is acceptable because it merely extends to others what some have already obtained and does not mark a new departure. Thus the use of comparability appears to compound considerations of fairness and convenience. In fact its effect on the movement of wages and salaries is twofold. First, it causes instability because it has no end; it generates an upward spiral of incomes because the process of granting increases comparable to those which have already been conceded is circular. Secondly, and central to the subject of this paper, it preserves existing wage relativities by moving all wage levels by the same proportion.

The objectives of incomes policy in Britain have required a weakening of the force of comparability and a deliberate change of wage structures. The statement of the government's 'Prices and Incomes Policy' said that 'comparisons with levels or trends of incomes in other employments' are one of the factors to which 'less weight than hitherto will have to be given'. The factor to which more weight must be given is the national rate of productivity growth.

While the policy was intended to reduce the force of crude comparability, it admitted the use of refined comparisons in exceptional cases. The statement said that 'where there is widespread recognition that the pay of a certain group of workers has fallen seriously out of line with the level of remuneration for similar work and needs in the national interest to be improved' there is ground for an exceptional pay increase. The policy therefore required that generalised comparisons should decline in significance and that comparability should only be used in exceptional cases. The exceptions would differ from the general in that the comparisons should be between similar jobs, that pay should have fallen markedly behind, that concern about this falling behind should go well beyond the industry affected, and that a case for restoring comparability could be made in the public interest.

The National Board for Prices and Incomes has found in its investigations evidence of the hold which the convention of comparability has over both sides of industry. It is used as a basis for wage settlement both within and between industries; workers in railway workshops have traditionally received wage increases of the same size as the railway operating staff, and London bus workers have in recent years had increases linked in part to the pay of certain grades of the same railway workers. While in all industries comparability plays a part, in some it has become a settled formula which is either the sole determinant or the dominant factor in the movement of wages and salaries. This was so in the industrial civil service whose basic rates were linked with the average increase in the basic rates of pay of certain categories of workers calculated at six-monthly intervals.

The main case against crude comparability, especially in some automatic form, is that it has extended settlements which exceeded the incomes norm laid down in the policy and therefore has fed the fires of inflation. But the contribution of comparability to the solidification of wage relativities and consequently to the erection of wage structures which act as barriers to change has also been emphasised by the Board. If wage rates in one industry move as they have done in others there is no prospect of the lowest paid ever ceasing to be the lowest paid or of the differentials in absolute terms between themselves and any other group being narrowed. Moreover, the re-ordering of wage relativities in response to changes in the occupational structure of the labour force or in order to obtain more flexible allocation of labour between jobs is inhibited.

Indeed, in recommending the abolition of formulae providing automatic comparability the Board has directed attention towards the need for the construction of wage structures which are tailored to the needs of each industry. Pursuing the example of the industrial civil service, the Board recommended the grouping of establishments on the basis of homogeneity of processes and products and the negotiation of a wage structure for each group. A general weakening of the hold of comparability on both sides in industry means the strengthening of pressures for the reform of wage structures according to agreed principles.

Comparability, subject to the qualifications which limit its use to exceptional cases, has figured only twice in the Board's recommendations, the pay of railway clerks and industrial civil servants being found to have fallen 'seriously out of line' with that in comparable employment. Its place in the policy recognises that feelings of unfairness stemming from comparisons of pay increases are not the only component of a sense of inequity and that such feelings need to be strong, widely shared and firmly based in refined comparisons before they can be accepted as a justification for a wage increase.

The use of comparability has specially serious implications in relation to productivity agreements. Such agreements provide deliberately large increases in pay in return for changes in working practices making possible large increases in productivity. The productivity element of the government's policy finds its expression in the acceptance of such agreements as exceptions from the incomes norm. The benefits to the community as a whole of the large productivity gains which can be made under such agreements warrant exceptional pay increases. The danger is that other workers in other industries or plants will use the argument of comparability to secure the exceptionally large wage increase without being expected, or perhaps without being able, to make equivalent changes in their working practices which unlock commensurately large productivity increases. Such extensions of the pay without an offsetting reduction in labour costs would damage the incomes policy by making incomes rise faster than productivity and would also reduce the attractiveness of productivity agreements for those who are willing to exchange alterations in working practices for increases in pay. It is necessary for the success of an incomes policy that such productivity agreements be insulated against the force of comparability.

Yet a productivity agreement can bring about changes in wage relativities both within an industry and between industries on such a scale that care has to be taken not to generate irresistible pressures for compensatory treatment from those who feel that their relative position has been worsened. In the electricity supply industry a productivity and status agreement affecting manual workers gave management greater freedom in the deployment of labour by making it possible to match working hours more closely to the needs of output and maintenance and in return workers received higher basic pay, with greater security of income, and a reduction in hours worked. As a consequence, white-collar workers in the industry felt that the differentials between them and the manual workers, both in pay and conditions, had been unfairly narrowed. The Board came to the conclusion that the wage relativities had been disturbed to such an extent that some compensatory payment was justified.

This example had two lessons. A productivity agreement in an enterprise which alters wage relativities cannot cover some workers and ignore others ; the changes in the pay structure need to be made as a result of drawing as large a proportion as possible of the labour force into the scope of the agreement. While initially all workers may be receiving more than their basic rates, workers on the same rates earn different sized supplements and some workers on lower rates than others achieve higher earnings.

Although this may not be typical of the whole of British industry, the Board has found that the most important element in the superstructure of earnings in the industries which it has examined has been overtime. In the baking industry where there is no payment by results, overtime and nightwork are the chief sources of earnings supplementary to the basic rate. Not only were average weekly earnings for the main group of workers £19 7s. 3d. for about 51 hours compared with a basic rate of £11 10s. for 40 hours but one-sixth earned more than £22 and one-fifth less than £16. The unevenness of overtime working strongly affects the earnings structure.

The extent and size of supplements to the basic rates is determined at plant level and so the departure of the earnings structure from that of rates is brought about by plant bargaining. The structure of rates provided by industry-wide agreements has been extensively modified by plant bargaining which distributes supplements among employees according to different criteria from those which govern rates. As plant bargaining has grown away from the industry-wide agreements and has come to display inconsistencies and failures of control the structure of earnings has become more disorderly. Imperfect control over the wages structure has meant imperfect control over wage costs and hence over prices.

The Board has had two objectives in this matter. First, it has made recommendations designed to reduce the dependence on overtime earnings and so reduce the gap between rates and earnings. In the baking industry, for example, the Board recommended, on the basis of the enquiries it carried out, that hours of work could be reduced without loss of output if certain working practices were changed making possible stable unit costs, maintained earnings and shorter hours. Secondly, it has sought to provide greater security of income by reducing the proportion of earnings which is dependent on local supplements. In baking it recommended a guaranteed minimum earnings level determined by a realistic length of the working week — 46 hours — instead of by the standard working week of 40 hours. These proposals in baking would reduce the gap between rates and earnings from almost 100 per cent. to about 30 per cent. of the rates.

Both productivity agreements and the closing of the gap between rates and earnings involve reforms of pay structures. A third pressure for reform comes from enquiries into the efficiency of existing structures. The reference of pay questions to the Board has led in two cases to the discovery of faults in pay structures and recommendations for improvements. The Board found that the banks were operating a single salary scale for the vast majority of their non-managerial staff although its employees fell very clearly into two main groups, those who performed relatively routine work and those who progressed through more responsible positions. An unwillingness to admit that these were two quite distinct groups of employees had held up the establishment of separate pay structures for each group. In the industrial civil service the pay structure had been refined to a point where there were hundreds of categories and separate rates of pay for semi-skilled workers, and in this case a simplified structure was required.

The improvement of wage structures has to be preceded by knowledge of what those structures are. The Board's enquiries have had to include surveys of earnings and hours of work because so little was known about the wages being paid in the industries referred to it. In a number of cases management did not possess the facts on which to base a critical examination of wage relativities until the Board gathered them. If, in the interests of the incomes policy, there is to be greater concern about wage relativities, it will have to begin with a more systematic collection of earnings data.

Chapter 11

INTERNATIONAL TRADE UNION CO-OPERATION AND NATIONAL STABILISATION POLICIES

BY

NAT WEINBERG [1]

PRACTICAL international trade union co-operation in collective bargaining matters is still so new as to make the subject a highly speculative one. It is useful, however, to describe four types of international trade union action which either have been undertaken already or which seem likely to be taken in the future.

The first involves individual national unions moving separately towards a common goal. An illustration is the drive of the International Metalworkers' Federation (IMF) for a reduction of the workweek of members of affiliated unions, which started at a meeting in Konigstein, Western Germany, in 1955. All of the IMF affiliates in attendance pledged themselves to make a reduction of the workweek one of their top-priority demands in the metalworking industries in their respective countries, the ultimate goal being the 40-hour week. I believe that all of the IMF affiliates in Western Europe (except France) and in Canada have since made good their pledges, at least to some degree. The workweek has been reduced and, in certain cases, additional paid holidays or longer paid vacations have been obtained. The 40-hour week is already — or soon will be — a reality for significant numbers of metalworkers in several of the countries.[2] It can be argued that the workweek would in any case have been reduced, but there is reason to believe that the IMF action significantly accelerated the process. Once the pledges had been

---

[1] The views expressed in this paper are the writer's and not necessarily those of the UAW.

[2] In the United States, where the 40-hour week was already in effect, working time has been reduced in the automobile industry, for example, by lengthened paid vacations and additional paid holidays (the gains in these areas in 1964 alone being equivalent to a reduction of the workweek by more than one hour) together with greatly increased paid rest time for workers on the assembly line and similar jobs, and substantial financial encouragement in voluntary early retirement.

given at Konigstein, the affiliates were asked to report on their progress at each subsequent IMF meeting. There was thus created the equivalent of the OECD's 'country examinations' which, experience indicates, do affect national policies and actions. In addition, each IMF affiliate was able to proceed with greater confidence because it had reason to believe that parallel moves in other countries would prevent it from being at a disadvantage in international competition.

A second type of situation is that which involves the joint negotiation, by several national unions, of a single agreement the terms of which are applicable across national boundaries. The European Economic Community (EEC) seems likely to generate such agreements. Inevitably, as trade barriers are eliminated and as the free movement of labour across country boundaries is permitted and encouraged, the horizons of national unions must be widened. There become relevant, as standards of comparison, not only wages and working conditions within each separate country, but those in all other countries within the Common Market as well. The Rome Treaty provided for the upward harmonisation of social benefits within EEC. It is only a short step from there to the upward harmonisation of wages and to collective bargaining agreements that cut across national boundaries.

The shape of things to come is indicated in a recent publication of the European Coal and Steel Community. It calls upon employers and workers in the Community to aim at 'the conclusion of European collective conventions' and continues: 'these conventions, which would constitute a major step towards the harmonisation of conditions, could not take a rigid form. They would be framework or reference agreements — model conventions allowing for all the possible variations justified by particular situations in any of the member countries. The minimum terms of employment set out in the European conventions would be revised periodically to take account of economic developments.'[1] I think it is quite likely that such conventions will be negotiated. If they are, they will in time tend to become more comprehensive, embracing an increasingly wider range of subject matter, and will tend to allow for a decreasing degree of variation from country to country.

A third type of situation involves a single national union, representing workers in two or more countries, negotiating either a single agreement, or practically identical agreements, for workers in the various countries. Such a situation arises out of the recently nego-

[1] ECSC, *Social Policy in the ECSC.*

tiated agreement between the United States and Canadian Governments providing for limited free trade in motor vehicles and motor vehicle parts.[1] The workers on both sides of the border belong to the same union, the UAW. They work for the same companies and they use the same technology to produce the same products for the same North American market. Yet the Canadian auto workers are paid up to 40 cents per hour less than those in the United States, and, despite this wage differential, cars sold in Canada, whether made in the United States or Canadian plants, are priced higher (even after allowance for differences in taxes) than the identical cars sold in the United States.

This is an intolerable situation from a union standpoint, and the UAW is determined to wipe out this wage differential. It is true that the general levels of Canadian wages and living standards are below those in the United States, but the common interests of auto workers on both sides of the border make imperative the elimination of the wage differentials within the auto corporations. Canadian auto workers want the same living standards as United States auto workers and they know their productivity makes that possible; United States auto workers see the elimination of the wage differential as essential for preventing a loss of their jobs to Canada. Of course, the elimination of the international wage differential would change inter-industry wage differentials in Canada and this may create some problems for Canadian authorities concerned with any stabilisation policy. But there is no practical alternative for a union confronted with the situation described.

The fourth type of situation arises out of the growth and spread of international corporations. In this situation separate national unions actively co-operate and co-ordinate their efforts, aiming towards common goals within individual international corporations wherever the latter may operate.

The international corporation is already an important phenomenon in the auto industry and in a number of others. The Chairman of the Board of the General Motors Corporation has stated: '. . . I have wanted to call attention to a development which in some ways is creating a new kind of capitalism. It is the emergence of the modern industrial corporation as an institution that is transcending national boundaries. These great concerns of the Free World both

---

[1] So long as the corporations comply with Canadian requirements as to the volume of production in Canada, they can ship parts and components across the border in either direction without payment of tariffs. Free trade applies to automobile companies, not to consumers.

here and abroad, are no longer adequately described as Dutch, German, French, Italian, British or U.S. corporations.' The President of the Ford Motor Company predicted the future of the world automobile economy when he said : 'Maybe one day we can have a giant body-making plant in Japan and a giant engine-making plant in Australia and maybe a carburettor plant somewhere else, and swap parts around our assembly plants throughout the world.' The President of the Chrysler Corporation described the dominating motive of the international corporation when he said : '. . . being a profit-making organisation, in competition with other profit-making organisations, a multi-national company has no other choice than to work for maximum efficiency by using the simplest and most economical means to get the desired results'. Henry Ford II, Chairman of the Board of Directors of the Ford Motor Company, made essentially the same point in more explicit language when he stated some years ago : 'American industry and European industry must, and I am certain will, increasingly source abroad and shop the world for the most economical values not only in finished products but, just as importantly, in parts, materials and accessories.' The railroads and shipping lanes of the world are becoming extensions of the automobile corporations' assembly lines.

In practice, the policy of world-wide 'sourcing' proclaimed by Mr. Ford is often a policy of buying human labour in the cheapest market and selling the product in the dearest. The trade union movement, however, as a matter of fundamental principle, rejects the notion that human labour is just another economic resource like raw materials or machinery to be bought as cheaply as possible and used as efficiently as possible. Through the IMF, therefore, the unions of the Free World which represent automobile workers have organised what are known as 'world-wide corporation councils' to co-ordinate the efforts of all IMF affiliates bargaining with each of the major international automobile corporations. Such corporation councils have been established, for example, for General Motors, for Ford, for Volkswagen-Mercedes, and for the Chrysler-Simca-Rootes complex.

One of the declared objectives of these councils, set out when several of them met in June 1966 in Detroit, is : 'upward harmonisation of wages and social benefits to the maximum extent permitted by the technological development of the industry in each country'. This objective will not be achieved overnight, but the world-wide corporation councils are already working toward it : a UAW Regional

Director has participated in government wage arbitration proceedings in Australia affecting General Motors workers in that country ; and UAW staff members have sat at the bargaining tables in at least two countries in Latin America to negotiate for workers employed by branch plants of United States auto corporations. Such kind of help will be furnished through the IMF in each case only where the national affiliate requests it. Each national affiliate will formulate its own demands, but a network of communications has been established that will enable each national affiliate to know what the particular international corporation with which it is concerned has granted to workers in other countries. That knowledge will undoubtedly influence the nature of the union's demands. Thus, horizons are being broadened, standards of comparison are cutting across national boundaries.

Such international trade union co-operation is an inevitable result of the rise of the international corporation. The labour relations policies of the international corporations are centrally controlled and co-ordinated throughout the world. The separate national unions bargaining with those corporations are compelled, in self-defence, to develop, on a voluntary basis, the highest possible degree of co-ordination among themselves.

As the efforts of the world-wide corporation councils progress, wage differentials between workers employed by the same corporation in different countries will be narrowed. The goal is not international uniformity of wage rates as such, but rather uniformity of unit labour costs, taking into account inter-country differences in technology and productivity. Trade unions believe that uniformity of unit labour costs is essential for preventing international corporations from playing off each national group of workers against all the others, particularly in situations of slack markets and excess capacity. The difficulties of international union co-ordination being as great as they are, it is unlikely that absolute uniformity of unit labour costs will ever be achieved on an international scale. Nevertheless, the pursuit of that goal will narrow international wage-rate differentials.

Another result will be the widening of wage differentials as between workers employed by the international corporations and other workers in the same country. The full range of consequences of such a widening of intra-country wage differentials is difficult to foresee. Undoubtedly, problems will be created for governmental authorities concerned with price stabilisation, as workers outside the international corporations strive to maintain or restore their relative wage position. However, there is a distinct possibility that the difficulties created for a stabilisation policy by this widening of wage differentials might be more than offset by important gains to the affected nations. For instance, higher wages paid to workers employed in branch plants of the international corporations might benefit the national balance of payments by reducing the profits that would otherwise be repatriated to the headquarters country of the international corporation. Other possible gains, social and political as well as economic, can readily be visualised ; but it is idle to speculate about them.

The point is that it is altogether too easy to jump to the conclusion that the effects of widening wage differentials within a country are entirely negative. Very little is actually known about the subject. Increasing trade union co-operation on an international scale makes the impact, both international and intra-national, of wage differentials a question that should be studied intensively.

Chapter 12

CLOSING STATEMENT

BY

PIERRE MASSÉ

THIS statement cannot, of course, be considered as a final pro-
nouncement on the subject matter of the Symposium. The Symposium has come to grips with a large problem. It is a problem
which, there can be no doubt, will remain to the fore for a decade
or perhaps even for a generation, and one which is rendered particularly difficult by the diversity of the situations in our respective
countries. The United States faces problems that hardly arise in
Western Europe ; and even between the countries of Western Europe
there are political, institutional and social differences that vary with
the parties in power, the trade union structure and the machinery
of economic policy. We have, in particular, had the privilege of
hearing Mr. Aubrey Jones refer to the work of the National Board for
Prices and Incomes and Prof. Giersch speak of the activities of the
Council of Economic Experts in the Federal Republic of Germany.
And I have myself described how, not long ago, we in France came
to establish a Costs and Incomes Study Centre, which is obviously
concerned with the subject matter of this Symposium. In such a
complex situation it would have been miraculous if, within three
days, conclusions had emerged ; the miracle, like the Trojan War,
did not take place.

I am not making a report on the Symposium. So much of interest
was said in such a short time that to do so would be impracticable.
I shall merely present my personal reflections on the discussions ;
what I say commits myself alone. However, I hope that our discussions will have helped to clarify the problem and to promote our
mutual understanding. That alone would be a great achievement in
a very short time, and would represent considerable productivity.

What I have just said is perhaps rather pessimistic. Let me now
strike a more optimistic note. Despite the differences, our countries
have a great deal in common. First, we are all from industrialised
market economies — even if, as in the case of France, that same economy is guided by a plan. Next, we all share certain aspirations which,

although they are now commonplace, bear repetition ; as much freedom of behaviour as the interdependence of modern affairs and a
concern for efficiency permit us to retain; full employment of workers
and — as far as possible — of equipment ; economic expansion, both
vigorous and lasting, which is protected from sudden depression ; a
high and rising standard of living ; a desire for social justice, with
priority for an improvement in the conditions of the less favoured
groups (a desire which exists, even if not always fully realised).

During the Symposium we have spoken a great deal of incomes
policies. Why, one may ask first of all, has that term only recently
been coined, although concrete expressions of the idea of an incomes
policy, such as income tax and social security systems and even — in
a sense — full employment, have in fact existed for a considerable
time in various countries, including, of course, France ?

A general answer has been provided by Prof. Sturmthal, namely :
'because in the nineteenth century manpower was abundant and in
the twentieth it has grown scarce'. I would be more precise and say
that we have deliberately made manpower scarce by adopting full
employment as one of the fundamental aims of our society. The
scarcity is not due, or is only to a minor extent due, to technological
progress, the spread of automation and large-scale capital investment
etc. ; in the main, it is intentional. So we must learn to live in comparatively new conditions of labour scarcity. As the author of one
of the papers has said, 'this fundamental demand for full employment
provides a new background for collective bargaining, one that was
unknown to the parties only a few decades ago'. Indeed, a kind of
mutation is occurring.

Some new approach must be discovered and it is by no means
abnormal that there should be a wide-ranging debate of the objectives
to be set, of the instruments to be used in reaching them, and of the
integration of incomes policies within a more broadly conceived
economic policy.

I shall start with the last point, which seems more simple than the
others. The views expressed have more or less favoured incomes
policies, but I think no one has argued that an incomes policy is a
panacea which alone would suffice. Its advocates regard it as a
complementary element in a wider economic policy, as a part of the
whole.

What, then, is an incomes policy? As a new concept, it is still
imperfectly defined. I shall accept, for the present, the definition
given by Mr. Saunders in his paper, namely 'any way of deliberately

controlling the development of (incomes) by government, or by organised labour or management, or by some form of joint control'. I have changed a word, replacing 'wages' by 'incomes' because everyone at the Symposium has recognised that an incomes policy would be neither fair nor rational, and would have no chance of success or even of acceptance, if it were nothing but a wage policy and failed to relate to every kind of income.

I know that Mr. Weinberg, in his vigorous statements, has expressed the view that prices should be handled first and that if price control could be effected, the rest would be less difficult. But it is my impression that this doctrine was not endorsed by the majority of participants, who regard an incomes policy rather as one which applies to incomes of all kinds.

On a related point, I think we were wise not to go far into the question of who is responsible for inflation. Not that this is an unimportant question ; but it is a difficult one, and I believe that it needs to be the subject of careful study by economists before it is discussed by a Symposium such as ours. It is a difficult question because, as Mr. Aubrey Jones has pointed out, inflation is an economic, social and institutional phenomenon, due in particular — he told us to the weakness of the consumer compared with other groups that wish to share in the fruits of higher productivity. Furthermore, it is perfectly possible that a reply to the question will not be the same in all countries and at all times. Lastly, I think enquiries into the responsibility for inflation are not a good way of establishing the atmosphere of co-operation which is desired.

As for our conceptions of what an incomes policy should be, I think that by simplifying somewhat one may distinguish three principal views which underlay the discussions. One is that an incomes policy would be useless save in exceptional circumstances ; that the machinery of the labour market operates efficiently enough for the trade unions, in their own interest, to regard it normally as adequate.

But this view presupposes a condition : if the operation of the labour market is to be compatible with a fair degree of stability, the trade unions must use, but not abuse, the relative strength conferred upon them by virtually full employment. That condition is fulfilled, Dr. Markmann told us, if you have a responsible trade union movement — which I regard as a highly important statement. Even so, would it not be better if the temptation to abuse a position of strength could be avoided ?

This temptation exists, in my view, if it is certain that in any circumstances full employment will be given priority over the other objectives of economic policy, and particularly over the competitiveness of industry and a satisfactory balance of payments. But I do not believe that this *is* certain. Experience seems to show that although, on the whole, full employment is a permanent objective of Western society, momentary lapses from it are sometimes accepted as a means of avoiding difficulties with foreign payments. So perhaps it would be more accurate to say that the combination of a responsible trade union movement, to use Dr. Markmann's expression, and a perfect strategy on the government's part would render a permanent incomes policy less necessary. But this is asking a great deal of both trade unions and governments ; also it would require the formulation of a criterion for distinguishing between use and abuse, and this would not, I think, be very easy.

The second view is to regard incomes policies as an instrument of a long-term policy, being implemented — for preference — by persuasion. Let me quote a passage from Dr. Crijns's paper,[1] introduced by Mr. Fehrs :

> There is no question of trying to abolish the independence of any part of this machinery, but there is a need to establish a procedure by which mutual persuasion can succeed, firstly, in relating total distributed income to the size of output, and secondly, in ensuring a more equitable distribution of income amongst all sections of the community, while achieving a relationship between consumption and investment that avoids any threat to the future development of the economy.

I think everyone will endorse this combination of objectives, which amounts to the ideal conception of an incomes policy. However, success by persuasion is conditional on acceptance of the ideal by the parties concerned ; such acceptance depends on the subjugation in the minds of these parties of the less elevated but more attractive immediate advantages. And that is probably a long process.

Mr. Le Brun had in mind a more systematic variant of this same concept when he proposed that an incomes policy should be part of an economic and social development plan, formulated by democratic process, having precise objectives, matched by a system of *programmation en valeurs* and implemented by a system of contracts or quasi-contracts. I can hardly quarrel with this solution because I tried, in connection with the French Fifth Plan, not so

---

[1] Chapter 5, p. 68.

much to put it into effect, of course, as to take an initial step towards it.

I now come to the third view, brilliantly advocated by Mr. Aubrey Jones. I do not think it is misrepresenting him to say that he regards an incomes policy above all as an instrument for long-term action. He told us, however, that inflationist behaviour is so deeply rooted in some countries that persuasion can only be effective if it is allowed to start working under the shelter of strong, long-term controls. I confess to being in two minds about this view. I do not like compulsion. As has often been said, it is a good example of the *provisoire qui dure*. Once present, it is hard to throw off ; and, if it lasts too long, it may cause violent reactions. On the other hand, I do agree that if controls are relaxed too soon, there is a risk of losing ground already won. The same problem arises in France, where we have had many years of inflation but — unfortunately in a sense — never the monetary disaster which cures people of that disease for a long time. Our Minister of Economic Affairs and Finance was entirely right when he said (I quote from memory) : 'to unfreeze prices is no problem — the difficulty lies in not having to freeze them again in six months' time'.

I would add one thing. Controls — compulsion — are necessarily clumsy instruments which lose their precision as time goes by. Price freezes are severely criticised because they prevent a necessary — or allegedly necessary — rise in certain prices. My own criticism is different. I would say that a price freeze soothes the conscience of every firm which maintains prices it could perfectly well reduce ; frozen prices hamper the adjustment of the economy to technical and economic progress.

It seems to me that we are entering a field in which experience must be the judge, and that we shall only find a satisfactory solution by cautious experiment and calculated risk. Nevertheless, I shall tell you what I think of the problem. In my opinion, an incomes policy consists of a set of fairly elaborate and specific measures aimed at exerting a long-term effect. The term 'incomes policy' should not be applied to the straight forward, comprehensive measures which may be required, in the short-term, to deal with some urgent situation. For instance, action of the classical sort to influence aggregate demand in order to restore the foreign payments balance does not properly belong to an incomes policy, although these two kinds of action can supplement each other, as several of the participants have said. There is no sharp dividing line between them ; but each should have its own particular field.

I spoke just now of *experience*, but I think I must also speak of *study* ; empiricism and reason should be made to interact and throw light upon each other. I now turn to a topic which requires further study.

Whichever view one may adopt from among those that I have just reviewed, the time will come when a decision has to be made about, in particular, what is reasonable and what is not. Dr. Markmann's responsible trade unionism must appreciate where the dividing line lies between use and abuse. The *ad hoc* committee charged with making proposals and the government which must be able to produce a decision, each eventually have to make up their minds. If possible, such decisions should be based on common criteria : if there are none, the dialogue which follows will not lead to a mutual understanding, for each group will refer to its own criteria. Thus the problem of defining such *evaluation criteria* is bound to arise. We have not really faced it in the Symposium, rightly so I think, because before these criteria can properly be discussed they require to be studied.

In my experience, an understanding of the problem as it exists at the macro-level is facilitated by national accounting. Let me give a small example. The Fifth Plan provides that *per capita* farm incomes shall increase more rapidly than wages and also more rapidly than the gross income of individual farmers. This relatively rapid progress seemed both desirable and possible : desirable because farm incomes stand at a low level ; possible because the common agricultural policy and the reduction in the numbers of farms yields greater productivity. It was decided to include this 'catch-up' element in the quantified projections of the Fifth Plan, though this was not easy. Indeed it was extremely difficult to reach agreement about which selective increases for large income groups are reasonable, but we did it, more or less successfully.

This example leads to a still more difficult problem, the question of the disparities within the farm income category. There are large prosperous undertakings and small marginal ones ; and the average figures in the Plan do not make sense for either group. If no action is taken to redistribute income within agriculture, the rich will become richer and the poorer will hardly become less poor. The marginal farms will disappear, and whilst this process may be considered desirable on purely economic grounds, a balance must be observed and perhaps compensation afforded if social inequalities are not to be increased. In Europe, a very important industry, the coal industry, is faced with a rather similar problem. The solution proposed by any economist with no compassion would simply be to reduce the industry's output fairly quickly. The social, the human attitude, cannot, of course, be the same.

So we see that it is impossible to be content with an evaluation of the position at the national or even at the industrial level. A true incomes policy should also take account of what is reasonable at the firm level. It is not economically desirable to restrict all enterprises to the same average norm. The leading firms should be able to pay wages, and to make profits, in excess of the average, in order to attract labour and capital. Moreover, they are usually in a position to do this because they make great improvements in their productivity. I know that this view has been challenged. I know that statistics can be quoted which suggest that above-average wages and profits do not attract resources. I have the greatest respect for statistics, but when they are contrary to my personal experience and observation some doubt arises in my mind and this is a question on which I prefer to suspend final judgment. Undertakings with low productivity, I may add, are in precisely the opposite situation. With the wages they can afford increasing at less than the average rate and their profits being squeezed they are eventually obliged to raise their prices.

Therefore the average norm should not be applied too strictly; but excessive inequality must also be avoided. This problem was raised by Mr. Mattei, who asked what standard should be taken for alignment, global productivity, or productivity in the undertaking ? One cannot decide which is most reasonable without a thorough background knowledge of how the profits of an undertaking are shared between workers, consumers, shareholders and resources for self-financing, etc.

Indeed whilst the productivity criterion is often advocated, those who refer to it do not always indicate precisely what they mean. Moreover, the basic concept of productivity is an ill-defined term, to which each speaker attaches a meaning that suits him best. So an intellectual and terminological job remains to be done. I have proposed the use of the term 'surplus' in this connection,[1] though this idea is only to a minor extent my own. Other concepts may be proposed and I would be prepared to accept the best. But I very much hope that the meaning of the various terms used in this field will be clarified. The French Costs and Incomes Study Centre intends to play its part in this field, in the coming months.

[1] See Chapter 1.

If we assume that such clarification has been obtained, we arrive at the following questions : What results would stem from an evaluation of conditions at the firm level ? How can we combine these results with the target figure which derives from an evaluation of circumstances at the macro-level ? What relative weights should be given to these two types of observations — one specific, one global — when the decisions are taken ?

The latter question is a fundamental one. Firstly, from a philosophical point of view (which I will mention only briefly since we drifted into philosophical questions more than once during the discussions), the distinction between specific and global characteristics suggests a clash between independence and solidarity, two extremely important notions, for there can be no social life without solidarity and no personal life without a minimum of independence. Moreover, in practice, this question is related to the highly controversial problem of central versus decentralised negotiations. He who regards the global situation as decisive will tend to stress negotiations at the centre ; and, in contrast, a preference for taking cognisance of more specific features implies a preference for decentralised negotiations. In Mr. Saunders' paper, there is a highly interesting analysis of the results obtained by one or the other method ; the results are perhaps semi-conclusive — three-quarters conclusive I might even call them in some cases. Of course such an analysis is difficult to carry out because the fact that the procedures were centralised or decentralised is not the only relevant consideration ; many other factors also play a part. It is because of this multiplicity of factors that I cannot regard this analysis, interesting as it is, as entirely conclusive. Even so, I believe that central negotiations yield a more homogeneous result.

If, as I believe, evaluations of circumstances at both levels have to be combined, with greater weight being attached to the global approach, we must consider how the different levels of decision can be linked ; or, as Prof. Sellier puts it, what is the optimum level of negotiation ?

The topic to which I have just referred is far from being the only one that requires study. There are others ; and it seems to me that any advances in the theory of growth would facilitate future discussions of these problems. For instance, Mr. Weinberg referred to the rising return to capital, whereas in the last century people spoke of the diminishing return. This is a fundamental change ; and I believe that the theory of growth — and more particularly certain questions connected with the yield from capital — needs further development. But that is not all. Our deliberations revealed another field which merits research, namely those sociological and even political problems posed by incomes policy which Prof. Sellier emphasised. A perfectly balanced incomes policy would be to the advantage of all economic and social groups and therefore no 'preconditions' should, in principle, be required for its acceptance. However, it would be quite unrealistic not to recognise that there is, at the outset, prejudice against incomes policies. In particular, incomes policies are sometimes regarded as a cover for what in effect are pure wage policies, and these in their turn are viewed as a cover for what might be called a system of wage policing. Since prejudice exists, it must be borne in mind, and so certain 'preconditions' may have to be met, at least during an initial period.

Prof. Pen, in his paper, makes a very complete analysis of the compensatory measures which have been viewed as possible counterparts for moderation in seeking wage increases. This paper contains a general review of what has been considered in various countries and a critical evaluation which I found extremely interesting. In addition to the compensatory measures listed there, reference was also made, in this connection, to public capital investment, i.e. the allocation of a larger part of the national income to public works. Because, in France anyway, no distinction is made between the rich and poor as regards the use of certain collective facilities (such as schools), all benefit equally from them. Of course, the roads — also a collective investment — are useful only to those who have cars, not to everybody ; but the motorised section of the population is large and ever growing. Indeed, I would say that in addition to the personal use made of such investments, they help to create a collective way of life and have an undeniable value in this sense.

A second compensatory measure which was mentioned in the discussion is a relative rise in low wage levels. I think we all subscribe to this principle. My own experience is that such a relative rise is easier to propose than to achieve, though that is no reason — on the contrary — for not trying to bring it about. Also, I believe that much can be done to encourage savings by wage-earners, which Mr. Le Brun has urged.

Two other problems in the same field were touched upon, and rather divergent opinions expressed about them ; the problems of the sliding scale and of long-term contracts. These are, of course, closely connected. I think that the use of sliding scales did not elicit much support. Yet without such an arrangement, long-term contracts would have to include revision or adjustment clauses because of possible rapid changes in the situation.

Several participants stressed the inadequacy of statistical information in their respective countries. I hasten to join that group, for during the seven years which I spent at the Planning Office I suffered from the same shortcoming. On several occasions I urged that the gaps should be filled, and progress is now being made. I remember also that nine years ago Prof. Kenneth Arrow, the distinguished American economist, in his inaugural address at Cleveland as president of the Econometric Society, stressed that investment in statistics yields a very high return. I would say that the return is diffuse and takes time, and that governments are therefore often disinclined to appreciate its value. I believe it is important that this question has been raised.

I have reviewed several differences in our approaches. Now let me stress two points of agreement, with a single dissentient voice in the case of one of them. First, there was agreement about the desirability of an active manpower policy, that is to say, vocational guidance and training schemes, a search for greater fluidity in the labour market and the encouragement of the workers' mobility. In this field an outstanding role has been attributed, almost unanimously, to the State — so often feared and criticised in other fields. No one objected to the State making the necessary efforts in this case. As Dr. Markmann says, public manpower policy 'is unchallenged by both the trade unions and the employers' organisations, for in no way does it impair their autonomy with regard to wage policies'. That is one point on which, I think, everyone agreed.

Secondly, an overwhelming majority, desirous of more contact between employers' and workers' organisations and a clarification by these organisations of certain problems, wished them to be asked to state clearly how they consider that wage movements and wage differentials should change in order to reflect the requirements of economic efficiency and social equity.

However, I would not overlook the important consideration that, in Prof. Pen's view, contact sometimes leads to conflict. There is an element of truth in this apparent paradox, but this does not prevent me from sharing the opinion of the large majority. Acknowledging the element of truth in Prof. Pen's reservation, I would reply that the necessary meetings must be carefully prepared and difficult questions approached, frankly, of course, but also prudently. I would add that it is not always wise to try to avoid conflicts at any cost, for sometimes they yield a positive result. I believe that the optimum approach lies between the two extremes, though I would myself place it nearer to the principle of consent than to conflict. A society with 20 per cent. of conflict and 80 of consent, or only 10 per cent. of conflict — like the salt in the porridge — and 90 of consent, might be the optimum. After all, much progress is achieved through conflict.

I now come to a problem about which I would not have liked to be the first to speak, for reasons which are easy to understand. But it has been raised by others and I do not see how I can avoid saying a few words about it. The opinions of several of the participants are influenced by whether or not there exists an overall economic plan — a delicate matter since some of our countries have implemented plans of this kind whilst others have not. But I think we should be failing in our duty — to evaluate experience in different countries — if we avoid this problem because it may divide us. I find it a particularly delicate matter to express my personal opinion about this question, but I shall do so all the same because I feel that enough time has elapsed since I was Planning Commissioner for me to speak quite freely. In any case, mine is a moderate opinion. You will see that I have expressed many moderate opinions in the course of these final remarks, but it is not my fault if extreme opinions are hardly ever entirely reasonable.

I think that the advocates of the two opposing views held about the value of economic planning should take a step towards each other's position. In my opinion, those who have no faith in planning should concede that, since a plan is the quantified expression of a medium-term policy, it may be a convenient way of rendering that policy more specific, of providing an occasion for discussing particular questions, and affording a means of eliminating the ambiguities which persist when policies are couched in literary terms. Thus a Plan makes the relevant discussions more precise and clear and those who do not generally support planning procedures might at least admit this. On the other hand, those who advocate planning also have something to concede. They must admit that a hard-and-fast programme cannot be traced out five years in advance, that the best-laid plans are subject to cancellation, and that all plans must therefore be endowed with a degree of flexibility. This was the approach that I tried to adopt when preparing the French Fifth Plan, which provides 'indicators' for giving preliminary warning of changes. Thus, if we agree to the need for more precision in medium-term policies and for a greater degree of flexibility in planning, perhaps the opposing views about the value of planning could be finally married, for there would then no longer be a great deal of difference between them. This opinion was not expressed during the course of the Symposium and, of course, it commits no one but myself.

A subject touched upon but, although it is very important, was not discussed in depth, is the international impact of wage and incomes policies. Some very interesting statements were made about this. If the main lesson of the great depression of the 1930s was the need for full employment, no doubt it will be said in the future that the primary economic development of the post-war years in Western Europe was the opening of economic frontiers and the recognition of a need for international competition. A wage or incomes policy must therefore take account of international considerations. It has been rightly pointed out that the principle of fixed rates of exchange is greatly modified in practice by a whole series of devices which are indispensable if excessive rigidity in exchange rates is not to have very serious social consequences for particular countries. But I think that this large question was merely broached by the Symposium and that a discussion of it could be fruitfully continued in the future.

I have reached the end of these final remarks. I have not been able to refer to all that I have heard, or even to all that I have noted, and I should certainly have welcomed an opportunity to re-read certain passages in the papers. But that is the duty of the *rapporteur* of the Symposium. Nevertheless I would ask the forgiveness of those who have not found any reflection in my statement of what they said. I can assure them that the memory of this Symposium which will remain in my mind is much more substantial than the above necessarily rapid and incomplete review of the proceedings.

I would like to thank the participants for attending the Symposium and the International Institute for Labour Studies — Mr. Cox and his staff — for organising it. My last word is an echo of what I said at the outset: may the close of this Symposium, and these final remarks, be not an end but a beginning.

Chapter 13

AN ANALYSIS OF THE PROCEEDINGS

BY

ANTHONY D. SMITH

I. THE LABOUR MARKET AND INFLATION

1. Introduction

IT is a corollary of the statement of the problem given in the Introduction that inflationary pressures in the labour market of the kind with which the Symposium is concerned can be broadly classified into two kinds : negotiated or arbitrated wage increases at a central level that are considered to be too high ; and the frustration of acceptable centrally negotiated wage increases by wage drift at lower levels of wage determination. Action to limit centrally negotiated wage increases to an adopted norm is largely a matter of implementing at that level a wage policy, the acceptance of which raises wider issues that are examined in the second part of this chapter. However, it has been suggested that regardless of whether a central wage policy is being pursued, means exist by which unions might be persuaded to make smaller wage claims. These measures, which relate to certain labour market practices, are examined in section 4 below.

But whether or not a policy for guiding centrally determined wage rates has been adopted, wage drift can constitute an inflationary element in the operation of the labour market. It was the primary task of the Symposium to examine certain aspects of this phenomenon and to determine how it might be treated in order to render the operation of the labour market less inflationary. An analysis of these deliberations is the subject of sections 2 and 3 below.

2. The Inflationary Mechanism of Wage Drift

The causes of wage drift have been briefly described in the Introduction. However, prior to reviewing the Symposium's deliberations on the vexed and difficult question of how wage drift might be moderated, it is useful to record the views expressed about the wage-drift mechanism.

The Labour Market and Inflation

There are various ways in which the several elements of wage-drift interact and differences in the sequence of collectively bargained increases and wage drift. Broadly two typical situations can be distinguished, both involving a fairly rigid wage structure in the short to medium term. In the first case such a rigid wage structure stems from a set of collectively bargained increases in wage rates that vary between industries and to which are added a set of wage-drift elements that also vary between industries but in such a way that they tend to offset the differential increases in bargained rates. Some observers believe that these inter-industry differences in wage drift result from the ubiquitous desire, on the part of workers, to maintain the wage structure by offsetting previously bargained differential increases in basic rates ; [1] in short, wage drift is linked with the widespread use of the comparability criterion. But others, as pointed out in the paper by Mr. Eskilsson,[2] believe that differential degrees of wage drift appear first and are eventually countered by differential increases in negotiated rates to yield the stable wage structure ; by this thesis, competitive bidding and systems of remuneration are the initial causes of wage drift.

In the second case, neither collectively bargained wage increases nor wage drift differ very much between industries, but the relationships between the various elements are rather more complex. Mr. Saunders outlined this hypothesis and we can do no better than to quote his remarks in full.

Inter-industry comparisons suggest that wage drift . . . does not greatly modify the wage structure, rather its effect is to stabilise inter-industry wage differentials over time. Such a result can be interpreted as reflecting the essentially tripartite nature of the wage determination mechanism. First, unions agree with employers on a certain set of wage increases. Secondly, particular employers in their search for labour of the desired quality offer additional remuneration. Thirdly, and this is the factor that seems to predominate in the end, the worker's desire for equal pay for equal work — and in practice this seems to be a preference for existing differentials — is given effect, either formally through the unions or shop stewards or by informal pressures on employers, and the pre-existing differentials restored by a further degree of

---

[1] Thus it has been claimed that, in the United Kingdom and Denmark at least, 'wage drift appears to have operated to maintain differentials in cases where rates movements would have implied a deterioration of position, i.e. there has been a tendency for payments above nationally negotiated rates to be highest in occupations where standard rates have lagged'. (OECD, *Wages and Labour Mobility*, Paris, 1965, p. 38.)   [2] Chapter 9, p. 105 ; *Discussion*, p. 228.

wage drift. Thus individual employers' attempts to attract labour by using wage drift to bid for labour is frustrated and the net effect is not a change in inter-industry wage differentials but an upward shift in the whole structure.[1]

In short, given roughly uniform increases in centrally negotiated rates, an inflationary process builds up from the interaction of *two* elements of wage drift — competitive bidding and the application of the comparability criterion.

In principle, it should be possible to determine which mechanism operates in each economy by examining the facts in each country. That this is more difficult to accomplish than to prescribe is largely due to the problem of separating earnings increases into contractual and drift elements, a matter touched upon at several points in the debate. But like some other difficulties involved in analysing the inflationary process — the demand-pull, cost-push controversy for example — an inability to disentangle with any precision the various causal relationships may not be too serious a handicap to the search for policy solutions. In the following two sections, we simply assume that both competitive bidding and the use of the comparability criterion are each in some measure responsible for inflationary pressures in the labour market, without attempting to apportion the blame.

It is important to qualify the foregoing, very simplified, references to the wage-drift mechanism in one respect. In addition to competitive bidding, piece-rate systems of payment are notorious for the way in which, between formal revisions of the rates, they cause earnings to rise.[2] The use of the comparability criterion means that wage drift from piece-rate systems is spread as much as that from competitive bidding, when hourly-paid workers seek a restitution of the pre-existing earnings differentials.

There was disagreement about the relative importance of competitive bidding and piece-rate systems as a source of wage drift. Both Mr. Eskilsson and Dr. Markmann recognised that the labour market situation and its reflection in competitive bidding is an important cause of wage drift, but they also attached much weight to the role of piece-rate systems. In contrast, Mr. Meidner was of the opinion that piece-rate systems as a cause of wage drift should receive relatively less emphasis and market forces more.[3] None the less, the participants were in general agreement with Mr. Eskilsson that,

[1] *Discussion*, p. 226.
[2] The manner in which this occurs is described by Mr. Eskilsson. (Chapter 9, pp. 108 *et seq.*)
[3] See Chapter 9, pp. 107 *et seq.* ; and *Discussion*, pp. 219, 220, 230 and 232.

regardless of the exact degree to which piece-rate systems are responsible for inflation, means by which they might be made less inflationary and the possibility of switching to 'mixed' payment systems, are worth further consideration.[1]

3. Action against Wage Drift

(a) *Competitive Bidding*. Many of the participants were of the opinion that, in the short to medium term at least, competitive bidding for labour supplies is neither very successful nor very necessary. Competitive bidding cannot be very successful in attracting labour to expanding units in the economy, when workers in other units very quickly claim and are granted comparable wage increases. That this is a probable result is suggested by the remarkable medium-term stability of inter-industry wage differentials, to which the OECD report, *Wages and Labour Mobility*, has drawn attention.[2] But even if it were the case that competitive wage-bidding is not frustrated by the use of the comparability criterion, it would probably still have limited success in attracting workers. For given the importance of non-pecuniary considerations in workers' choice of jobs, wage differentials would need to be excessively large in order to have the desired effect.[3]

In any case, it was agreed — and again largely on the basis of evidence presented in the oft-quoted *Wages and Labour Mobility* — that despite the absence of frequent and large changes in wage differentials, there is in fact a great deal of mobility in the labour market, much of it towards expanding firms and industries. Indeed, an interesting paradox was revealed : labour mobility can be triggered off as much — and perhaps even more — by a rigid wage structure as by a flexible one. More precisely, a rigid wage structure, by preventing marginal firms being 'featherbedded' by means of relatively low wages, helps to bankrupt them and release their workers for employment in the more dynamic units.[4]

---

[1] See Chapter 9, pp. 108 *et seq.*   [2] *Op. cit.*
[3] See the statements of Messrs. Rehn and Stein, *Discussion*, pp. 214, 223 and 224. It has been suggested that a worker requires an income increase of about 10–20 per cent. even when higher pay is the motive for changing jobs. (K. O. Faxén, 'Incomes Policies in Sweden : Problems and Developments', *The British Journal of Industrial Relations*, November 1964, p. 343.)
[4] See the statements of Prof. Sellier and Mr. Stein, *Discussion*, pp. 197 and 223. These two mechanisms could be qualitatively very different. Workers who are attracted to expanding units by higher wages are *ipso facto* likely to be much more mobile, and probably more efficient, than workers who are coerced into

It was generally agreed, however, that in the longer term, the emphasis placed, especially by Prof. Sturmthal and Mr. Mattei, on the necessity of changes in wage differentials that accord with the required redistribution of the labour force, is justified. Whether or not these differentials in fact emerge in the longer term depends on the durability of the comparability criterion and, if a wage policy is being implemented, on the nature of the provisions, if any, for differential wage increases. We return to these questions in the following section.

When dealing with economic problems that have long proved intractable, there is a natural tendency to seize upon novel policy suggestions for their solution. Yet even when allowance is made for this, the enthusiasm voiced at the Symposium for active manpower policies as a means of making the operation of the labour market less inflation-prone, is remarkable. Why are active manpower policies expected to be so effective in this respect and why do they command such widespread support ?

Prof. Sturmthal traced the inflationary operation of the labour market to the fact that whilst full employment is now an accepted and practicable goal in developed economies, the husbanding of labour resources which this requires has not been developed to the same pitch as, for instance, the administration of capital.[1] If this diagnosis is correct, then active manpower policies which improve the administration of labour by promoting and accelerating its structural redistribution in both the short and long run through measures that influence the patterns of demand for and supply of workers can do much to make the labour market less inflationary. In the present context the most relevant impact of active manpower policies is that, by channelling supplies of labour to those parts of the economy which need them, they remove the motive for competitive bidding. But their disinflationary impact does not cease there. By reducing structural unemployment they allow the general level of demand, and thereby inflation, to be kept lower than it would otherwise need to be for sustaining full employment. Furthermore, some active manpower policies — retraining programmes for example — are such that they make periods of transient unemployment more tolerable. This means that there need be less of a bias, when determining the government's future expenditure policy, to over-correct

such moves by redundancy and who, in the last resort, may not in fact be mobile at all.
[1] *Discussion*, p. 211.

for anticipated recessions, thereby avoiding cyclical periods of excess demand and consequent inflation.[1]

Unlike most of the measures discussed by the Symposium, active manpower policies have a universal appeal because they are seen not as crude intervention in and suppression of the labour market mechanism but as a means of making it function more smoothly and perfectly. Moreover both trade unions and employers favour active manpower policies as a means of improving the operation of the labour market, since they in no way interfere with their autonomy in wage determination.[2] That active manpower policies have probably nowhere been attempted, as yet, on a scale — and at the cost — where they could be expected to have a substantial effect, means that we must wait to see if all this enthusiasm is justified.

(b) *The Comparability Criterion.* To the extent that inflation in the labour market is due to the invocation by trade unions of the comparability criterion in wage negotiations, social factors are at its root. For in their attempts to maintain a given set of wage and salary differentials, the various groups of workers are motivated by a desire to preserve what they regard as their proper social position in the earnings scale. More simply, it is hard for any working man to accept that he should get a smaller wage increase than others. Mr. Aubrey Jones was of the opinion that inflation in the labour market stems mainly from this source.[3]

There is no doubt that the amount of inflation caused by the use of the comparability criterion is considerable. Moreover, the indications are that, if it is left unattended, inflationary pressures from this source will grow. In the first place, inflation generated by the comparability criterion has no end. Wage and salary rates for different groups are not determined simultaneously, so that there is a continuous process whereby some groups claim wage rises in order to restore previous differentials but which, in turn, are regarded by other groups as disturbances to the wage structure that need to be countered by further wage increases.[4] This wage-wage spiral is likely to receive further twists as a consequence of the tendency for militant unionism, and the power to claim compensatory salary increases, to move up the social scale.[5]

---

[1] For a description of the role of active manpower policies see the statement of Mr. Rehn, *Discussion*, pp. 213 to 218.   [2] See Chapter 8, p. 90.
[3] *Discussion*, p. 230.   [4] See Chapter 10, p. 115.
[5] Attention was drawn to claims for compensatory — and frequently overcompensatory — salary increases for workers at the upper end of the social scale, in Sweden and the Netherlands, by Mr. Meidner and Prof. Pen. (*Discussion*, pp. 192 and 233.) See also the statements of Mr. Aubrey Jones, *Discussion*, pp. 224 and 231.

Secondly, there is a natural tendency for unions when negotiating wage increases to make comparisons with the higher wage rises that have recently been granted. The inflationary impact of this feature, too, will tend to be progressively accentuated for Western Europe, as the more highly skilled occupational groups look increasingly to the higher salaries they can command in the United States.[1] Mr. Aubrey Jones' apprehensions about this extension of the comparability criterion across national frontiers are largely confirmed by Mr. Weinberg's paper on ' International Trade Union Co-operation and National Stabilisation Policies'.[2] Whilst the international co-ordination of collective bargaining by an international trade union organisation — sometimes as a defence against the activities of international corporations — brings certain benefits to low-wage countries,[3] it can also have tremendous inflationary repercussions on internal wage structures. The harmonisation of national wage levels in a regional grouping of countries at approximately the same stage of development, would have less dramatic implications. Wage levels in each member country would probably not in any case differ wildly, and a harmonisation of their wage policies could be conducted alongside the harmonisation of their whole economic and social structures. Moreover, the internal wage structure would probably be disturbed to a less extent than the general wage level. Yet even in this case, as Prof. Giersch pointed out, it is important to take some account of regional productivity differentials when harmonising wages.[4]

In theory, the simplest way of breaking the continuous wage-wage spiral caused by the invocation of the comparability criterion is to stipulate, simultaneously and for a common period, a uniform wage rise for all workers, taking account of drift due to such factors as piece earnings during the previous period. In effect most of the wage policies that have been attempted approximate to this, not on account of any intrinsic desirability of uniform wage increases, but because of the conceptual and practical difficulties encountered in the formulation of a more flexible policy. This approach, as Mr. Stein pointed out, is feasible in the short and medium term given the compatibility in such a period of a rigid wage structure and labour mobility, a consideration which goes far towards explaining why short-term wage policies are practicable.[5] Yet, as previously pointed out,[6] there must be certain changes in the wage structure that accord with

[1] *Discussion*, p. 231.   [2] Chapter 11.   [3] *Discussion*, p. 238.
[4] *Discussion*, p. 239.
[5] See the statement of Mr. Stein, *Discussion*, p. 224.
[6] See above, p. 143.

the required long-term reallocation of the labour force. To this requirement must be added those longer-term changes which the community desires as a matter of equity, a relative increase in the lowest earnings being the most common.

It seems essential, therefore, that a policy for breaking the wage-wage spiral, if it is to be accepted on a lasting basis, must make some provision for changes in the wage structure. Several of the participants, especially trade unionists, were quick to point out that the wage policies that had been tried, policies relating to a *centralised* bargaining procedure with a basic national norm as the principal criterion for wage rises, conspire against the development of necessary wage differentials.[1] If crude comparability is to be abandoned, what can be put in its place ? Reference was made in the Symposium to three possibilities : micro-productivity changes, job evaluation systems and the priorities and preferences of the trade union movement. These are listed in an order which is the reverse of the support they received.

It is, of course, generally recognised that the exclusive use of micro-productivity criteria — tying wage increases, percentage point for point, to productivity improvements in the firm or industry in question — is a nonsensical basis for a wage policy. Such a policy has no conceptual foundation and would be quite impracticable since wage differentials would very soon become unwarrantedly and unacceptably wide.[2] What is debatable, however, and received due attention in the Symposium, is whether micro-productivity criteria — especially at the industry level — can be used to indicate in which direction and to some extent by how much (though certainly not point for point) certain wage increases might be allowed to deviate from a national norm — say the rise in national productivity — to yield longer-term changes in the wage structure. This device has a certain appeal. There is usually a fairly strong positive correlation, especially within the manufacturing sector, between inter-industry differences in productivity increases and labour force changes, so that, to some degree, a wage structure which develops in line with micro-productivity changes roughly matches the requirements of the market. Moreover, it might be considered in a sense 'fair' that

[1] See the statements of Messrs. Markmann, Keinzl and Meidner, *Discussion*, pp. 197, 203 and 229.
[2] Mr. Weinberg thought that the use of micro-productivity criteria for determining wage increases is legitimate in cases where firms refuse to translate higher than average productivity improvements into lower prices (*Discussion*, p. 192). The use of micro-productivity criteria in price policies is referred to in the second part of this chapter.

factors in industries where productivity has risen most should enjoy above-average increases in their remuneration.

In fact current opinion — and the Symposium was not exceptional in this respect — does not favour this device. Its unpopularity can largely be traced to experience in the Netherlands, where the use of micro-productivity differentials for this purpose has been cited as a completely unworkable feature of the wage policy.[1] Certainly it is a method that has serious disadvantages. Primary among them is the difficulty of establishing how much weight should be attached to an industry's productivity change relative to the national average. Undoubtedly most weight should be given to the national norm [2] and it is probably important that, unlike in the Dutch system, the prescribed relationship should be simple if approximate. Secondly, productivity measurement at the industry level poses conceptual and statistical problems of considerable complexity.[3] Thirdly, as stated, the pattern of productivity changes only approximates the pattern of structural changes in the distribution of labour. The relationship is by no means exact. Fourthly, to the extent that a rapid productivity improvement in a certain industry is the result of scientific or technological discoveries that happen to affect its processes, it can be considered inequitable that the factors employed in that industry should reap most of the benefits.

Many of the participants considered that basing a wage structure on the kind of job evaluation systems described by Mr. Eskilsson is at least worth a try.[4] Without being 'scientific', job evaluation at least substitutes systematic consideration of comparative job contents, and changes therein, for mere custom and tradition. And it meets the strong desire for 'comparative equity', by careful comparison of the difficulty and attractiveness of different kinds of work. Nevertheless, some scepticism was expressed about whether such schemes could, in fact, do the job. Such scepticism has its root in two considerations ; the fact that job evaluation systems are not completely 'objective' and allow a certain margin for bargaining about wage rates ; and because, although the resulting wage structure might be regarded as 'equitable', it need not provide the differentials that would accord with the required short-term reallocation of the labour force.[5]

[1] See Chapter 2, p. 19, Chapter 4, p. 54 and *Discussion*, p. 190.
[2] See, for example, the statement of Mr. Massé, *Discussion*, p. 190 ; and Chapter 12, p. 134.   [3] Chapter 4, pp. 54 and 55.   [4] Chapter 9, pp. 111 to 113.
[5] These doubts were raised by Mr. Weinberg, Prof. Sturmthal and Mr. Meidner, *Discussion*, pp. 227, and 230. Of course, by concentrating on the difficulty and

The Labour Market and Inflation

Mr. Saunders expressed surprise that trade union movements (and management), have not paid more attention to problems connected with the distribution of income, particularly since the position of influence in which post-war economic conditions have placed them might enable them to implement their chosen priorities.[1]   Mr. Aubrey Jones also called on the unions to resume their traditional concern with the distribution of incomes and to prescribe priorities for the wage claims of different groups of workers.[2]

The trade union participants responded to these challenges. They not only agreed that the establishment of such priorities and the development of a more rational wage structure should be a major function of the union movement, but claimed that it is so.[3]

They argued, however, that the union task in this field is made difficult on two counts. First, the effective implementation of a set of priorities determined by the trade union movement presupposes the existence of a central union organisation with sufficient power to screen and schedule the claims of the various member unions and groups of workers ; [4] we return to this question below. Secondly, it is impossible for unions to consider changes in wage differentials in isolation from the wider questions of income distribution, and in particular, from the distribution of income between labour and property. For if a highly paid worker is to be persuaded to forgo a wage rise in order to benefit a low-wage worker, there must be an assurance that the benefit will, in fact, accrue to the latter worker and not be appropriated by the former worker's employer in the form of larger profits.[5] This consideration suggests, as Mr. Aubrey Jones pointed out, that if the unions establish and implement a set of wage priorities, their action will need to be bolstered and safeguarded by government measures concerned with the global distribution of incomes.[6]

A further difficulty is that a set of differentials established by the unions might tend to be based on principles of equity rather than on economic requirements. The union principle of 'solidarity' points

attractiveness of work, job evaluation does relate the wage structure to relative supplies of labour in different occupational categories, and thus may well provide major rational criteria for the long run restructuring of patterns of wage relatives that the Symposium thought necessary.

[1] Chapter 2, pp. 19 and 20, and *Discussion*, p. 180.
[2] *Discussion*, p. 232.
[3] See the statements of Messrs. Meidner, Weinberg and Keinzl, *Discussion*, pp. 229, 233 and 234.
[4] See the statement of Dr. Keinzl, *Discussion*, p. 233.
[5] See the statement of Mr. Weinberg, *Discussion*, p. 233.
[6] *Discussion*, p. 235.

to a uniform wage for a given occupation regardless of industry ; whilst the industrial redistribution of the labour force might require a long-term change in inter-industry wage differentials. Also, union principles frequently favour a narrowing of occupational differentials, whilst shortages of skilled manpower might require the opposite.[1]

Clearly, each of the three methods — micro-productivity criteria, job evaluation schemes and a system of trade union priorities — is in some way unsuited to the task of guiding changes in the wage structure. Indeed, for some, the limitations of these devices are sufficiently serious for them to be rejected in favour of differentials as determined by 'the market'. Mr. Mattei thought that more consideration needs to be given to the question of whether, in fact, a centralised wage system is necessarily better than a market-orientated decentralised determination of wage differentials, even if the latter proves to be inflationary.[2] However, the general feeling of the Symposium was that nothing could be lost and much might be gained in a search for a system of criteria that would guide the longer-term development of wage differentials and which could be integrated into a wage policy.

(c) *The Control of Decentralised Wage Determination Procedures.* Experience suggests that attempts to influence plant-level wage determination from a 'centre' — be it a trade union federation, an employers' organisation or the government — are doomed to failure[3] if the pressures behind the factors causing wage drift — especially competitive bidding and the use of the comparability criterion — are not substantially moderated. Yet because of the lack of any quantitative evaluation of their impact — a gap emphasised by Mr. Rehn in the case of active manpower policies [4] — it is impossible to know whether measures of the type examined above could reduce wage drift to such an extent that they would make a significant contribution to the prevention of inflation. Almost certainly they could not entirely supress wage drift of the kind in question. Therefore, where an attempt is being made to guide wage increases by a centrally devised norm, further measures will almost certainly be needed if the outcome of wage determination procedures at the periphery are

---

[1] When it eventually becomes fully operative, experience with the system whereby the British TUC examines the wage claims of its member unions will provide an interesting postscript to these deliberations of the Symposium.
[2] *Discussion*, p. 221.
[3] Unless, of course, they are backed by legal sanctions.
[4] *Discussion*, p. 216.

to conform with this norm.[1] Such influence or control could, in principle at least, be effected through one, or a combination, of three instruments : the trade union movement, employers' organisations or the government.

There has been a tendency to believe that trade union movements in developed countries, if structurally modified, can do most to ensure the implementation, at the plant level, of a centrally agreed wage policy. Whilst this question was broached in the Symposium the discussion bore disappointingly little fruit — though perhaps in view of the contentiousness of the problem and its ramifications well beyond the subject matter of the Symposium, this is hardly surprising. None the less views were aired which would need to be taken into account whenever the question is examined in its wider context, and which are therefore recorded.

When a central trade union organisation has agreed upon the elements of a wage policy, whether or not in conjunction with other groups in society,[2] it normally finds it difficult to implement the policy at the plant level via the union system. In part, lack of sufficient central control can be ascribed to the fact that not all unions are necessarily affiliated to the central federal movement ; in part it is due to the insufficient influence of a given union on plant-level wage determination in its domain.

A central federal union organisation is obviously unable to control the wage policy, at the national or plant levels, of the non-affiliated unions. This is especially important in the case of non-manual workers' unions. In addition, however, the freedom of each outsider to pursue a more aggressive wage policy is the envy of member unions, and weakens their resolve to follow the chosen policy. In this way the political division of the French trade union movement does much to explain the importance of local- and plant-level wage determination in France.[3] Yet even in those countries — such as Sweden — which are usually regarded as having a strong centralised union movement,

---

[1] Mr. Aubrey Jones was particularly emphatic that it is necessary for society to effect some form of control over wage determination procedures. See, for example, *Discussion*, pp. 224–225.

[2] Conditions for securing trade union support for a nationally conceived wage or incomes policy are examined in the second part of this chapter.

[3] See Chapter 7, pp. 83 to 85, and the statement of Mr. Le Brun, *Discussion*, p. 219. In the case of France, it is particularly important to distinguish between plant-level collective bargaining and plant-level wage determination. There is relatively little of the former reflecting, as Mr. Le Brun points out, the paucity of collective bargaining at higher levels. There is, however, much of the latter, in the form of wage decisions taken unilaterally by employers. This makes for a very decentralised system of wage determination.

there may in fact be several important union federations and little co-ordination between their wage policies.[1]

Prof. Pen, Dr. Markmann and Prof. Sellier drew attention to the trade unions' preference for less centralised systems of wage determination in the Netherlands (now if not previously), Western Germany and France.[2] To some extent this can be ascribed to traditions of autonomy in individual industrial and craft unions. But union preference for industry or plant-level bargaining is also based on hard economic calculation. More precisely, in his paper, Prof. Sellier suggests that employers prefer the use of macro-economic criteria in wage bargaining whilst trade unions place more emphasis on micro-economic criteria.[3] The thesis certainly has some substance. The use of macro-economic wage norms, especially when unaccompanied by any effective price regulations, places employers in a strong position in wage negotiations. For employers in firms where productivity is rising quickly may limit wage rises to the nationally prescribed norm, by invoking public opinion, and appropriate the excess productivity gains as profits.[4] In contrast, in firms where productivity rises slowly, employers may simply not have the resources to grant a wage rise as high as that prescribed in the national norm, and workers are faced by the choice of wage rises below the norm or redundancy.

Of course a union preference for decentralised wage determination procedure does not imply that wage determination will in fact be a decentralised process. Indeed, according to Prof. Sellier, employers are often in a position to enforce their own preference in this matter, choosing a level of negotiations where, relative to the union, their position is strongest. Since this level differs from industry to industry, so does the pattern of collective bargaining.[5] Nevertheless, it is possible to generalise about, and to compare, the systems of wage determination in different countries, on the basis of broad assessments of the relative importance of centralised and decentralised decision-making processes. The French system is largely decentralised, whilst the West German system is much more centralised — though as Dr. Markmann shows by no means completely so.[6]

[1] See the statement of Mr. Meidner, *Discussion*, p. 192.
[2] Chapters 8, pp. 92 and 93; and 6, p. 72. See also *Discussion*, pp. 205 and 220.
[3] Chapter 6, p. 72.
[4] See the statements of Mr. Weinberg : *Discussion*, p. 193, and Chapter 3, pp. 30 and 41.
[5] *Discussion*, p. 228. [6] Chapter 8, pp. 94 and 95.

The Labour Market and Inflation

In any case, a preference for, or even the fact of, decentralised wage determination, whilst it might complicate the implementation of a wage policy accepted centrally by the union movement, in itself does not render it impossible. What is required is some form of *control* which the central union organisation can effect over negotiations at other levels. It is at this point that the discussion necessarily spills into other fields, for the question of control is intimately connected with the problem of the optimum structure of the trade unions, a problem which, as Prof. Sellier indicates, is not merely or even mainly a matter of their size but also of the homogeneity of their objectives.[1] It is also a question of the relative extent of the participation of union officials from different levels — full-time and plant-level representatives — on the various collective bargaining bodies.[2] Given a formal union framework that apportions, coordinates and controls the kind of wage negotiations which can be undertaken at various levels, there seems to be no fundamental reason why fairly decentralised negotiating machinery could not be effectively controlled from the union centre.

Certainly the trade union participants did not consider that decentralised wage determination procedures are necessarily incompatible with the implementation of national guidelines,[3] but if this is to be achieved, almost certainly there needs to be an effective central control of bargaining procedures at the various levels. The lack of such central control, in the United States for example, makes it uncertain whether effective compliance with national guidelines could be ensured through the union movement.[4]

Yet, if such control can be provided, a degree of decentralisation in wage determination procedures would be an extremely useful feature of wage-policy machinery. It would allow the policy to be much more flexible, and in particular would acquaint the trade union movement with those wage differentials, dictated both by equity and the needs of the market, which, as was proposed above, it might need to promote. The flexibility which a degree of decentralisation affords would also be regarded by trade unions as a safe-

---

[1] Chapter 6, p. 74.   [2] Chapter 8, p. 91.
[3] See the statements of Mr. Le Brun and Dr. Markmann, *Discussion*, pp. 219 and 222.
[4] Chapter 3, p. 25.
That is, it might prove difficult for the wage policies of individual unions to be centrally co-ordinated. The frustration of central guidelines by wage-drift elements seems less probable in the United States, largely because of the institutional framework — individual unions controlling plant-level bargaining much more stringently — but also because a basic pressure making for wage drift, labour shortages, has been much less pronounced in the United States.

guard against actions by recalcitrant employers of the type previously referred to, and would therefore make a system of national wage guidelines more palatable.

There was no reference in the Symposium to the implementation of national wage norms, at industry or firm level, through the medium of employers' associations, in a manner analogous to that prescribed for the unions. This does not reflect a lack of balance on the part of the participants, as much as a recognition that the nature and structure of employers' organisations is generally such as to make this approach unthinkable. However, there was some discussion of three instruments which the *government* might use to bring employers' wage decisions into line with the chosen policy : price controls, fiscal measures and enterprise-state contracts.

One reason for the introduction of price control in Norway, the Netherlands and France, for instance, has been to limit the wage increases which employers can concede.[1] The major problem is to prescribe, for any firm or industry, the appropriate price change given that their rates of productivity increase are not uniform ; this question is more conveniently examined in the second part of this chapter.

Prof. Sellier and Mr. Saunders urged that consideration should be given to the use of fiscal measures for limiting wage increases negotiated at the firm level.[2] In this connection, special attention was devoted to Steuer's proposal that where prices are raised, wage increases should be effectively blocked and profits taxed at a higher than normal rate. Many variants of such a scheme with different degrees of complexity can be envisaged. For all of them difficulties would be posed by the nature of the existing fiscal systems on to which they would need to be grafted, and also, no doubt, by conflicts between the various objectives of fiscal policy.[3] Nevertheless, the concensus seemed to be that fiscal measures merit further attention.

The French Government has negotiated contracts with certain enterprises on the basis of which, in return for the various forms of public facilities which they enjoy, these firms try to adhere to the investment, export and price objectives of the national economic plan. Mr. Le Brun proposed that the firms in question, as part of the contract, should also be required to negotiate and adhere to collective agreements containing wage clauses that accord with the

[1] See Chapter 2, p. 21.
[2] Chapter 6, pp. 75 and 76 ; and Chapter 2, pp. 21 and 23.
[3] See the exchange between Dr. Markmann and Prof. Sellier, *Discussion*, pp. 196 and 197.

provisions of the plan.[1] Obviously the feasibility of such a system depends on the authorities being in a position to offer something in return for these commitments. The French authorities are in a special position in this respect for not only can they make public facilities a basis of such contracts but, in return for their negotiation, they have also offered relaxation of the price controls introduced in 1963. In the absence of such a *quid pro quo* it is not at all certain that the authorities in other countries could tie firms in this manner. However, the major disadvantage of the system is that by no means all firms, and probably not even a majority of them, could be covered by such contracts without the system becoming impossibly unwieldy. This might not be a serious disadvantage in the case of a price policy, since the existence of price leadership patterns means that contracts need to be signed with comparatively few firms.[2] In contrast, when there is fierce competition for labour supplies a very comprehensive series of contracts would be needed to implement a wages policy by this means.

In principle, at least, the authorities can, of course, control the outcome of decentralised wage determination procedures by employing legal sanctions that allow only those wage increases conforming to the stipulated criteria or norm. Statutory powers for this purpose should be clearly distinguished from the statutory imposition of an incomes or wage policy itself.[3] Given that a wage policy has been agreed upon by most unions and employers then the use of legal sanctions to ensure that recalcitrant groups — individual unions or firms — adhere to the central guidelines, is 'a perfectly normal function of the law'.[4] The adoption of statutory powers for this purpose is essentially an extension of the instrument by which contractual provisions concerning terms of employment are made legally binding on groups which are not a party to the immediate contract.[5] Moreover, Dutch experience with the enforcement of a wage policy suggests that if statutory powers are used in this relatively limited way, they are acceptable for more than a short period. Dutch experience with 'black' wages also indicates, however, that even legal enforcement cannot be completely effective if the basic causes of wage drift are not suppressed.

[1] Chapter 7, p. 87, *Discussion*, p. 195.
[2] In this context see Chapter 3, p. 44, and the statement of Mr. Weinberg, *Discussion*, p. 235.
[3] The wider issues connected with the compulsion of a trade union centre to accept a government-formulated wage policy are touched upon in the second part of this chapter.
[4] Chapter 2, p. 20.   [5] See, for example, Chapter 7, p. 84.

4. Moderating Wage Claims

Social tension, the antagonism of one group in society for another, can create inflationary pressures in the labour market by two routes. Tensions exist between the various groups of workers that are largely defensive in nature and seek an outlet in attempts to preserve the existing wage and salary structure and, especially, occupational differentials. This effect, the inflationary impact of the use of the comparability criterion, has already been referred to. Secondly, however, social tensions — ranging in nature and intensity with the type of economic and political system — also exist between workers as a group and the recipients of other forms of income, and this tension may give rise to rather more aggressive behaviour and wage claims which seek to enlarge labour's share of the national product. We now turn to this kind of inflationary pressure and consider whether it might be moderated by labour market policies which try, directly or indirectly, to ease the tensions.

Obviously, the roots of social tension are many and varied, and the Symposium could only consider causes and appropriate counter measures for those elements which appear to have an inflationary impact, and by no means all of these. Three relevant topics were, in fact, referred to : the political flavour of the government ; the use of long-term wage contracts ; and the introduction of profit and capital sharing schemes and investment wages.[1] In all cases the Symposium came to clearly negative conclusions.

Far from there being any consensus about the *size* of the impact on wage claims of the government's political leanings, agreement could not even be reached about the *direction* of the relationship. On the one hand, government by left wing parties was a common feature which Mr. Saunders detected in the six countries implementing a wage policy,[2] and Prof. Pen thought that only a left wing government can introduce a successful incomes policy.[3] In contrast, Dr. Kienzl believed that the arrival of a government sympathetic to labour's interests might cause higher than average wage claims ; and in Mr.

[1] Mr. Aubrey Jones suggested that the greater degree of security that accompanies a salaried status might moderate wage claims if it were extended to all workers. (*Discussion*, p. 204.) It would have this effect, he claimed, by making income more certain and by helping to remove the tensions which exist between management and labour. In general — and especially as revealed in answers to the questionnaire — the other participants were not very enthusiastic about this approach.
[2] And, as his data suggest, wage policies in these countries do seem to have had some moderating effect at the *central* level. (Chapter 2, p. 14.)
[3] *Discussion*, p. 203.

Massé's view, the intensity of the relevant social tensions are largely independent of the type of government in power.[1] In fact, of course, the nature of this relationship is largely irrelevant to policy options — except in so far as it influences the electorate in its choice of government. A change of government is unlikely to rank highly among the policies which the ruling party consider in their attempts to combat inflation!

The Symposium examined the possibility that long-term wage contracts, by giving workers a feeling of security about the level and development of their earnings for some years ahead, could provide for smaller wage increases than would otherwise be acceptable. Prof. Pen considered long-term contracts in his paper and concluded that, in certain circumstances, they might help to moderate inflation.[2] However, he conceded that, in practice, they may not make for much stability and, indeed, are even harmful on occasion.[3] This was the general feeling of the Symposium.

It is tempting to blame the inadequacies, in this context, of long-term contracts on two of their major features. Long-term wage contracts are generally only acceptable to trade unions if they contain both an 'improvement' element — whether or not it is called that — and an 'escalator' clause.[4] Frequently the improvement element is tied to the growth of national productivity, and given that the contracts are long-term,[5] there may also be a need to provide for differential wage increases based on micro-productivity criteria; the problems associated with the use of micro-productivity criteria have already been referred to.[6]

Escalator clauses are needed in order to offset cost-of-living increases during the currency of the contract. If used in conjunction with national productivity changes — on a point for point basis — they ensure that labour's share of the national income does not fall. But because of the extra twist which escalator clauses may give to the wage-price spiral they are widely regarded with considerable disfavour by both economists and governments; and employers, too, give reasons for disliking them.[7] Trade union attitudes seem to be more ambivalent. Thus, unions have misgivings about escalator clauses on account of their lack of precision and flexibility, and

---

[1] *Discussion*, pp. 203.   [2] Chapter 4, pp. 53 to 56 and 63.
[3] *Discussion*, p. 203.
[4] See the statement of Mr. Weinberg, *Discussion*, p. 207.
[5] 'Long-term' wage contracts are usually of the two to three years' currency. With the time horizons normally used in economics, 'medium-term' would describe them more accurately.
[6] See pp. 146 and 147.   [7] See Chapter 4, pp. 53 and 54.

because, by being automatic, to some extent they take wage decisions out of the hands of union officials. In West Germany, deeply rooted fears of hyper-inflation contribute to the trade unions' opposition to their use.[1] Yet, despite the recognised deficiencies of escalator clauses, only long-term contracts which offer the workers such protection will normally be acceptable to labour. Indeed, in his paper, Prof. Pen prescribed productivity changes *plus* cost of living increases as the basis for wage increases, stressing the realism of such an approach.[2] It is certainly the case — as Mr. Weinberg went to some lengths to show — that the failure of the United States system of guidelines to provide workers with protection from cost-of-living increases, did much to make the policy unacceptable to American trade unions.[3]

Yet probably the basic shortcoming of long-term contracts and the reason why they are not more widely favoured is that they aim at a form of automatic increase in one economic variable, wages, in a world where related variables are not controlled, and of the variations in which — the cost of living apart — no account is taken. In short, the economic conditions in which the contract is negotiated change during its currency. Thus West German trade unions are opposed to long-term contracts because the economic situation can change significantly even over a period of as little as two years.[4] And in both the Netherlands and the United Kingdom, long-term contracts have made provision for large wage increases in years when they have proved to be quite inappropriately high.[5] Much of the discrepancy between wage increases provided for in long-term contracts and those that are fitting in the circumstances eventually experienced, lies in the difficulty of forecasting the medium-term rate of productivity increase.[6]

Whatever the cause of the discrepancies that can occur between the contractually prescribed wage increases and those which would be appropriate in the new set of circumstances, the discrepancies give rise to restiveness and pressures to change the terms of the

---

[1] See the statement of Dr. Keinzl, *Discussion*, p. 203 ; and Chapter 8, p. 100. Mr. Mattei stated that in Italy, too, workers are not entirely happy with all aspects of the widespread use of escalator clauses. (*Discussion*, p. 206.)
[2] Chapter 4, pp. 50–53.   [3] Chapter 3, pp. 31–33 ; and p. 38.
[4] Though in Western Germany there is no protection against cost-of-living changes. See above and the statement of Dr. Markmann, *Discussion*, p. 208.
[5] See the statements of Prof. Pen and Mr. Aubrey Jones, *Discussion*, pp. 203 and 204.
[6] Forecasting problems are compounded where price as well as productivity changes are taken into account. See the statements of Dr. Keinzl and Prof. Pen, *Discussion*, pp. 202 and 203.

contract.[1] These pressures may prove sufficient for the contract to be changed — trade unions, for example, invoking the 'living document' concept [2] — or for it to provide for *ex post* adjustments. It has even been suggested that the terms of long-term contracts be amended annually to accord with revisions to the national plan.[3] Yet if the terms of the contract can be formally or informally changed during its currency, it is difficult to see how it remains a long-term contract. If their terms can be revised, what becomes of the certainty and security which they are supposed to offer to workers and which, it was thought, might be traded for smaller wage claims ?

It is generally agreed that the profit-sharing, investment-wage and capital-sharing schemes described and evaluated by Prof. Pen, may in the long run reduce income inequalities, promote a feeling of labour-management partnership and improve the status of workers in economic activity.[4] Such consequences will eventually help to reduce social tensions, and to the extent that these influence wage claims, they will help to moderate these too, but this impact is very much a long-term one, and its size cannot be foreseen.[5] Furthermore, investment wages and capital-sharing schemes, which defer the payment of a part of labour's total remuneration, may be useful in combating inflation by reducing *demand* pressure, though profit-sharing schemes, by which workers receive a cash payment from profits in the year when they are made, do not have this effect.

However, in Prof. Pen's view, and those participants who expressed opinions about this matter were in general agreement with him, such schemes would have very little moderating effect on cost inflation, either by reducing wage claims or by giving additional remuneration to workers in such a way that employers choose not to pass it on as price increases. In particular, employers *do* tend to regard payments made to labour under these types of scheme as costs, and they will be reflected in the prices they charge. This is likely to be most pronounced in the case of investment wages, and rather less so — but by no means to a negligible extent, despite the teachings of economic theory — in the case of capital- and profit-sharing schemes.

[1] See the statement of Dr. Keinzl, *Discussion*, p. 202.
[2] See Chapter 4, p. 54 and *Discussion*, p. 203.
[3] See the statement of Mr. Le Brun, *Discussion*, p. 209.
[4] For a description and an evaluation of these schemes see Chapter 4, pp. 56–63 ; see also the statement of Dr. Markmann, *Discussion*, p. 207.
[5] Because of the special conjunctural experiences of the West German coal and steel industries, it is difficult to establish whether or not relatively low wage increases in these sectors have been due to the system of 'co-determination' which they employ. See the statements of Dr. Markmann and Mr. Weinberg, *Discussion*, pp. 208 and 209.

Moreover, the introduction of such schemes implies a deterioration in capital interests relative to those of labour in the firm in question, which means that there will eventually be an increase in the firm's capital costs that will also be translated, to some extent, into price increases.

Two factors militate against any significant moderation of wage claims as a consequence of the use of these schemes : one is peculiar to profit-sharing schemes, whilst the other applies to investment-wage and capital-sharing schemes, too. Prof. Pen demonstrates [1] that whilst a profit-sharing scheme may moderate wage claims in the year of its introduction, its effect thereafter is likely to be infinitesimal. This once-for-all benefit is a very telling limitation of profit-sharing schemes as a means of limiting wage claims. More generally, a gradual introduction of any of these schemes, or the existence of unsuitable conditions in some industries and firms which prevents them from attaining economy-wide coverage,[2] would probably lead to higher than normal wage claims by non-covered workers as a compensation for their failure to benefit.

II. SOME ASPECTS OF WAGE AND INCOMES POLICIES

1. Incomes Policies and Demand Management

In the Introduction, it was stated that a symposium having the objectives of the present one could only have meaning if it is accepted that factor returns, and particularly wages, are not completely determined by market forces. In other words, it is a basic creed of the Symposium that unions and firms have a certain power to raise wages which is largely independent of the demand for the products and workers in question. In the papers presented at the Symposium there is an explicit or implicit acceptance of this assumption.[3]

Also the discussion itself revealed a consensus that the oligopolistic market positions currently enjoyed by many firms and trade unions allows them, within limits, to raise wages and pass on the cost increases to the consumer. Naturally enough, there were divergent views about the size of this freedom of manœuvre which

---

[1] Chapter 4, pp. 57 and 58.
[2] In Western Germany, for instance, investment-wage schemes tend to be operated only in industries — such as construction — where special characteristics favour their use. See the statements of Dr. Markmann, Prof. Giersch and Mr. Weinberg, *Discussion*, pp. 208 and 209.
[3] Most attention is paid to this assumption by Prof. Pen, Chapter 4.

oligopolistic market positions confer on unions and firms. At one end of the scale, Mr. Aubrey Jones believed that the wage-fixing powers enjoyed by unions and firms are a major explanation of inflation.[1] At the other, Mr. Mattei thought that the margins are very narrow — certainly narrower than those suggested in Prof. Sellier's paper.[2] It was also suggested that the size of these margins varies considerably between industries, but is indeed very narrow in some sectors. Yet, given the widespread use of the comparability criterion, it is difficult to believe that the use of oligopolistic powers to raise wages (and prices) even in a relatively few industries, will not be eventually transformed into a fairly general rise in the wage (and price) level.

Prof. Sturmthal believed that such an abuse of oligopolistic power could hardly account for much inflation, given that whilst unions and firms have for long enjoyed such powers, the inflationary problems to which it is alleged this gives rise have appeared only comparatively recently.[3] However, two new factors that might have a bearing on more recent developments can be identified. First, Mr. Aubrey Jones drew attention to the tendency for unionism to move up the social scale, a development that was echoed in other parts of the debate.[4] Secondly, and perhaps more important, the exercise of such oligopolistic powers probably requires full or nearly full employment — a contemporary condition — and in such circumstances wages rise faster than they would have done with the same level of employment but in more perfect product and factor markets.

This leads naturally to the next question : whether the treatment of inflationary processes requires both measures of the kind which are the subject-matter of the Symposium and appropriate policies — budgetary, fiscal and monetary — for the management of the general level of demand. A reading of the papers and discussions reveals that the participants were at one in a belief that whether or not appropriate labour market and income policies can make a substantial contribution to the prevention of inflation, they need to be implemented, as Mr. Massé stated,[5] within the framework of wider economic policies that are also directed towards this goal.

However, this consensus masked divergent views about the degree of complementarity which should exist between demand management

---

[1] *Discussion*, p. 224. [2] *Discussion*, p. 190 and Chapter 6.
[3] *Discussion*, pp. 211 and 227.
[4] See the statements of Prof. Sturmthal and Mr. Aubrey Jones, *Discussion*, pp. 211, 224, 227, 228 and 231 ; and above, p. 144.
[5] Chapter 12, p. 128.

and incomes policies. Indeed, no less than four distinct views of this matter were revealed if not, in each case, supported by the Symposium. At one end of the scale are those who, because of their bent towards a 'deterministic' view of income formation,[1] believe that an incomes policy can have but limited success in curbing inflation. Correspondingly, adherents of this view think that from time to time, and in the apparent absence of any third policy alternative, it is necessary for the government to pursue a deflationary policy in order to halt or retard the rise in incomes and prices.[2]

A more constructive approach can be discerned in a statement of Prof. Giersch.[3] In effect, the policy proposals of the West German Council of Economic Experts, to which Prof. Giersch referred, advocate a measure of disinflation as a means of retarding or halting a rise in prices. In this way a disinflationary, or indeed, deflationary demand policy could be used as a *precursor* of an incomes policy, to provide by means which would not be tolerated for any length of time, conditions — in the form of inherited price stability — that would greatly favour the introduction of a more permanent incomes policy.[4] Such action could probably make a major contribution to the viability of an incomes policy. In Sweden, for example, it is obvious that the *anticipation* of a continued price rise has itself severely undermined action to limit wage increases.[5] In general, a springboard of the type implied by this policy would enable the realistic approach advocated by Prof. Pen to be implemented without it being a vehicle by which inherited inflation is carried forward.[6] The pre-existence of only a small degree of inflation in the United States probably helped to make the wage guidelines effective for a while.

The demand policy which commanded most support as a complement to an incomes policy is that which aims at a level of demand which just avoids any general surplus demand for labour.[7] With total demand set at this level, pockets of structural unemployment will necessarily appear. Mr. Rehn emphasised that not only must social policies be pursued in these circumstances to compensate for

[1] See Introduction.
[2] Mr. Mattei drew attention to the fact that in Italy some unemployment had been chosen as a means of reducing inflation ; and, in his view, the measures taken in 1966 by the British Government were tantamount to the same policy. (*Discussion*, p. 221.) [3] *Discussion*, pp. 184 and 185.
[4] The British deflationary measures taken in 1966 could be interpreted in this light, though their effect in this direction is masked by the simultaneous price freeze which achieves the same result more surely and directly.
[5] Chapter 9, pp. 102 and 103. [6] Chapter 4, pp. 48–53.
[7] See, for example, the statement of Mr. Rehn, *Discussion*, pp. 213 to 218.

unemployment, but active manpower measures must also be implemented. These measures must seek, on the one hand, to reduce structural unemployment and, on the other, to prevent the appearance of inflationary pressures in bottleneck areas, not only by promoting the redistribution of the labour force, but also by providing for selective demand policies.

The fourth approach is the one which industrialised countries have adopted in recent years but are now trying to avoid : a crude — as opposed to a selective — demand policy which ensures sufficient total expenditure to provide full employment, but does so only at the expense of considerable excess demand for labour, and, via such mechanisms as competitive bidding, gives rise to inflation. Experience suggests that, when supported by demand management of this sort, a wage policy either collapses as a result of the tensions which arise in the union movement, or is not very successful in restraining increases in labour costs. And not only can the consequent 'wage explosion' lose much, perhaps all, of any ground gained during the currency of the wage policy, but also faith in the viability of wage or incomes policies is badly shaken, perhaps to the point where their future use even in short-term emergency situations is jeopardised.

It is not possible to single out any one of the above varieties of demand policy as being universally the best for combination with a wage or incomes policy. Much depends on the economic situation at the time when the policy is chosen. Thus, whilst the disinflationary policy described by Prof. Giersch may be suitable where the initial position is one of full employment — as in the case of West Germany — it would be much less acceptable in the United States.[1] And the coincidence in 1963 of an unusually rapid rise in the size of the labour force and the approach of a balance of payments crisis prompted the French authorities to deal with the problem more by measures affecting incomes (in this case a price policy) than by deflationary demand policy.[2] Moreover, different demand policies may not be mutually exclusive. In particular, there would appear to be scope for experimenting with the 'disinflationary' and 'avoidance of excess demand for labour' approaches described above, the former preceding the latter in a systematic attempt to avoid inflationary pressures from the demand side.

---

[1] See the statement of Mr. Weinberg, *Discussion*, p. 187.
[2] See Chapter 1, p. 4 ; and the statements of Mr. Aubrey Jones and Mr. Massé, *Discussion*, pp. 188 and 189.

Whatever type of demand policy is chosen to complement an incomes policy, their integration raises difficult technical problems. Obviously, if the common aim of both the incomes policy and demand management is a greater degree of price stability, the measures undertaken to influence the level and structure of demand should conform to this objective. Thus, attempts to implement a disinflationary policy by reducing the budget deficit, if based on a rise in indirect taxes, may clash, in their effect on prices, with the aims of an incomes policy.[1] More generally, the demand policy chosen for combination with an incomes policy might well need to promote, simultaneously, four objectives : a general level of demand which avoids excess demand for labour ; a structural distribution of demand that avoids the development of bottlenecks in the economy ; a balance of the various categories of expenditure which takes account of the effect of planned or expected increases in incomes (especially wages) on consumers' expenditure ;[2] and an expenditure pattern which over the longer term will maximise the growth of national productivity and thereby lessen inflationary pressures on this account.

There would seem to be much scope for further consideration of and experimentation with various combinations of demand management and incomes policies. Industrialised countries have frequently resorted to policies of temporary disinflation — the well-known 'stop-go' approach — but such periods do not seem to have been systematically used for launching an incomes policy. And nowhere have active manpower policies been developed to a pitch where the level of demand can be restricted to a point where it implies no excess demand for labour, whilst ensuring full employment or, in Mr. Rehn's phrase, making deviations from full employment socially acceptable.[3]

2. Wage and Incomes Policies : Objectives and Conditions

A cursory look at the proceedings could easily suggest that the wider deliberations of the Symposium reached the following impasse : wage or incomes policies may be implemented in the short run, but there are no short-term problems to which they are suited ; whilst in the long run there may be economic and social problems which they could usefully treat, but it is impossible to sustain them. A

[1] See the statement of Mr. Aubrey Jones, *Discussion*, p. 188.
[2] Mr. Massé described an exercise in which this effect was reconciled with other plan objectives. *Discussion*, pp. 195 and 196.
[3] *Discussion*, p. 218

closer inspection of the proceedings — and also the later reflections of the participants [1] — suggests that the outlook for these policies is by no means so bleak. A wage or incomes policy can serve a useful purpose in the short run ; and, if certain conditions are fulfilled, it could prove feasible as a permanent instrument of economic and social policy. We will examine each of these possibilities in turn.

(a) *The Short Term.* It was felt that the only major short-term problem which a wage policy might be called upon to solve is a balance of payments deficit. However, scepticism was expressed about the efficacy of a wage policy in this role because, as Mr. Saunders pointed out, there is a lack of association between inter-country differences in changes in unit labour costs and the development of their balance of payments situations. This is due, in the first place, to the consideration that factor returns other than wages influence price changes. Secondly, Mr. Saunders pointed out that even if a measure of success is achieved in stabilising the general price level, export prices may continue to increase and the trade balance, therefore, deteriorate.[2] Thirdly, as Mr. Weinberg stated, balance of payments difficulties can arise as a result of adverse capital flows [3] even when there is no deterioration in the trade balance.

In effect, this means that a wage policy would not necessarily deal with the basic cause of a balance of payments problem. Whilst this is true — and has important 'equity' implications — an effective wage policy would nevertheless tend to counter the unfavourable effect of the factors at the root of the problem, though, of course, it would not necessarily offset them completely. Moreover, the implementation of an *incomes* policy by influencing a wider range of costs would avoid many, if not all, of the shortcomings of wage policies in this respect. In any case, the almost universal consensus that wage policies, if successfully implemented, can do much to achieve price stability eventually [4] prompted the participants to regard their contribution to a solution of balance of payments problems in a much more favourable light.

To the extent that uncertainty persists about the efficacy of wage or incomes policies in this role, it can probably be explained in terms of the nature of the balance of payments problem that needs to be dealt with. In brief, it seems likely that whilst a wage or incomes

---

[1] As contained in their replies to the questionnaire ; see Introduction.
[2] *Discussion*, p. 200.   [3] Chapter 3, p. 25.
[4] This was revealed in replies to the questionnaire.

policy can make little impression on a pre-existing balance of payments crisis, they can help to stave off such a crisis if implemented in time. Obviously there will be a lag between the introduction of a wage or incomes policy and the time when it begins to bite, a delay which the economy perhaps can ill afford, and the government may be obliged to turn to other policies — deflation or devaluation — on this account alone. Secondly, even the introduction of the most stringent wage and incomes freeze may have little impact on the balance of payments problem where the crisis is of such proportions that only a *reduction* in wages and incomes would have any significant impact.[1]

In contrast, it is very probable that a wage or incomes policy which slows down the rate of increase in both labour costs and the general price level can do much to ward off balance of payments difficulties, even though, by itself, it could not guarantee their prevention. Such anticipatory action seems to have been successful over a relatively long period in the case of the Netherlands, and, as pointed out by Mr. Massé, over a relatively shorter period in France.[2] Prof. Giersch emphasised the value of an incomes policy as a means of avoiding a balance of payments problem in a country 'embarking' on an expansionist policy,[3] and, for example, the United States guideposts were intended to play this role. Mr. Zoeteweij pointed out that if wage policies are used in connection with balance of payments problems, the fact that they need not strive for absolute price stability and the possibility of relaxing their stringency from time to time according to the balance of payments outlook, would make them much more palatable;[4] this would apply equally to more widely conceived incomes policies.

(b) *The Long Term.* We now turn to the proposition that in the long term there exist objectives which an incomes policy could usefully pursue, but such a policy is not viable on a permanent basis. The proceedings revealed two important objectives which it was thought long-term incomes policies could do much to attain. First, even if the authorities are successful in avoiding excess demand, full employment nevertheless gives rise to creeping inflation which can eventually cause both internal problems and balance of payments difficulties;[5] an effective incomes policy could help to prevent this.

[1] See the statement of Mr. Mattei, *Discussion*, p. 221.
[2] *Discussion*, p. 188. The French policy took the form of price controls, but these were also intended to restrain wage increases.
[3] *Discussion*, p. 201.   [4] *Discussion*, p. 200.
[5] See the statement of Mr. Stein, *Discussion*, p. 224.

Secondly, incomes policies could be the instrument for achieving the desired long-term changes in income distribution — both between labour and other factors and between different groups of workers. Indeed, this latter objective, which might also be viewed as a condition of a long-term incomes policy, is frequently accepted as its primary feature.[1] Why then is there so much scepticism about the long-run viability of incomes policies ? In the remainder of this section we shall try to answer this question by identifying the conditions which, if fulfilled, might make incomes policies permanently acceptable.

It is important to distinguish between dissatisfaction with incomes policies that derives from defects in their formulation and more deeply rooted problems. The major defect of formulation which has led to the relaxation or collapse of some policies relating to incomes has been their lack of comprehensiveness ; they have been either price or wage policies but not incomes policies. For instance, the fact that the price controls introduced in France in 1963 were not accompanied by any measures to limit, directly, wage increases, pre-determined their current relaxation. For whilst these controls were also intended to restrain wage increases, their full impact could not be transferred in this way and, as a result, profits, investment and the future productivity potential of the economy, suffered.[2]

The more usual shortcoming, however, is that policies of restraint have frequently been limited to wages. The trade union views expressed in the Symposium, and wider appreciations of union attitudes to this question,[3] show that a long-term policy if it is to be one of restraint must certainly make provision for the limitation of non-wage incomes as well as of wages. United States experience, related by Mr. Weinberg, shows how a policy which is effective only in respect of, and bears inequitably on, wages, eventually loses the support of labour.[4]

For whilst the United States policy was widely conceived in the sense that guidelines were also established for price changes, these

---

[1] See Chapter 2, p. 18.

[2] See the statements of Mr. Aubrey Jones, Mr. Massé and Mr. Mattei, *Discussion*, pp. 188, 189 and 190. It should be emphasised that it was never envisaged that these price controls would be permanent.

[3] See, for example, OECD, *Non-Wage Incomes and Price Policy : Trade Union Policy and Experience*, Paris, 1966.

[4] Chapter 3. Since Mr. Weinberg's paper was written, the use of an explicit wage guideline has been abandoned by the United States authorities. In its stead the government has merely urged that, in 1967, wage increases should not exceed the rise in national productivity by as much as the cost of living rise. (United States Council of Economic Advisers : *The Report of the Council of Economic Advisers*, January 1967, p. 129.)

were not as effectively implemented as that prescribed for wages ; in particular prices failed to decrease in industries where productivity increased at more than the national rate.[1] That a form of wage policy has managed to endure in the Nordic countries in the absence of price controls of comparable severity, reflects to a considerable extent the lack of pronounced success of these policies in holding down increases in earnings relative to productivity increases.[2]

In practice there appear to be two principal means of directly influencing changes in non-wage incomes : fiscal measures and the joint use of price and wage policies. The disadvantage of fiscal measures is that whilst they could do much to ensure equity of treatment, they do so after the formation of primary incomes and, therefore, cannot moderate the impact of rises in factor returns on prices. The use of fiscal policy in this context was not considered by the Symposium ; [3] nevertheless it might well have an important role as a complement to an incomes policy. Some attention was, however, devoted to price policies.

Much can be said in favour of incorporating a price policy in an incomes policy. First, powers to limit price increases would help to restrain wage rises. For, on the one hand, a curtailment of the freedom to raise prices would make employers much more chary of bidding for labour supplies or of conceding wage claims ; and, on the other, wage claims would in any case tend to be lower as a result of the smaller, or non-existent, rise in the cost of living. Secondly, used in conjunction with a wage policy, the price level could be manipulated in such a way that profits would be squeezed, and, in principle at least, be made to develop in accordance with prescribed norms. Thirdly, price policies would act directly on the basic symptom of inflation, price instability, the reduction of which would be a major objective of a long-run incomes policy.[4]

During the discussion, however, as Mr. Massé pointed out in his closing statement, action with respect to prices received only mild support.[5]

---

[1] Chapter 3 and *The Report of the Council of Economic Advisers, op. cit.*, p. 128.
[2] See Chapter 2, Table 2. Price controls have been used fairly stringently in Austria and the Netherlands.
[3] The employment of fiscal policies for this purpose should be distinguished from their use as a means of limiting wage concessions.
[4] Mr. Weinberg stressed some of these advantages. (*Discussion*, p. 225.) Mr. Weinberg's support of price policies extends to the point where he considers that with their operation no special action — other than a requirement for trade unions to defend wage claims before public opinion — need be taken in respect of wages. (See also his statement, *Discussion*, p. 235, and Chapter 3, pp. 44 *et seq.*)
[5] Chapter 12, p. 129. In addition to the comments of Mr. Weinberg on price policies, see, for example, those of Mr. Aubrey Jones and Dr. Kienzl, *Discussion*, pp. 188 and 234.

But this too proved to be an occasion when the later reflections of the participants, as given in replies to the questionnaire, tended to change the picture, with considerably more support being given to price policies — though rather predictably, dissidents were still to be found in employer circles or among those who lean towards a 'deterministic' view of income formation. But whilst price policies eventually evinced a fair amount of support, an important qualification was attached to this. In brief, there was considerable agreement that rigid price control amounting to a price freeze could only be tolerated as a short-term emergency measure.[1] If they are to be acceptable over longer periods, price controls would certainly have to be used in a much more flexible manner. The difficulty of exerting sufficient influence on prices, whilst allowing a considerable degree of flexibility for changes in price differentials, is one of those fundamental factors affecting the long-term viability of incomes policies to which we now turn.

A major reason why French price controls and United States wage guidelines were eventually relaxed was that effective action was not taken in the case, respectively, of wages and prices. The collapse of the Dutch policy cannot *basically* be attributed to such a lack of comprehensiveness : action was taken with respect both to wages and prices.[2] If any one factor can be singled out for this collapse it is that whilst wage drift was to some extent suppressed by law, the pressures causing wage drift (a desire to undertake competitive bidding, etc.) persisted. The result was not merely 'black' wages, but more important, the development of tensions within the union movement as a result of the fact that union officials were prevented by law from claiming for their members wage increases at the plant level which employers would otherwise have been ready to concede. Eventually, therefore, the unions were forced by dissension among their members to withdraw their support from the Dutch wage policy. The Dutch experience, in broad outline at least, is by no means unique. Mr. Rehn recounted a very similar Swedish story.[3] There is little doubt that the pressures making for wage drift and its extension at the plant level, and the causes of these pressures, would need to be lessened if a wage, and thereby an incomes policy, is to

[1] This is, in fact, the normal practice in industrialised economies. For example, rigid price control was used in this way in Denmark and France, in 1963, and currently in the United Kingdom. Mr. Weinberg, too, held that rigid price control is only tolerable as a short-term expedient. (*Discussion*, p. 236.)

[2] See, United Nations, Economic Commission for Europe, *Incomes in Post-War Europe*, Part I, chapter iii.

[3] *Discussion*, pp. 213 and 214.

become permanently practicable. That is why the subject matter of the Symposium — as examined in earlier parts of this chapter — is so important.

The second basic difficulty encountered by a long-term incomes policy is that it must allow for a great deal of flexibility. Lessons drawn from the proceedings about the need for, and possible ways of achieving, long-term flexibility in wage differentials, have been examined in the first part of this chapter. A question that has not been examined — it was left open above — is how to formulate and implement a policy which avoids a maldistribution of resources by allowing price differentials to be sufficiently flexible over long periods ?

It should be recognised that in one sense the problem of prescribing long-term changes in price differentials is more difficult than allowing for long-term changes in wage differentials, since the former need to change much more than the latter. For this reason, if for no other, price freezes of the kind which governments have occasionally resorted to are out of the question as permanent policies. Yet the governments of Western Europe and North America have never adopted alternative price policies that have a coverage which is sufficiently large to be accepted by the unions as an effective counterpart to a wage policy. More precisely, governments have interfered with the price mechanism on a long-term basis only in the case of a few sectors (agricultural and housing for example) and for curbing monopolies and restrictive practices.

A more general method which has been tried is the use of micro-productivity changes for guiding price changes. If wage increases are uniformly tied to national productivity, this method prescribes that prices should fall in the industries enjoying productivity improvements above the average and be allowed to rise in others. However, as in the case of the use of micro-productivity criteria for guiding wage increases,[1] there are serious drawbacks to this method. In particular, the micro changes in unit *labour* costs which this method implies — a rise in sectors where productivity increases slowly and a fall elsewhere — do not necessarily reflect the size or direction of micro changes in unit *total* costs, the relevant concept for prices, and because of the conceptual difficulties of measuring changes in total factor productivity, these would be very difficult to gauge. Furthermore, over the long term, provision would need to be made for changes in wage differentials, and thereby a corner-stone

[1] See above, pp. 146 to 147.

of a micro-productivity price system shattered. Thirdly, American experience shows that, even over the medium term, this method is difficult to implement.[1]

A more promising approach would seem to require a rather less rigid system. In particular, a system of notification and scrutiny of prices, operated by a government or other public body and perhaps reinforced by reserve legal sanctions, appears to have a better chance of success. Such a system seems to have worked reasonably smoothly in the Netherlands.[2] And the work of the United Kingdom's National Board for Prices and Incomes also appears to have met with considerable success in its treatment of prices.[3] Mr. Weinberg's proposal for a Review Board falls within this category too.[4]

Criticisms of this approach usually centre on the 'scrutiny' stage, and are based on the consideration that the ministry or board in question could only hope to review a small proportion of product prices. Yet whilst, as stated, the problem of changes in price differentials is in some ways more difficult than that of wage differentials, the enforcement of a price policy probably is not. This is due, essentially, to the fact that currently competition for labour supplies is fiercer than competition in the product market. There are frequently systems of price leadership in the product market, as a result of which Mr. Weinberg believes that not more than one hundred corporations in the United States would need to be covered by his proposal for it to be effective.[5]

The third flexibility requirement is that provision must be made for relative changes in the major income streams, especially for changes in the shares of wage and non-wage incomes. References to this topic in the Symposium were associated with the question of the suitability and acceptability of changes in national productivity as a guideline for wage increases, the criterion on which short- and medium-term wage policies have usually been based.[6] Its appeal stems from the following relationship : if wages increase in proportion to national productivity, and the unit costs of other factors remain unchanged, the price level will be stable and labour's share in the national income constant.[7] Thus, at one and the same time, the

---

[1] See Chapter 3. [2] *Incomes in Post-War Europe, op. cit.*, Part I, chapter iii.
[3] See the statements of Mr. Aubrey Jones, *Discussion*, pp. 235 and 236.
[4] Chapter 3, pp. 44 *et seq.* [5] *Loc. cit.*
[6] For example, this was the basis of the United States guidepost system, and it is the criterion towards which British policy (the wage freeze apart) has moved. See Chapter 3, p. 26, and Chapter 10, p. 116.
[7] This statement needs qualification in several respects, some of which are mentioned below.

application of this criterion aims directly at price stability and, in principle at least, gives labour some assurance about its share.

Yet the proceedings revealed that it is a criterion which is not greatly favoured by trade unions. It can be objected to on the grounds that, in practice, it guarantees neither price stability nor a constant share for labour. This is due firstly to the fact that whilst the trend rate of productivity improvement may be relatively easy to forecast, current actual changes may well diverge from it.[1] Secondly, other factor costs (and import prices) may not remain unchanged. Thirdly, the use of this criterion only ensures price stability if prices are reduced in industries where productivity rises at more than the national rate. Because these are far from minor qualifications, the price level and the cost of living may well continue to increase and, as a consequence, labour's share fall. United States experience suggests that such consequences are by no means unlikely.[2] But the principal trade union objection to the use of this criterion, especially as an element of a long-term incomes policy, is that it would prevent a rise in labour's share, a major union objective.[3]

Given the trade union opposition to the use of this criterion over the long term, can any substitute be found for guiding changes in wages relative to other factor incomes ? Obviously the choice of alternative criteria would depend on the principles adopted for determining in what circumstances and by how much the share of wages should be allowed to change. This goes to the very crux of the problem since these principles depend, in turn, on how, and by which parties, the long-term incomes policy is formulated. We return to this question below. At this juncture suffice it to say that the trade union participants were by no means alone in their insistence that decisions about the rates at which incomes, and especially wages, should change in the long run will need to be much more pragmatic, and based on a much wider set of data — profits, relative changes in the various categories of final expenditure, the rate of economic growth, etc. — than has been the case in shorter-term policies. This implies a much closer integration of incomes policies with — where these exist — economic planning procedures, and a switch from 'physical' criteria to criteria expressed in value terms ; [4]

---

[1] See, on these questions, the statements of Dr. Kienzl and Mr. Meidner, *Discussion*, pp. 202 and 229, and Chapter 3, pp. 27 and 28.
[2] See Chapter 3.
[3] See the statement of Mr. Meidner, *Discussion*, p. 228.
[4] See Chapter 5, p. 67 ; Chapter 6, p. 72 ; Chapter 7, p. 86 ; and Chapter 8, p. 89. See also the statement of Mr. Le Brun, *Discussion*, p. 209.

Mr. Massé's venture in this field suggests that when required, it should be possible to formulate such criteria at the micro-economic as well as the macro-economic level.[1]

The third basic difficulty derives from social and political objections to the permanency of compulsion, although controls are frequently tolerated as a means of implementing a short-term incomes or wages policy. Opposition on this score is scarcely surprising, especially when it comes from trade unions and employers. For if an incomes or wages policy is thrust upon these groups, it means in effect that they relinquish a major traditional function, the determination of wages. As Prof. Sturmthal pointed out, in such circumstances, the whole *raison d'être* of, especially, the trade union movement, would be called in question.[2] Indeed, Prof. Sturmthal was very much of the opinion that not only is permanent compulsion in connection with incomes policies unacceptable to unions and employers but that it is undesirable *per se* because it contains seeds which, if they grow, can endanger democracy. Mr. Massé gauged that most of the other participants favoured implementing an incomes policy by persuasion.[3] The only obvious exception was Mr. Aubrey Jones, however, who favoured an element of compulsion on a longer-term basis, on the grounds that action by employers — and especially those in mono-polistic and oligopolistic market situations — and by individual trade unions, are a primary cause of inflation and can only be curbed if the government wields powers that have the same restraining effect as the forces of competition in former times. Moreover, he con-sidered that only such compulsion will have the necessary shock effect and arouse the community from their acceptance of continued price instability — an acceptance which, in itself, feeds the fires of inflation.[4]

If, therefore, a permanent incomes policy is acceptable only when it is voluntarily supported by the most closely affected groups, this implies that employers and unions [5] especially must be *persuaded* to agree to the principles on which the policy is based and to the way in which it is to be implemented.[6] There would appear to be two basic conditions for obtaining such support. First, the incomes policy would need to relate to all incomes. Secondly, provision

---

[1] Chapter 1, pp. 5 to 8.   [2] *Discussion*, p. 211.
[3] See Chapter 12, p. 130.   [4] *Discussion*, pp. 188 and 224.
[5] Though the support of other groups in the community would also need to be enlisted.
[6] The need for such persuasion was emphasised, especially by Dr. Crijns ; see Chapter 5.

would have to be made for the participation of the various groups in the formulation of the policy.

In the latter connection the Symposium revealed an attitude that could have considerable significance during the next few years. In the papers, discussion and replies to the questionnaire, many participants expressed the view that a longer-term incomes policy can only properly be formulated within the context of a national economic plan. Support for this view came particularly, but by no means exclusively, from the trade union participants.[1] On a political level it derives from the fact that the affected parties feel that by participating in the planning procedures and machinery they will have the necessary influence not only on incomes policy but also on much wider, if related, social and economic policies ; Mr. Le Brun was quick to point out that such participation is not yet realised.[2] On a technical level, and as previously stated, many appreciated that a longer-term incomes policy would need to be shaped by a wide variety of social and economic variables and in turn would have ramifications throughout the economic system, and that the necessary integration of incomes policies with other economic and social measures could only properly be accomplished within the framework of a comprehensive national plan.

If it is the case that the fate of incomes policies and economic planning are closely linked, then the type of *rapprochement* of views referred to by Mr. Massé,[3] between planning and non-planning advocates, could have important repercussions on the development of incomes policies. In particular it could prove vital whether or not the current trend away from formal and detailed plans to more flexible indicative programmes proves to be mere camouflage for an abandonment of economic planning or a move towards a more realistic and effective system for guiding the development of the economy and providing a framework for policy decisions.

3. *International Aspects of Incomes Policies*

A discussion of certain international implications of incomes policies grew out of two hypotheses contained in a statement by Prof. Giersch : that with a system of fixed international rates of exchange,

---

[1] Indeed, to the extent that a pattern of support can be discerned, it seems to be largely a geographical one, the 'continental' participants in general urging the need for the integration of incomes policies and economic planning, whilst the 'Anglo Saxon' and Scandinavian participants were largely silent on the question.
[2] *Discussion*, p. 194.   [3] Chapter 12, pp. 137 to 138.

incomes policies are doomed to failure in small, export-dependent countries; and though potentially viable in the larger countries where exports are less important, their implementation is likely to aggravate international disequilibria.[1] Prof. Giersch asserted that in smaller countries, a normally high dependence on exports means that any initial success which an incomes policy might have in achieving price stability is soon lost as a result of wage drift when firms in the export sector attempt to attract resources in order to supply the world market where prices continue to rise. To a considerable extent, this hypothesis is borne out by the statistics assembled by Mr. Saunders and Mr. Eskilsson.[2] Mr. Saunders' data show that the effectiveness of centrally devised wage policies is largely frustrated by wage drift; and Mr. Eskilsson's findings suggest that, in Sweden at least and if the building industry is left out of account, wage drift may be higher in the export sector than in the domestic sector.[3] It is in fact likely that such wage drift would arise if competitive bidding and the use of the comparability criterion cannot be contained.

The second hypothesis is that if a country (most likely a large one with a relatively small export sector and therefore little 'imported' wage drift) successfully implements a wage or incomes policy, it will give rise to international economic disequilibria in the form of a balance of payments surplus that will probably accrue *vis-à-vis* the rest of the world. This possibility has much wider implications. In the first place the adoption and pursuit of such a policy might be criticised because it has a 'beggar my neighbour' effect.[4] But, at the worst, as Prof. Ulman pointed out,[5] whilst income policies, if they have this result, beggar one's neighbour by appropriating their exchange reserves, they avoid harming one's neighbour by exporting unemployment and stagnation as a result of the pursuit of the deflationary policies which the treatment of domestic inflation might require in the absence of an incomes policy. The second relevant observation, also made by Prof. Ulman, is that in practice incomes policies are frequently adopted to stave off balance of payments

[1] *Discussion*, pp. 185 and 186.
[2] See Chapter 2, Tables 1, 2, pp. 17 and 18, Chapter 9, pp. 106 and 107; and *Discussion*, p. 185.
[3] However, this result is by no means conclusive. Mr. Eskilsson has set out to test the opposite hypothesis, that wage drift is higher in domestic industries that are sheltered from foreign competition, than in those that are exposed to foreign competition and such a testing requires that domestic industries exposed to imports as well as export industries, be included in the 'exposed' sector.
[4] *Discussion*, p. 186.   [5] *Discussion*, p. 197.

difficulties and to that extent they will, in fact, help to correct international disequilibria.[1] Of course, it is by no means inconceivable that incomes policies might be adopted in particular countries to deal with the purely internal impact of inflation, and if there is neither international co-ordination of such policies nor a system of flexible exchange rates, it is not impossible that such incomes policies could cause international disequilibria.

This leads to a more positive question : given the general reluctance to change rates of exchange for correcting international disequilibria,[2] can incomes policies be used for this purpose. That Prof. Sellier was able, in his paper, to draw an analogy between the State's former manipulation of the gold value of its currency and the contemporary use of wage policies suggests the possibility of using incomes policies in this role.[3] Moreover, Mr. Zoeteweij drew attention to the fact that twice when considering how to raise the price level in order to align it more closely with world prices, the Dutch authorities had regarded a wage increase via wage policy and a revaluation of the guilder as alternatives and in fact had opted for the former.[4]

It is difficult to believe that incomes policies could succeed in this role without a degree of international co-ordination of the objectives adopted in each country — a procedure analagous to the rules of the game as prescribed by the IMF in an attempt to avoid, for example, competitive devaluations. Precisely what coverage, in terms of countries, would be practicable and what form such international co-ordination of incomes policies might take, it is difficult to imagine. One possibility is that it might be effected, on a limited scale, within the framework of regional groupings of industrialised countries which seek to harmonise a wide range of economic and social conditions.

Dr. Crijns, in his paper, drew attention to the steps which have been taken in this direction by the European Economic Community.[5] That both the principles on which co-ordination might be based and the methods for achieving it have as yet only been formulated by the Community in very general terms, reflect, as Mr. Fehrs pointed out, the fact that attention has only recently been directed toward this aspect of incomes policies.[6] Further consideration of the

---

[1] See also above, pp. 164 and 165.
[2] Mr. Mattei and Prof. Sturmthal emphasised that practices exist which mean that exchange rates are not as inflexible as they would appear to be. *Discussion*, pp. 221 and 223.   [3] Chapter 6, p. 70.   [4] *Discussion*, p. 199.
[5] Chapter 5, pp. 68 *et seq.*   [6] *Discussion*, p. 237.

international repercussions of income policies, advocated by Mr. Massé,[1] would seem to be desirable.

III. CONCLUSIONS

Within the field of inflation and incomes policies the Symposium was intended to consider whether certain measures, if taken independently, would help to make the operation of the labour market less inflationary, and whether they could be used as part of an incomes policy. The Symposium has done little more than screen some measures that fall within this class, separating those that would bear further scrutiny and experimentation from those that promise little in this context. Long-term contracts, profit- and capital-sharing schemes and investment-wages appear to fall in the latter category. In contrast, a number of measures that seek to limit wage drift rather than to restrict formal wage claims, promise to make the operation of the labour market less inflationary. Thus, the use of active manpower policies — by lessening competitive bidding — and changes in systems of remuneration, might limit initial wage drift ; the replacement of the comparability criterion by job evaluation schemes or a system of trade union wage relativity preferences, might do much to prevent the spread of wage drift ; and influence on decentralised bargaining procedures through the union movement or by means of fiscal, price or statutory measures would, in varying degrees, help to underpin the limitation of wage drift that would stem from these measures.

Two considerations need to be borne in mind when considering these measures. First, whilst each might help to make the labour market less inflationary, even the approximate size of their impact is not known. There is much scope here for quantitative research. Secondly, the fact that these measures offer to limit inflation even in the absence of an incomes policy does not mean that each of them would be *acceptable* in the absence of such a policy. In particular, measures to improve the control of decentralised wage negotiations through the medium of the trade union movement, or the statutory limitation of the results of such negotiations, are unlikely to be feasible unless much more comprehensive policies are implemented.

This leads to the question of the extent to which such measures provide a basis for an incomes policy. Undoubtedly, their adoption

---

[1] Chapter 12, p. 138.

would contribute to the viability of such a policy — though in the absence of quantitative assessments of the kind referred to above it is impossible to gauge the size of this contribution. If they were used as precursors to a wage or incomes policy, they would improve its chances of success simply by limiting the rate of inflation that the policy would need to tackle. But more important, experience suggests that a wage or incomes policy is unlikely to succeed over a long period, if the pressures that make for wage drift are allowed to persist in full force, so that such measures would need to be pursued alongside the wage or incomes policy.

The proceedings reveal, however, that while measures that make the operation of the labour market less inflationary are a necessary condition for a longer-term wages or incomes policy, they are by no means sufficient. It seems that a lasting policy with respect to incomes would also need to be comprehensive in its coverage, to provide for changes in the major income shares as well as in wage and price relativities, and to make suitable provision for the participation, in its formulation, of the various groups in the community. These matters were not a primary concern of the Symposium, though the proceedings were useful, in this connection, in that they identified certain policies which at one and the same time could be used to make the labour market less inflation prone, and help to ensure the wider conditions for incomes policy ; price and fiscal policies come within this class.

Finally, in the case of even wider policy issues, the results are instructive if paradoxical. It was emphasised, in particular, that incomes policies are closely related to two other major policy fields : the manipulation of exchange rates and demand management. In the case of exchange rates, a suggestion that the reluctance to change currency parities may undermine an incomes policy was developed into the thesis that incomes and exchange rate policies might, in fact, be regarded as alternative means of attaining a given objective — equilibrium in the balance of payments. In contrast, the view that incomes policies and demand management are in some degree alternative methods of achieving a given objective, price stability, received less attention than the consideration that if the level and structure of demand is not managed in an appropriate fashion, it can undermine an incomes policy.

A SUMMARY OF THE DISCUSSION

I. Objectives, Conditions and Instruments for Incomes Policies

A DISCUSSION on the basis of the papers prepared by Mr. Saunders, Prof. Sellier and Mr. Weinberg.

Mr. Saunders, referring to his paper, wished to emphasise that he had not intended to suggest that the sole objective of an incomes policy is to keep the rise in labour costs within the limits of the increase in national productivity. This is just one test which is very commonly applied by governments, economic journalists, international organisations and academic economists.

In Mr. Saunders' view an incomes policy means that some organisation should be in a position to control rather directly and to co-ordinate the major lines of development of money incomes. One purpose of such control is to influence the rate at which, in the aggregate, costs and prices rise. The objective need not necessarily be complete stability in the price level; such stability may be impossible or undesirable. There would simply be an attempt to achieve some defined aim in respect of the rate at which costs and prices rise. The second purpose of such control should be to promote the growth of real income and improve the efficiency of the economy. And a third purpose is to promote what may be described as social justice — that distribution of income among industries and between profits and labour, occupations and social classes, which seems about right to the majority of people. Like most of the major aims of policy in the economic field these three purposes are almost certainly ambiguous and, in most circumstances, incompatible with each other, and, for example, it would be undesirable to use an incomes policy to obtain efficiency and growth, much less price stability, at the expense of social justice. The best use of an incomes policy is to try to move a little further towards each of these three desirable objectives.

Mr. Massé has distinguished the following two aspects of an incomes policy: whether there should be an incomes policy and what its general aims should be; and how it should be implemented. The answer to the second question is bound to differ from one country to another. But certain common elements seem to be necessary in every country if an incomes policy is to be implemented, and Mr. Saunders had tried to explore these common elements by posing a series of questions in his paper.

A Summary of the Discussion

The first necessary element is some degree of co-ordination of formal wage bargaining. This does not necessarily mean complete centralised bargaining in the sense of one central bargain determining a part of all wage changes, but it does mean that there should be control of the bargaining by a reasonably powerful centre on both the management and trade union sides ; there must be some central body in which wage policy can be crystallised. Secondly this control by management and unions must extend, to some degree, to the level of the enterprise — a major issue for the Symposium. How can such control be exercised and what margin, if any, should be left for the 'local' determination of inter-firm wage differences ?

Thirdly, the government, as the representative of society as a whole, must be able to have a sufficient influence on wage determination. Government control of wages may take the form in which it existed in the Netherlands during most of the post-war period, in principle the statutory control of all wages, or it may be used as it has just been developed, at the other extreme, in the United Kingdom — to be used as a last resort in an emergency and to prevent what the government considers to be anti-social action by certain minority groups. In fact there is a wide range of possibilities between these two extremes. There is a case for the government promoting impartial investigations, such as those now conducted in the United Kingdom by the Prices and Incomes Board, not just to settle disputes but to provide answers to wage or price problems that are in accordance with the national interest as well as with the views of the social partners immediately involved. Unfortunately such investigations can only be carried out on a very small scale ; the experience of Mr. Aubrey Jones's Board is that to produce convincing answers in a specific case is a very big task and that it would be impossible to do this on a really comprehensive scale. It is hoped that an examination of a few cases will yield a set of principles that can readily be applied to others.

The government cannot satisfactorily play its part unless there is a reasonable consensus in society about what the distribution of income roughly ought to be. Certain elements of conflict and of harmony, about which Prof. Pen has written, are required in a successful society. Probably most people feel that there is a need for rather more harmony and rather less conflict. This problem of arriving at a social consensus is probably the most difficult task for the trade union movement in many countries. It is particularly difficult in countries where the unions regard the government as a political opponent, and even presents problems in countries where the authorities are in political harmony with the trade union movement.

Fourthly, and this is an extremely important common element in any kind of successful incomes policy, each of the parties immediately concerned — the government, unions and management — should have an explicit interpretation of the main objectives of the policy. In particular, they must translate the economic efficiency and social justice objectives into requirements in the wage structure. No matter what is said about the need for more incentives or about the desire for solidarity or for equal pay for equal work, in the end, from all these principles there seems to have emerged a wage structure which remains virtually constant, in which wage relativities hardly change even over quite long periods.

Mr. Saunders attributed this rigidity to the fact that neither unions nor management are prepared to propound a policy about the distribution of income, to say specifically, for example, how much the difference between skilled workers and unskilled workers ought to be (or indeed whether it should be greater or less than the current margin) or what should be the relationship between the standard pay of, say, a clerical and a semi-skilled worker. Similarly they refuse to face the problem of how much it is worth offering by way of incentives in particular occupations or enterprises in order to secure the benefits of greater efficiency. This conflict between justice, however we define it, and efficiency, has never been resolved and representatives of management and of unions have not attempted to define what we mean by these terms ; they have not tried to state what they mean by an incomes policy in terms of the distribution of income. Perhaps it is impossible. But it seems to be one of the subjects that should be discussed in the Symposium. It is a problem on which the unions in most countries could make a definite set of propositions that would stand a reasonable chance of acceptance since the history of wage determination in the past few years suggests that the initiative lies very heavily with the trade union movement in most western European countries. That is, one can interpret the situation as being to some extent essentially one of aggression on the part of the trade union movement, with employers and management reacting, on the whole, rather passively, and in these circumstances it is unfortunate that trade union movements have not tried to define a set of propositions which, given this background, would have a good chance of acceptance.

Prof. Sellier said that, in the section of his paper concerned with the economic conditions for active mediation, he had tried to show that decisions about the wage level had become essentially monetary and that a mediator plays the role of arbiter between the interests of major groups — workers, employers and society as a whole. Government intervention through a mediator certainly affects the outcome of wage negotiations, but it is not possible for the State to determine the level of wages as precisely as it can fix the value of its currency. In an economy where the supply of credit is flexible and where competition is more or less monopolistic in nature, there are wide margins within which wage rates can be negotiated, margins that the State cannot completely close. Moreover, government intervention in wage determination procedures can never be complete. Income policies do not fully eliminate wage drift, though the data presented by Mr. Saunders suggests that this was almost achieved in the

A Summary of the Discussion

Netherlands, a rather exceptional case. Also, incomes policies cannot be limited to wages but must also take account of other incomes — certain agricultural incomes and social security benefits are the most important ; state intervention, imperfectly effective even in the case of wages, must relate to the formation of all incomes and thereby to prices.

State intervention needs to be active in some degree ; in the case of 'passive' mediation, the mediator limits his role to that of a helpful intermediary, in the case of 'active' mediation he tries to influence the terms of the agreement. In the latter capacity he has three functions : to provide the negotiating parties with information ; to influence the timing and duration of the negotiations ; and to affect their outcome. The provision of information is a basic task of a mediator, though in the case of a passive mediator the information relates only to the desires and intentions of the negotiating parties. An active mediator is distinguished by the fact that he introduces into the negotiations information which perhaps one, or both, of the parties would rather ignore. In France, there is provision for a type of active mediation at the firm level which permits the mediator to examine the circumstances in which a certain wage claim could be conceded. For this purpose he may wish to evaluate the firm's capacity to pay and as a result this type of mediation is not welcomed by employers and is little used.

In France, active mediation has recently been used on the occasion of major conflicts and when attempts have been made to implement an incomes policy. In fact, the provisions of national indicative economic plans of the kind adopted in France have important implications for the determination of the equilibrium level of wages and constitute one type of information used in active mediation. Data taken from the plan is more effective than simple productivity information, since it takes account, at the macro-economic level, of the interdependences of all prices and incomes. However, whilst such information is very important, it may have little impact on the determination of wages at the plant level.

Prof. Sellier said that it is important to realise that the effect of mediation, even passive mediation, on the timing of wage negotiations is not neutral. As pointed out in his paper, mediation tends to benefit workers when the economy is moving into a recession and employers when it approaches a boom. The importance of this effect can be gathered from Keynes' assertion in 'How to Pay for the War' that economic equilibrium could, at that time, have been restored if wage claims were only delayed for three to six months.

The third objective of active mediation is to alter the outcome of the wage negotiations. In this connection it is important to understand how mediation is received by the parties immediately concerned, a consideration that is closely linked with the question — given much attention of late [1] — of the optimum level and structure of wage negotiations. It is

[1] Prof. Sellier cited, as an example, H. A. Turner and H. Zoeteweij, *op. cit.*

frequently debated whether central negotiations have the best results, reference being made to the Dutch and Swedish systems. But when the union movement itself lacks a centralised structure it is unlikely that central wage negotiations will be possible. The situation in France, where wages are negotiated essentially at the firm level, is a good illustration of this. Prof. Sellier alluded to an OECD group of experts [1] who had suggested that the size of trade unions might usefully be reduced. He thought that, in the present context, the homogeneity of the structure of the trade unions and their aims are more relevant than their size.

In connection with the degree to which the active mediator can affect the outcome of the negotiations, Prof. Sellier drew attention in his paper to proposals made by some economists for incentives that might influence the negotiations in the required direction and narrow the limits within which employers and unions find that they can negotiate wage rates. For in an expanding economy with a flexible money supply and oligopolistic competition, the margins within which the wage can be negotiated are very wide, and as a result, large wage differentials, reflecting different capacities to pay, occur. Thus, there is a need for some device that acts as a substitute for more competitive conditions and for a tight credit situation. One such proposal is that employers who grant too high wage increases should be penalised by fiscal measures. Unfortunately such measures would need to be flexible in their provisions between industries and firms if they are to be effective, posing administrative problems that would make it difficult to use them in the short term.

The primary sociological implication of an incomes policy is that an active mediator tries to persuade certain groups in society, employers and workers, to accept a major macro-economic goal ; that is he tries to persuade them to integrate and reconcile their individual interests with an objective adopted by society as a whole. When an incomes policy is based on voluntary support and not on any measure of control, in effect, the classical choice between the alternatives of the maximum degree of freedom and the maximum degree of effectiveness is avoided in preference to a certain combination of these two features. The ideal of a harmonious society, and its parallels at the firm level — works councils and incentive payment systems — have, as their goal, the substitution of co-operation for conflict. Whilst at the firm level little success has been achieved in this direction, at the level of society as a whole there are better prospects since the mediator, whilst he does not ignore the immediate goals of the negotiating parties, is external to their conflict and can seek the acceptance of a wider objective. In France, active mediation has proposed two such common, wider goals, the promotion of the growth of total consumption and the improvement of the economy's international competitiveness.

It is the mediator's task to persuade the negotiating parties to participate actively in such a policy, otherwise it will fail. In effect, this means

[1] OEEC, *The Problem of Rising Prices, op. cit.*

that he must persuade them to sacrifice present consumption in favour of the greater material well-being that would accompany, in the long run in this case, an improvement in the economy's competitiveness. Another major obstacle to the success of this policy is the very different degrees to which individual employers support the common goal. In an economy where each employer is a dynamic, efficient exporter, the common goal would have the same implications for all, and their uniform response would itself help to secure the necessary co-operation from workers. But, with contrasts between firms in respect of their efficiency rating and export characteristics, the mediator's goal can be far removed from those of individual entrepreneurs, considerably weakening labour's faith in its achievement. In these circumstances it is legitimate to ask whether the basic sociological requirement for a successful incomes policy should be to improve certain conditions, first those affecting employers and secondly those influencing workers, in order to change and make more harmonious the plans of individual firms.

In this connection, attention can be drawn to the revision of minimum wages in France. Would not a rise in minimum wages have the effect of raising the participation of the more dynamic and efficient firms, and of workers, in the pursuit of the common goal ? For, in effect, such an increase would threaten only the marginal firms, which in any case — and subject to satisfactory social safeguards — is one element of the common goal ; the efficient firms would not oppose such a rise. The French textile industry provides a good illustration of co-operation between unions and the more efficient managements for fighting those enterprises that can only compete on the basis of low wages. The sociological condition for the success of an incomes policy is that it be based on a national consensus, but in order to achieve this it is necessary that the individual goals of employers and workers conform more closely to the wider common objective established by the mediator.

Mr. Weinberg said that the essence of his paper could be stated very simply. First, the United States guideposts died because they were improperly formulated, being promulgated from on high rather than being developed by the parties that were expected voluntarily to carry them out. Secondly, they died because they were inequitably applied as between wages and prices and because, in particular, no action was taken against prices that were excessive to begin with and which should have been reduced. The guideposts died because they constituted, essentially, a wage policy and not an incomes policy in a country where, as the data presented in Mr. Weinberg's paper show, wages were not the source of inflation. Recent price increases are due partly to shortages of foodstuffs — and this is likely to be a temporary problem — and partly to an abuse of administered pricing power. There has been a wages policy in a country where wages were not the problem and no incomes policy where rises in incomes other than wages were inflationary.

The Labour Market and Inflation

There are three basic requirements for a sound incomes policy. First, efforts should be made to minimise inflationary pressures. This can be done partly by means of manpower policies and partly by efforts to direct demand away from and capital into the bottleneck areas of the economy, etc. Secondly, if inflationary pressures cannot be completely eliminated, it is important to develop policies that will avoid inequities as a result of inflation. Thirdly, if inequities nevertheless do occur, then other mechanisms such as tax measures must be used to correct these inequities. Only if equity is assured can an incomes policy be maintained. It should be emphasised that from a trade union point of view equity does not simply mean the preservation of the *status quo* in the distribution of income. It requires that increments in the gross national product be distributed in such a way that they contribute to a greater degree of social justice.

Prof. Giersch reported about his experience as a member of the Council of Economic Experts in West Germany (Sachverständigenrat zur Begutachtung der gesamtwirtschaftlichen Entwicklung). This body, which is an official institution but is independent of the government as well as of employers' associations and the trade unions, has the task of analysing economic conditions and alternative policies. Unlike the United States Council of Economic Advisers it can seek to influence government policy only through its reports and their impact on public opinion. As far as wages are concerned the Council did not advocate a simple productivity guideline. Instead, they formulated a rule which takes into account — besides productivity — changes in capital costs, in the terms of trade, in the structure of employment and deviations from internal and external equilibria. In its second report the Council was quite specific in taking account of inevitable price increases which must be expected as a result of past developments. In 1965 there had been a rise in the cost-of-living index of about 3 per cent., roughly in line with the experience of other European countries. In these circumstances, the Council of Economic Experts adopted an approach which can be described by a quotation from Robert Solow : 'But suppose prices have been rising, and suppose that it is very unlikely that they can be made to level out in one year. Then it is difficult for labor to acquiesce in a figure for money wage increases which would give the right real-wage increase only if prices were constant. That would be to acquiesce to a subnormal increase in real wages and a supernormal increase in profits. On the other hand, to add the current rate of price increase to the rate of productivity increase would be to throw the entire burden onto profits or, more likely, guarantee that prices will continue to rise. What is needed is some target pace for slowing down the price trend over a couple of years.' [1]

The Council suggested that an initial rate of inflation of 3 per cent.

---

[1] See Robert M. Solow, 'The Case against the Guideposts', in *Guidelines, Informal Controls and the Market Place*, edited by G. P. Shultz and R. Z. Aliber, Chicago and London, 1966, p. 54.

might be reduced to 2 per cent. in 1966 and to 1 per cent. in 1967. To reach this target without stagnation it appeared necessary to eliminate, gradually and simultaneously, the 3 per cent. rate of inflation that had become standard in all the components of effective demand, as well as in interest rates and expected wage increases. The proposal was based on an annual growth of productivity and potential GNP of 4 per cent. plus a margin for price increases, falling from 2 per cent. in 1966 to 1 per cent. in 1967. Rises in the wage level compatible with this course were about 6 per cent. in the first year and about 5 per cent. in the second.

Many people in Germany considered this approach to be acceptable, since it left the distribution of income untouched and avoided the danger of a stabilisation crisis. However, the Federal Government and some employers' associations preferred productivity-guided wage increases ; they therefore rejected it.

Apart from lessening the danger of inflation and unemployment, the gradual approach urged by the Council had the advantage of reducing the likelihood of an external disequilibrium — which, in the case of Germany, would mean a persistent and growing balance of payments surplus that sooner or later could wreck the whole stabilisation policy. Prof. Giersch placed a great deal of emphasis on this point. He explained that, given the present monetary system and world-wide price rises, an individual country is bound to surrender its internal stability, unless it is prepared to abandon the principle of constant exchange rates. Any guideline for wage increases which is directed at stabilising the national cost level will be frustrated by the market unless the exchange rate can be correspondingly adjusted or is free to move.

To demonstrate how price rises can be internationally transmitted through the wage mechanism, Prof. Giersch pointed to the problem of wage determination in the export industries. If export prices are rising or if export industries are not forced by foreign competition to pass on, in the form of lower prices, productivity increases which are substantially above the national average, these industries are likely to bid up wages or to grant wage increases in collective bargaining which would go beyond what would be compatible with a constant national cost level. To understand the full implications of this mechanism it has to be realised that in these circumstances trade unions find it advantageous to start a wage round in the export-oriented industries and make these industries pace-setters for subsequent negotiations in the other industries.

In connection with the notion that market forces may prevent the operation of a guideline, Prof. Giersch was not surprised to observe in Mr. Saunders' paper that relatively small countries with central control of wage bargaining have a large wage drift.

It could be argued that a national incomes policy might be easier in a large country with a relatively small export sector. But this would be true only for the country in question. If it were successful, the incomes policy would cause correspondingly greater balance of payments problems in smaller countries, which would force upon them disinflationary policies and, possibly, temporary stagnation. From this it follows that with a system of fixed exchange rates, national incomes policies must be co-ordinated on an international level. This complicates matters considerably. More flexibility of exchange rates would permit individual countries, where the conditions for an incomes policy are relatively favourable, to prove that such a policy is feasible and to no one's disadvantage provided that it is based on a comprehensive co-ordination of macro-economic decisions.

Finally Prof. Giersch said that incomes policy had to be understood and supported by the general public. This condition is far from being fulfilled at present, and, judging from German experience, to cultivate the right attitude in the community may take years, if not a generation.

Mr. Massé said that even if international co-ordination succeeded in yielding an annual price increase of the same order of magnitude in each country thereby avoiding many international trade problems, inflationary price increases would still pose serious internal problems. Also, Prof. Giersch's proposals for retarding price increases were global and budgetary and concerned essentially with the level of demand, rather than with incomes policies.

Prof. Giersch emphasised that an incomes policy unsupported by an appropriate budgetary policy would be doomed to failure. Why should trade unions follow a guideline directed at stabilisation, if governments pursue policies contrary to this objective ? If, for example, the authorities base their tax estimates on the assumption of a 3 per cent. rate of inflation, the trade unions can hardly be made to believe that price stability is around the corner.

Prof. Sturmthal agreed with most of what Prof. Giersch had said. However, he thought that whilst it is the task of the professional economist to determine when the total of projected investment, consumption and governmental expenditures is likely to exceed total probable output, to decide where the cuts in expenditure should occur is a value judgment and the subject matter of politics, and a uniform cut of one percentage point in the increase in each item, as proposed by Prof. Giersch, may not represent the preferred pattern.

Prof. Giersch agreed that it is the responsibility of the competent authorities to decide where to make the cuts in expenditure. The proposal of the German Council of Economic Experts was simply intended as a starting-point for discussion. Its report pointed out, for example, that an increase in the government's share in GNP would still be compatible with a stabilisation policy, if the inflationary effects of an accelerated rise in public expenditure were compensated by measures to slow down the rate of increase in private consumption and investment. Higher tax rates could do the trick ; in certain circumstances a budget surplus might be required. To launch an incomes policy for stabilisation, it may be necessary to adopt as simple a concept as possible. This was the notion behind the principle of simultaneous and proportionate action with regard to the individual components of aggregate demand and factor prices. A simple set of rules, which show that all sectors have to make proportionate contributions to stability, has a greater chance of convincing the general public that an incomes policy is not necessarily aimed at changing the distribution of incomes.

Mr. Rehn thought that the definition of incomes policy used by Mr. Saunders — the regulation of the wage level by the State or by the labour market institutions — should be adhered to. Prof. Giersch seemed to imply that budgetary policy could also be considered as an element of an incomes policy.

Mr. Weinberg said that Prof. Giersch's statement raised two questions about the situation in the United States. First, a disinflationary budgetary policy can be adopted in Germany because the initial position is one of full employment. This would not be appropriate in the United States where the unemployment rate, measured in terms of United States concepts, is about ten times the West German rate — though regrettably there is still talk about cooling off an over-heated economy in the United States.

Secondly, the United States situation has important international implications. Alarm about inflation in the United States was grossly exaggerated, there being none until very recently and then it has been partly due, as mentioned already, to temporary phenomena. In any case the United States balance of payments difficulties were not attributable to a trade deficit but to other factors which require special policies. Indeed, a high official of the United States Government had pointed out that if the United States substantially increased its trade surplus, difficulties would be created for other countries. To this extent therefore the degree of price increase experienced in the United States may have been internationally helpful.

Mr. Aubrey Jones was of the opinion that budgetary and incomes policies complement each other since there are both economic and social elements in the inflationary problem. Turning his attention to Prof. Sellier's distinction between passive and active mediation, he pointed out that the United Kingdom has a long tradition of the former and that a current major problem is whether the passive mediator or arbitrator should be transformed into an active mediator or arbitrator. Should the mediator who, by tradition, has taken into account only the interests of the parties immediately involved now take account of a wider set of considerations when giving his judgment ? Mr. Aubrey Jones thought that such a change asks too much of the mediator. When, for instance, there is a threat of a strike, it is almost impossible for the mediator to do other than take into account solely the interests of the two parties. It is preferable to entrust the role of active mediator to some other body or bodies, government, quasi-government or otherwise, to which the judgment of the passive mediator could be referred in order that wider considerations be taken into account. In any case, in the long run, the interest of the parties and the public interests may well coincide. For instance, a company is faced by the problem of whether to maximise profit in the short run at the expense of research, development and long-term investment, or to take account of its profit record over longer periods. A trade union has a similar choice — whether to obtain the maximum wage rise now, or to secure a greater stability and therefore a steadier increase in incomes over a longer period.

If the longer-term interest is to be taken into account by some quasi-governmental institution, then the problem posed by Mr. Saunders must be faced : should the necessary influence be exercised by persuasion or by some element of compulsion ? It is not possible to wait the generation that Prof. Giersch has suggested may be necessary for cultivating the appropriate changes in the community's attitudes. For two reasons, therefore, some element of compulsion may well be needed. First, a country introducing an incomes policy is invariably faced by an economic crisis and the situation — as it is now in the United Kingdom for example — is usually too serious to allow it to rely solely on persuasion. Secondly, the problem is in part an institutional one. Trade union officials are driven by their members to seek maximum wage increases, so that, especially if the industry is oligopolistic, employers tend to distribute higher productivity to workers in the form of higher wages than to consumers in the form of lower prices. Such an institutional problem needs to be solved more quickly than by persuasion over the course of a generation, and some element of compulsion seems to be required.

Mr. Aubrey Jones agreed with Mr. Weinberg that efforts to influence prices are just as important as efforts to influence wages, and a degree of compulsion must be exercised in respect of both. In this connection it is pertinent that whilst, as Prof. Giersch had pointed out, an incomes policy must be supported by an appropriate budgetary policy, the latter can imply an increase in prices in certain conditions. The British budgets of 1965 and 1966 sought to limit the increase in living standards which from a general point of view were rising too rapidly, by raising indirect taxes and thereby prices. Mr. Massé had said that without the stabilisation policy, which applied to prices rather than to wages, a greater degree of budgetary deflation would have been needed in France. Yet is there not some concern that this French price policy had been detrimental to profits, and thereby to investment and future productivity ?

Mr. Massé, replying to Mr. Aubrey Jones, said that when the stabilisation measures were introduced in September 1963, the damage was already done, the French economy was overheated. Nevertheless they were in time to halt the rapid deterioration in the French balance of payments. Given that devaluation was virtually impossible at that time, there were, in fact, only two policy options for dealing with the balance of payments crisis : classical deflation by means of budgetary and credit measures or a composite policy embracing the classical approach but including, also, price controls that would themselves influence, indirectly, wages. The government chose the latter course. The reasons for this can be found in some features that were peculiar to the French economy at that time. More precisely, with one million people entering France following Algerian independence, the government feared that general economic measures which might have retarded the economy too much would have created unemployment and made the reabsorption of this labour force particularly difficult. Consequently, the authorities chose the policy that would have least adverse effects on production.

It is true that this policy had some undesirable results, in particular a reduction in profits and investment. This reduction could have retarded the rise in productivity, although priority was given to productivity improving investments, but it is difficult to be precise about this. In any case, measures have been taken to stimulate investment again, to encourage high productivity industries, to develop training schemes and, in general, to promote growth and minimise the effects of the reduction in profits.

Mr. Mattei, commenting on Mr. Saunders' paper, said that he did not think that the classification of countries that it contained, based on whether or not they had a centralised system of wage determination, is quite correct. More precisely, Italy has enjoyed an adequate degree of centralisation since the Second World War, with a central employers' organisation co-ordinating the terms of the contracts of the various sectors and with several contracts — for example, that stipulating the relationship between the wages of men and women — being negotiated at the national level.

Mr. Mattei stated that he was also opposed to policies that make the wage structure too rigid. In Italy, for example, the sharp increase — within a period of three or four years — of wages in the textile industry and other similar short-term developments has completely changed the wage structure.

It is also vital for a distinction to be drawn, and a choice made, between tying wage increases to productivity increases on the one hand, at the industry or firm level and, on the other, at the national level. Mr. Mattei thought Mr. Saunders' paper a little confused on this point.

The various papers presented to the Symposium do not seem to pay adequate attention to the relationship, in different countries, between incomes policies and escalator clauses. Indeed, there is a tendency to refer loosely to wage rises without stipulating whether they are in real or money terms.

Price controls are referred to by Mr. Saunders as a means of limiting wage increases. But it is overlooked that such controls also reduce profits as can be seen from French and Italian experience in recent years. How can price controls prevent wage increases when, in fact, they are frequently granted *before* the introduction of controls ? What are the consequences of price controls on investment and, above all, on the international competitiveness of the economy, given that they can hardly moderate those wage increases determined by forces external to the firm ?

Unlike Prof. Sellier, Mr. Mattei did not believe that there exist wide margins within which wages can be determined. Because of international competition this margin is very narrow and varies with the degree of development, technological achievement and capitilisation of a given country, factors that change little in the short run. In this connection, the extent of monopolistic or oligopolistic pricing — and therefore the flexibility of wage concessions — is also exaggerated. Conditions vary greatly between industries. In labour intensive industries — such as textiles — where, it is true, wage rises can have a particularly strong inflationary impact, the degree of competition is greatest, and, therefore, the margin within which wage rises can be granted, narrowest. Obviously, pricing policies in, say, the chemical industry can be more flexible, but in any case wage increases in this sector have less impact on the general monetary equilibrium of the economy.

Mr. Saunders, replying to Mr. Mattei, said that he had used a very simple test in his paper, the relationship in various countries between productivity increases as measured by statistics relating to total industry — an average of an enormous variety of productivity increases in different enterprises — and the over-all average increase in wages. Very little is known about the dispersion of productivity changes between enterprises, but it is likely that it is extremely wide and that if increases in wages were to be governed by the productivity changes in individual enterprises they would differ greatly and after a few years would be quite unacceptable. In the Netherlands wages were for a time governed by productivity developments in individual industries and it seems to have led to dispersions that proved unacceptable.

Mr. Mattei said that he had simply wanted to draw attention to the fact that whilst in certain industries, electricity for example, productivity is increasing, in others such as city transport where urban congestion has reduced the speed of traffic, it may actually decrease. Does this imply that wages should be reduced in this sector ? Productivity changes at the level of the firm must be rejected as a basis for wage increases since, for reasons of social justice, a certain minimum wage increase must be given to all workers and such other criteria as the rise in national productivity must therefore be used.

Mr. Massé expressed the opinion that at least three-quarters of any rise in wages should be related to the growth of national productivity, and the rest to productivity developments at the firm level in order to provide some incentive to those employers and workers whose productivity increases most. Also, it is important to realise that whilst labour productivity

A Summary of the Discussion

is a meaningful concept at the national level, within an enterprise it is more ambiguous. In the case of the Electricité de France, for example, investment and technical progress has caused in a ten-year period a rise in output per hour of 5 per cent. in the hydro-electric stations and 16 per cent. in the thermal power stations. But this does not imply that the quality of work has risen most in the latter section, simply that investment there has embodied particularly important new techniques. It is because of such difficulties that attach to the concept of labour productivity that Mr. Massé has suggested a concept of global factor productivity. The new French Costs and Incomes Study Centre has been charged by the government with examining developments in three or four particular firms and two or three industries. In fact, however, the Centre is also considering the question raised by Mr. Mattei, and which is central to an incomes policy: whether attention should be paid essentially to changes in national productivity or whether account should also be taken of conditions in individual firms.

Prof. Sellier noted that incomes policies seek to co-ordinate wage increases in such a way that inter-industry and inter-firm differences in capacity to pay and in the margin within which they might concede wage rises, are largely ignored. Even in the absence of an incomes policy the stability of the existing wage structure seems to be largely assured over the longer run — and Mr. Mattei's textile example is especially interesting since it is an exception in this respect. Yet in the short term there are sharp inter-industry and inter-firm differences in wage increases as a result of contrasts in their capacities to pay and in the margins within which they find that they can strike a bargain. A French study of the period 1954 to 1964 [1] shows that whilst the wage structure was stable over the period as a whole, there were very sharp contrasts between industries within the period, in quarterly wage changes. It is from the absence of a co-ordination of these short-term increases, and in the attempts of each group of workers to maintain the long-term structure, that labour market tensions stem.

Mr. Mattei said that he did not understand these short-term changes to which Prof. Sellier referred. In France, as in other countries, collective agreements terminated after one, two or three years.

Prof. Sellier replied that in France the wage provisions of collective agreements have little effect on actual earnings, and it was the latter that he had in mind.

Mr. Weinberg returned to the question raised by Mr. Mattei: which productivity changes, national, industry or firm should be used as the criterion for determining wage increase ? As a general principle, changes in national productivity are the most relevant. But this principle needs

---

[1] J. J. Silvestre, 'Les comportements cycliques de hausses de salaires dans les industries de transformation' (France, 1954–64), *Revue d'Economie Politique*, No. 2, 1966.

qualifying. If the fruits of productivity improvements above the national average are being passed on to consumers as lower prices by the industry or firm in question, then the trade union realises that resources are simply not available for providing a wage increase in the same unit much above the national rate of increase in productivity. But if the industry or firm is retaining these fruits in the form of profits, workers will insist that their wage increases be related to productivity improvements in the firm in question.

Mr. Fehrs agreed fully with Prof. Sellier that whilst in the short term there are very sharp differences in wage rises, in the long term the wage structure tends to be stable. However, there is one exception to the latter rule connected with the conjunctural situation of an industry. Where an industry is relatively depressed then regardless of the productivity performance of the industry wages rise less than the average. Thus the coal-mining industry in Western Germany — and in other countries — is now passing through a difficult period, with the result that whilst its productivity is increasing substantially wages are rising less than in the economy as a whole.

Mr. Meidner said that he was a little unhappy that Mr. Saunders had included Sweden in the group of countries which have some kind of incomes policy. Mr. Saunders' paper had identified four significant features common to the five countries with an incomes policy. In Mr. Meidner's opinion, two of these four features are not to be found in Sweden.

Firstly, there is no substantial co-ordination of wage claims in Sweden, since there is not just one powerful trade union federation but three and little real co-ordination between their policies. True there is no religious division in the Swedish union movement of the kind that exists in the Netherlands ; nor are there any basic political divisions. However, the Swedish trade union movement is divided into three social and skill groups, a situation that poses very serious co-ordination problems — as can be seen in the complete lack of co-operation that attended the teachers' strike. As a result of this lack of co-ordination the following sequence of wage claims occurs : manual workers, organised in the largest group (probably the group Mr. Saunders has in mind when he refers to the powerful trade union federation) obtain, say, a 4 per cent. wage increase, followed by the white-collar union with between 7 and 8 per cent. and finally the third group, the academic workers, claiming between 15 and 30 per cent. (the claim in this case representing an accumulation of claims over several years that were not conceded). This is a very approximate picture of what can happen, but it is sufficient to show that great care needs to be exercised when evaluating the degree of co-ordination in Swedish trade unions' wage policy.

Secondly, the Swedish Government exercises virtually no control over prices even by means of persuasion. The government merely urges that prices should not be raised too often and in a too unreasonable way, and then publishes data about the frequency of increases.

Mr. Saunders accepted Mr. Meidner's claim that there is not complete co-ordination of wage claims in Sweden, but pointed out that there is not complete co-ordination of wage claims in any country. Did Mr. Meidner feel that there is less co-ordination in Sweden than there is in the other Nordic countries, Norway, Denmark, Finland, none of which has perfect comprehensive co-ordination ? Mr. Saunders wished to distinguish between countries which have some degree of central control and those that do not, and it seems that Sweden, Norway, Denmark and Finland are in a different category in this respect to Western Germany, Britain, France and Italy. If the Swedish wage co-ordination arrangements are closer to those in Germany than to those in Norway then Mr. Saunders' classification is incorrect. Mr. Saunders accepted Mr. Meidner's contention that, apart from in the agricultural sector, there is no price control in Sweden.

Mr. Meidner replied that if Mr. Saunders had in mind the Confederation of the LO, it is probably correct to say that Sweden has the most centralised system of wage co-ordination in Western Europe. But the other Nordic countries do not have such a strong white-collar union and academic federation as Sweden, and this makes it difficult to give a clear answer to his question. The influence and membership of the white-collar groups are increasing in Sweden, and the problem of co-ordinating the three federations is much more pressing now than it used to be. The description in Mr. Saunders' paper is perhaps correct for earlier Swedish experience, but the scene is changing.

Prof. Pen greatly admired Mr. Weinberg's paper but wondered if it is very relevant to the problems being discussed, since the United States seems to be the only country where there has been no problem of wage inflation in the last five years. Nevertheless it is very important to know why this should be the case. What factors are at play in the United States that are absent in Europe ? Is it the relatively higher level of unemployment ? Is it the guideposts, dead or alive ?

Mr. Weinberg thought that a combination of unemployment and the guideposts had been responsible for holding down wages in the United States.

Prof. Pen pointed out that this suggested that the guideposts had been effective. Also, he wanted to know if all groups in the United States community were happy that wage inflation had disappeared. Do not some people welcome it ?

Mr. Weinberg replied that the guideposts had been effective to the extent that they allowed employers to mobilise public opinion on their side in wage negotiations. They have not been perfectly effective — and now that prices are rising they are ceasing to have any influence — and the level of unemployment in the United States bears much of the responsibility for restraining wage increases. Mr. Weinberg believed that there is a general concern over inflation in the United States, but conceded that if a choice had to be made between full employment and price stability, American unions would follow Europe in accepting a degree of inflation.

Mr. Le Brun said he wished to express the general feelings of French trade unionists about incomes policies. The worst basis for an incomes policy is the assumption that wage increases are the major cause of inflation. History shows that inflation, which has lasted in France for more than 40 years, has not benefited labour since in each inflationary surge price increases have preceded wage rises. The theoretical arguments advanced for explaining why wage increases are responsible for inflation are also challenged by the French trade union movement. For only by a round-about sequence of events can wage increases be blamed. Such indirect reasoning incriminates wage rises on the following basis : they have an impact on the distribution of national income (though, of course, other increases also influence this) ; which in turn affects the level of savings and their distribution between enterprises, households, and the government sector and this, finally, can affect the inflationary process by its implications for the finance of investment.

National planning was urged for the French economy by the Confédération Générale du Travail before the Second World War. It was with the unions' support that planning was included in the economic programme after the liberation and with their participation that the first modernisation and re-equipment plan was carried through. The French trade union movement, although at present divided, has continued to interest itself in the formulation of the plan — even if in a rather critical fashion of late. In any case, it is only within the framework of a national plan that workers and unions would be willing to support an incomes or wage policy. Moreover such co-operation would only be forthcoming if both the methods used for the plan's formulation and its contents were acceptable to the unions. Something has been done in recent years to increase union participation in the planning process, but they have still not been invited to present and defend their wage claims at the outset of the planning process, a form of participation that would to some extent ensure that such claims be planned and co-ordinated. By such a procedure wage changes could be considered more systematically and, especially, account taken of their impact on investment.

The attitude adopted by unions towards the plan, and therefore towards a wage policy, is determined by the extent to which it provides for such social objectives as the following : a high priority for collective investment, a relative increase in minimum wages, the achievement of full employment and a gradual reduction in hours of work. Within such a framework, the unions could be trusted to support the policy without the need for any change in their essentially democratic and decentralised structure.

The adoption by the unions of such an attitude both to the national plan and to a wages policy also requires — what has for too long been absent — the unity of the French trade union movement.

The principal instrument for implementing a wages policy should be the economic plan itself, couched in value terms. Given this, instruments and institutions designed specifically for a wages policy would probably not be required. However, the implementation of the wages policy probably does require the development of more democratic and decentralised planning procedures and a system of contracts — not only collective agreements at different levels containing wage provisions, but also contracts between the State and enterprises that coincide, and can be varied, with the plan. The French Government has already concluded certain contracts, or quasi-contracts, with firms by which, in return for state aid, they try to fulfil the investment, export and price objectives of the plan. However, there is a need for the provision of state assistance to firms to be systematised and provided, in the context of each contract, in return for the enterprise's negotiation of and adherence to collective agreements that accord with the plan's provisions for incomes changes. Such collective agreements would provide for wage increases the larger part of which would conform to the plan's norms, but which would also take some account of productivity changes.

In all periods when real wages have risen, the savings of the labour force have increased more than proportionately. In France, income from savings is largely tax free and it has even been proposed that tax relief should be given for new savings themselves. French trade unions would welcome tax relief on savings that are invested through savings banks or in a 'national investment bank' that has been proposed particularly for channelling workers' savings into projects that conform with the plan.

Also, it should be possible for the progression of direct taxation to be arranged in such a way that it would discourage the payment of incomes that are greatly in excess of the plan's norms.

Mr. Massé, replying to Mr. Le Brun's statement that insufficient account had been taken in the national plans of the views of French trade unions, said that perhaps the real fault lay in a failure of the planners to explain how the plans are formulated. Initial work on the Fifth Plan was directed towards achieving the following objectives : the financing of public consumption and investment from current receipts thereby obviating the need for government borrowing ; an equilibrium in the balance of payments ; no increase in the tax burden ; and a rise in the production index to $127\frac{1}{2}$ at the end of five years, in the index of public investment to 150 and in the index of social security benefits to 145 — these latter two rates of increase being much above that of national production. In fact it was found that these objectives could only be simultaneously achieved if real wages increased by no more than 2 per cent. per annum — a condition that was unacceptable. As a result the government agreed to reduce its public investment programmes and social security benefits and have some recourse to borrowing, thereby giving room for a planned rise of 2·8 per cent. per annum in the real wage, or about 3·3 to 3·4 per cent. when account is taken of structural changes in the labour force. In this way a balance was achieved, but perhaps the processes by which it was arrived at were not made known sufficiently clearly and widely.

The emphasis placed by Mr. Le Brun on a system of contracts largely presupposes the practicability of centralised negotiations. But in turn this requires the existence of sufficiently centralised and homogeneous groups of negotiating partners, including a centralised and united trade union movement.

Mr. Massé supported Mr. Le Brun's proposals for changes in the fiscal system, provided that they are introduced gradually.

Prof. Pen referred to the statement in Mr. Le Brun's paper that trade union actions, and the level of wages, are not responsible for inflation in France. This is a remarkable statement, given that according to Mr. Saunders' figures wages have risen faster than productivity in France, leading to a rise in labour costs of at least 3 per cent. per year — that is, wage inflation. It might be argued that whilst this is true prices rose even faster. But if that is the case the share of wages in the national income should be diminishing, and Prof. Pen thought that, in fact, it was increasing.

Mr. Le Brun said that there probably existed a terminological misunderstanding between himself and Prof. Pen. Mr. Le Brun did not consider all cost and price increases as inflationary, only those that interact and become progressively larger. Price increases of this type are caused, essentially, by excess demand, which in turn has as its roots not changes in primary incomes but such factors as a budget deficit, a surplus on foreign account and too much credit. As previously pointed out, wage increases can affect these elements too, but only indirectly.

When considering changes in the share of labour in the national income it is important to remember that it can rise not only as a result of wage increases but also because the number of wage and salary earners is increasing as the result of the tendency to classify many entrepreneurs in this category.

Dr. Markmann raised some questions connected with Prof. Sellier's paper. First, when Prof. Sellier says that a task of the active mediator should be to provide more information on the basis of which disputes can be settled he probably has in mind essentially circumstances in France. In Western Germany, for example, relevant information — including that provided by the Council of Economic Experts — is already taken into account at all levels of wage negotiation.

Secondly, Prof. Sellier calls for a greater degree of centralisation in collective bargaining as a means of rationalising wage determination procedures. Such a proposal threatens not only the role of trade unions and employers' organisations as bargaining partners, but also economic growth. If too much emphasis is placed on the desirability of a uniform wage increase — such as the famous 3·2 per cent. United States guidepost — the necessary structural shifts in the economy will not be encouraged. The wage differentials that result from a flexible system of collective bargaining play a role in steering labour to the jobs, firms, industries and sectors where it is most needed.

Thirdly, Prof. Sellier states that local union powers are strictly limited in Western Germany. In fact there is a considerable degree of flexibility in these powers, and local union officials may in fact deal with many problems that are the subject of collective bargaining.

Finally, Prof. Sellier draws attention to the proposal of M. D. Steuer that taxation be used to discourage firms from granting too high wage increases. Such proposals have been examined in Western Germany, but it is thought that the inflexibility of the fiscal system, the forecasting problems and the time lags involved make such a policy impracticable. What might be feasible is to use tax allowances as a means of encouraging workers to save.

Prof. Sellier said that by his reference to the mediator's introduction of new information he had in mind, principally, considerations relating to the general equilibrium of the economy, the type of information that is provided, for example, by the French style of indicative planning.

Obviously Dr. Markmann believes that too centralised a wage policy will hinder the allocative function of the labour market, although an OECD study [1] has suggested that this function of wage differentials may be greatly exaggerated. Nevertheless, it is true that employers do try to outbid each other for labour, and there is a need to replace this process by active manpower policies. Wage differentials could only be used in two ways. Either they could be widened even more in the hope that eventually they will induce the necessary redeployment of labour, or wage rates could be co-ordinated so that each firm must pay the same rate for a given type of labour, a situation that would force inefficient firms to modernise or to go out of business and release their workers for expanding firms.

Dr. Markmann had suggested that the rigidity of fiscal systems would cause too many administrative problems if they are used in the manner advocated by Prof. Sellier. But why are fiscal systems too rigid ; and why should their rigidity be accepted without any attempts to remove it ?

Prof. Ulman said that Prof. Giersch had made the interesting suggestion that if they are unco-ordinated, national incomes policies may have the undesirable effect of 'beggaring one's neighbour'. It should also be remembered firstly that a policy of deflation, undertaken country by country, can entail the same undesirable effects, and secondly, that some internal deflation can probably be avoided by using an incomes policy. The real significance of Prof. Giersch's point is that it draws attention to

[1] OECD, *Wages and Labour Mobility, op. cit.*

the very important question of whether or not the major objective of a national incomes policy should be to solve a balance of payments crisis. There are other objectives of incomes policies, and if a country independently embarks upon an incomes policy for reasons other than a balance of payments crisis, this might well entail undesirable international repercussions. But if it pursues an incomes policy solely to cure a deficit in its balance of payments, then presumably it would be remedying international disequilibria.

It should be appreciated that if, in fact, balance of payments crises are the only proper occasions for an incomes policy, the prevention of inflation may not necessarily be a primary objective. For instance the battered United States guidepost policy of 1962, undertaken in a period of price stability, could perhaps be defended on the grounds that the treatment of the balance of payments difficulties current at that time required a policy of price minimisation regardless of whether or not prices were actually rising.

This leads to the suggestion of Prof. Pen's that the United States guideposts may have been effective and, therefore, that their use has important implications for other countries. Some information can, indeed, be interpreted as evidence of their effectiveness. Econometric studies of the period 1961–1965, based on the Phillips Curve approach, but using such variables as changes in profits and the cost of living as well as the level of unemployment, predicted wage rises that are above those that in fact occurred, and it is tempting to attribute this disparity to the influence of the guideposts. In fact, of course, this result may simply be due to the lagged effect of previously higher unemployment levels. Therefore perhaps Prof. Pen must wait for an answer to his question of whether or not inflationary wage increases have disappeared in the United States.

It is true that manufacturing wage increases in the United States have been considerably below relatively high short-term increases in productivity which, in turn, have been due to the fact that the economy has been moving through an 'upswing' with a consequent rise in capacity utilisation. The rise in real wages in manufacturing industry has also been considerably below the rise in productivity, with the result that the wage share has tended to fall. The price increases that have retarded the rise in real wages can be attributed to the various factors to which Mr. Weinberg has drawn attention — increases in farm prices, which it is hoped will be temporary, and in various service charges and other incomes. There has also been a failure of prices to fall in industries with higher than average productivity improvements. Certainly price increases over the last year cannot be attributed to any significant extent to the outcome of collective bargaining, because there have been very few important new contracts.

Not only is it important to establish whether an incomes policy is having the desired economic effects, it is also important to enquire about the degree of compulsion that is necessary to produce these results. An incomes policy has two tasks to perform : to achieve the desired economic effects and moderate price increases ; and to do this with a minimum of compulsion — the problem which Mr. Aubrey Jones raised.

Prof. Ulman did not regret the absence of inflation in the United States either from the viewpoint of the community as a whole or in the context of its long-run institutional benefits to the unions. But a degree of inflation is undoubtedly a concomitant of full employment, and therefore the absence of a moderate degree of inflation in the United States is regrettable to the extent that it is connected with the absence of full employment and the consequent hardship of the most underprivileged people in the community, the Negroes.

Mr. Zoeteweij referred to the point raised by Prof. Ulman : namely, what should be the primary objective of an incomes policy ? Prof. Ulman had suggested that in practice the main objective seems to be the need to solve a balance of payments crisis so that, for instance, there might be more tolerance of moderate price increases than would result, if, for example, the productivity criterion were to be strictly applied. Mr. Zoeteweij thought that this suggestion is very pertinent since, in practice, there has been a fair degree of tolerance towards price increases in various countries as long as they do not give rise to balance of payments problems. In fact, on two occasions it has been debated in Holland whether wage policy should aim at actually maintaining current price increases or whether it should aim at stability in some other sense. Twice the country had been so successful in its wage policy that large balance of payments surpluses have appeared and, on both occasions, it was decided that rather than correct this situation by re-valuing the guilder (though this was done in 1960) wages and therefore prices would be allowed to rise.

If solving a balance of payments crisis is a more appropriate objective of incomes policies than price stability as such, then this would have some important implications for the conduct of an incomes policy and for the chances of its success. For instance, if greater tolerance can be shown toward some price increases, the difficult task of enforcing price reductions in industries where productivity rises faster than average might be avoided. Such a tolerance would also allow a reasonably large increase in the wage level. It has already been pointed out that where a country's productivity is rising by, say, only 3 per cent. per annum, then after various allowances have been made on account of wage increases resulting from changes in the structure of the labour force and other inevitable rises, the 1 or 2 per cent. which, strictly, is then available for wage increases may be considered too small by the trade unions. Moreover, if the balance of payments situation were the central objective of an incomes policy, it might be possible for the government, by drawing attention to the alternative policies, to persuade the parties immediately concerned with wage and price fixing that it is in their interest to support the incomes policy. For when the primary objective is to maintain or restore the balance of payments equilibrium, there is a very clear alternative to incomes policy, namely, the use of deflationary budgetary and monetary policies with consequent damage to the interests both of trade unions and of employers. It should be possible for a government to present this choice quite boldly to employers' and workers' organisations and to indicate that unless they are able to formulate jointly a reasonable wage and price policy it would take the appropriate deflationary measures.

Finally, if the balance of payments situation is to be the primary *raison d'être* of an incomes policy, both its introduction and its implementation might be easier since, normally, there would be no need for a continuing policy ; pressures that might build up in a period of wage restraint could be released in years when the balance of payments was satisfactory.

Of course, internal problems caused by price increases — such as those associated with the position of fixed income recipients — would remain. But it is quite possible that distortions in the distribution of income due to inflation could be corrected with less difficulty by alternative measures than by policies that need to influence wage and price fixing procedures in an attempt to achieve absolute price stability.

Mr. Saunders expressed scepticism about the suitability of incomes policies for correcting balance of payments situations. If it is believed that restrained increases in labour costs constitute the main factor in correcting balance of payments crises, then on the basis of data for the last five years presented in Mr. Saunders' paper it would be deduced that : by 1965 the West German balance of payments would be very bad (which in fact it was, though it is now improving) ; the French balance of payments would now be in a terrible situation ; the Italian balance of payments situation would be very unsatisfactory ; the Netherlands, Norwegian and Swedish balance of payments would be excellent ; the British balance of payments would be good in 1965 ; and the United States balance of payments would be perfectly wonderful.

The fundamental factor that causes inter-country differences in competitive ability — and this is the most relevant factor when examining balance of payments situations — is not the level of, or changes in, unit labour costs, but the level of and changes in industrial prices, or more precisely, exports prices. There is a close relationship between the level of export prices and the current balance of payments in merchandise, even when corrections have been made for changes in the general market situation and the structure of markets, etc. Competitive ability is related to export prices, not it seems to the general price level, so that the significant relationship in this context is that which obtains between industrial prices generally and export prices, the export premium, and this may or may not be affected by an incomes policy. Thus, although an incomes policy is frequently pursued simply for the sake of correcting a balance of payments situation, it cannot really be effective in this role.

Prof. Giersch agreed with Mr. Saunders that it is not possible to infer from changes in labour cost data the balance of payments positions of individual countries. There are factors other than unit labour costs that are relevant to the balance of payments ; capital movements and changes in the terms of trade are two examples. Nevertheless, incomes policies, by helping to resolve balance of payments problems, can be very useful to a country that wishes to embark upon an expansionist policy and to avoid having to correct a persistent tendency towards balance of payments deficits by 'stop and go' measures.

Returning to the international aspects, and more particularly to Prof. Ulman's point about 'beggar my neighbour' policies, Prof. Giersch re-called the possible 'beggar my neighbour' effects emanating from coun-tries that are determined to pursue a stringent stabilisation policy. Other countries, where less orthodox views prevail, may not welcome the im-portation of stability that is forced upon them.

In this connection Prof. Giersch recalled that in February 1966 a number of economists had suggested that the international monetary system be modified so as to allow individual countries to widen the margins attached to currency parities from two percentage points to eight or ten, and to allow the parities to be shifted by two percentage points per annum. This would give each country a choice between attaining price stability and tolerating a rate of inflation compatible with its national temperament, tradition and labour market institutions.

There are other possible approaches. Countries might be allowed to change their parity at very short intervals and at a fixed and predetermined rate. Countries aiming at a relatively large degree of stability would have to revalue their currencies *vis-à-vis* the rest of the world, whilst countries which tolerate a rather high rate of inflation would have to devalue permanently. International differentials in interest rates would adjust themselves to the different degrees of inflation and to the divergent de-velopments of exchange rates.

II. Measures for Moderating Wage Claims

A discussion on the basis of the paper prepared by Prof. Pen, introduced by Dr. Kienzl.

Prof. Pen said that the object of the classification of the variables in-fluencing wage increases and presented as a formula in his paper, is the following. If wage inflation is to be suppressed, the rate of increase of wages should equal the rate of increase in labour productivity. But this is not very realistic since if the cost of living rises at all, trade unions cannot agree to such a wage policy. Therefore, a more practical policy would be to try to limit wage increases to the sum of productivity and cost of living increases, to make such cost of living increases as small as possible and to minimise the part of wage increases that stems from social tensions by treating these tensions.

The weakest point in this approach is that it rests rather heavily upon the existence of sufficient central control over wage claims. A basic assumption in Prof. Pen's paper is that trade unions exert a strong influence over claims for wage increases and that there are various ways of inducing trade unions to behave in a less inflationary manner.

Dr. Kienzl, reviewing Prof. Pen's paper, stated that whilst he was in general agreement with its contents, he thought that certain points needed qualification. First, which changes in national productivity should be taken into account when determining wage increases ? The previous year's rise in productivity is not generally acceptable to unions, though some attempts have been made to use it in Austria. Potential productivity growth is more suitable, but there are tremendous forecasting difficulties involved. Secondly, if, as Prof. Pen proposes, the rise in wages should include an allowance for price increases, a parallel question arises : which price rise, last year's or the one forecast for next year, should be used ? The difference can be substantial. In 1966, Austrian prices rose by 2 per cent. compared with an anticipated 4 per cent. for 1967 — though price increases, along with balance of payments changes, have proved to be the most difficult economic variables to forecast in Austria. And the margins of error that attach to national income forecasts mean that the formula proposed by Prof. Pen need not, in practice, be inconsistent with an increase in labour's share of the national income.

Dr. Kienzl pointed out that long-term wage contracts, to which Prof. Pen had drawn attention in his paper, had some weaknesses. In particular, in Austria it had been found that after an agreement has lasted from one to one and a half years, union members become restive and present union leadership with the problem of avoiding a breach of its terms.

In the case of the question to what extent are high wage claims attributable to social tensions, it is necessary to distinguish between social tensions in a rather narrow sense and political tensions. In the case of the latter, the evidence suggests that the advent of a government with a political flavour that is particularly sympathetic to labour's interests, can give rise to higher than average wage claims. On the other hand, a government that is sympathetic to business interests might well be reluctant to throw away the fruits of its political victory in the form of a bargain with the unions of the type proposed by Prof. Pen. In the case of social tensions *per se* the workers who feel particularly socially frustrated are usually those — Negro, agricultural and some service workers for example — who, even if their frustration is channelled into large wage claims, are least well placed in terms of bargaining power for obtaining them. Some evidence is needed that social tensions are in fact instrumental in prompting high wage increases before the hypothesis can be accepted.

Prof. Pen points out that escalator clauses are regarded with disfavour

A Summary of the Discussion

by economists and employers. In fact, trade unions do not regard them very highly either. The methods used for calculating cost-of-living changes leave much scope for argument, and whether or not the results are realistic, workers' subjective impressions of how prices have changed rarely coincide with developments as shown by the cost-of-living index. The inflexibility of escalator clauses is also a serious disadvantage. If the trade union movement decides that the national economic situation is such that a wage pause is needed, previously negotiated escalator clauses may prevent them from implementing such a policy. Moreover, unions dislike such clauses simply because their existence can create a feeling among members that it is the clause and not the union which is protecting their interests.

Finally, a centralised wage policy, taken in conjunction with the solidarity that characterises the trade union movement, means that it is very difficult to bring about the changes in wage differentials that are required. Such changes would give rise to very strong tensions between branches of the union movement.

Mr. Massé agreed with Dr. Kienzl that social tensions appear regardless of the political flavour of the government.

Prof. Pen, replying to the points raised by Dr. Kienzl, stated that the trend increase in potential national productivity is relatively easy to forecast and, in the type of economy under discussion, is about 4 per cent. per annum ; and that union members are unlikely to be satisfied with wage rises based on assumptions about productivity growth that are nearer 2 per cent. per annum. Forecasting price increases does indeed pose more difficult problems. But compensation for cost-of-living rises might be set fairly low, say at 2 per cent. per annum, and adjustments made *ex post* for any price increases in excess of this.

Perhaps long-term contracts cannot bring a very great deal of stability to the system. After a while pressures to change their terms will arise, witness the development of the 'living document' concept in the United States. Moreover their effect can be positively injurious. In the Netherlands, many long-term contracts provide for a wage increase of 7 per cent. in 1967, and when allowance is made for the fact that comparable claims will be made in weaker industries and for wage drift, it seems likely that wages will rise by not less than 10 per cent. in the year.

Prof. Pen agreed that right-wing governments might find it difficult to offer trade unions the benefits that the latter consider adequate. As a result, it would seem that only leftist governments are in a position to launch a successful incomes policy. The actions of an unsympathetic government were, to some extent, responsible for the collapse of the Dutch wage policy.

Prof. Pen could understand that union officials disliked escalator clauses on the grounds that they had the appearance of limiting the extent to which the unions are responsible for their members' interests. Yet it is this very same militancy on the part of union members which it is necessary to dampen in order to limit wage demands, and his paper sought to examine various devices that might bring about the necessary change in attitudes. In any case, members' interests are not really served by a union policy that leads to wage inflation. Moreover, unless trade unions change their hardened attitudes about the desirability of existing wage relativities, then their desire to raise by a substantial amount the lowest living standards will necessarily imply a good deal of inflationary pressure ; if substantial minimum wages are to be set and wage inflation avoided, then the better-paid workers will, in a relative sense, have to suffer.

Mr. Aubrey Jones found it difficult to criticise Prof. Pen's paper. He agreed that social tensions, perhaps not so much between employer and worker as between worker and worker, were at the basis of many of the problems under discussion and he thought it might be impossible to eliminate many of them.

He, too, was very sceptical of the usefulness of long-term contracts as a means of stabilising the rate of wage increase and, in general, combating inflation. So much depends on whether expectations about the long-term increase in national productivity at the time at which the long-term contract is concluded prove to be correct. There existed a case in the United Kingdom of a contract concluded just prior to the government's July 1966 disinflationary measures, that provided for a wage increase of 13 per cent. per annum for each of the three subsequent years. What attitude should be adopted to this agreement after the end of the current wage freeze ? If it is left intact, how large will be its inflationary impact, given first that expectations about the growth of national productivity in the period when it was made are now unlikely to be realised for some time and, secondly, its impact on the wage demands of other workers ?

The basic objective of the various schemes — profit-sharing, investment wages, capital-sharing, etc. — examined in Prof. Pen's paper is to give the worker a sense of security and proprietorship. Another way of achieving this goal is to change the status of the worker in the direction of that of the salaried employee. In the United Kingdom, at least, a worker's expenditure commitments are becoming more inflexible over time as a result of the acquisition of consumer durables on hire purchase, whilst the structure of his earnings, a basic wage plus a large variety of variable supplements, is largely unchanged and leaves a sense of insecurity that is utterly at variance with the increasing certainty of his spending commitments. A second reason for giving workers a salaried status can be found in the changing role and position of management. In a large company the managing director is not in a very different position to the ordinary worker. He has a greater responsibility than the man on the shop floor towards the shareholder and the long-term interests of the organisation, but the old distinction is tending to disappear and it would be in accordance with this trend to change the status of the worker nearer to that enjoyed by the professional manager. Such an objective should be an inherent part of an incomes policy, though it would raise the problem of how it could be quickly achieved whilst preserving the incentive to work — a task more easily achieved by a wage-type remuneration than by a salary.

Prof. Sturmthal was not clear precisely what Prof. Pen meant by the term 'social tensions'. How can changes in social tensions be measured ? To measure them by the rate of wage increases is obviously inappropriate in the present context since this would be a tautology. Nor would strike statistics, for example, be suitable. Moreover, whilst the existence of social tensions can, of course, be very damaging to society, it is also necessary to be cautious about the desirability of excessive social harmony. Many undesirable acts have been committed in the name of the *volonté générale*. A degree of social tension is desirable.

Prof. Pen agreed that too much social harmony makes for sleepy societies and perhaps even worse. As for the measurement of social tensions, he thought it was far from impossible to construct certain index numbers that would measure this phenomenon. Research in the industrial relations field being carried out by such people as Hilda Behrend, relating to attitudes to wage relativities and social stratification, might provide suitable indicators. Status differences between management and workers may or may not, in fact, be disappearing — Prof. Pen thought there was little change — but certainly most people do not feel that there have been significant changes ; and inflation itself creates social tensions because virtually every group in society feels that it makes them worse off than others.

Mr. Fehrs noted that in recent years the Netherlands has abandoned the system of wage increases based on the type of formula presented in Prof. Pen's paper ; there has, in fact, been a wage explosion. One reason for this is that firms pay 'black' wages in excess of the wage rates fixed by collective agreement. Another is that some attempt has been made to allow Dutch wages to approach the levels reached in neighbouring countries. In the latter connection is it true that the Dutch authorities intend to allow the wage system to develop even closer to those operating in neighbouring countries ? Also, it would be very interesting to know a little more about the factors that have caused the sharp rise in the share of Dutch labour in the national product, referred to by Prof. Pen.

Prof. Pen said that in the Netherlands there are some groups that wish to preserve the existing system, others that would like to see it abandoned. Initially it was the employers who tried to get rid of the centralised wage policy, probably because it was at variance with their ideology, but now it is the largest trade union that is quite openly advocating that the system be abandoned. The outcome is uncertain and may not be known for some time, but could well resemble the Swedish system.

Whilst Dutch wage policy probably enjoyed rather more success in the 'fifties than Mr. Saunders' figures would imply, it has achieved very little in the last seven years. The wage explosion of about 15 per cent. per annum has meant that the share of wages in national income has increased. This simply reflects the validity of the Solow production function which postulates an elasticity of substitution between labour and capital of less than one, in fact, about 0·6 ; in these circumstances a wage explosion automatically implies a rise in the share of wages in national income.

Mr. Mattei drew attention to the very effective minimum wage system in Italy. By this system minimum rates negotiated by collective bargaining are legally enforceable and are applied to all workers in the relevant sectors, whether or not they are members of organisations signing the original contract.

If Prof. Pen's formula is adopted, it would result in a continuous rise in the share of wages in national income, except when unemployment is sufficient to change this trend. Because of this, a wage policy based on such a formula would not be satisfactory. For the basic economic problem now facing governments in industrialised countries is how to encourage new investment and improve the competitiveness of their economies. (In the latter connection, a reduction in the degree of protection may, for example, be useful.) Yet if the share of wages in national income is to rise, where will the resources necessary for this investment come from ?

In Italy, escalator clauses in wage contracts have been widely used since the end of the Second World War, and whilst neither employers, nor workers nor the government are entirely happy with every aspect of the system, it is the general opinion that given continued price increases, long-term contracts would be unacceptable unless they contained escalator clauses. Of course, the nature of the escalator clause needs to be considered carefully and in the current attempt to formulate a three-year contract covering the main industrial sector, it may be necessary to abandon the system whereby changes in the cost of living are considered every three months, since they allow seasonal agricultural price variations to have a substantial inflationary effect. There are grounds for accepting changes in the cost of living as the minimum minorium for wage increases, rather than the rise in national productivity as suggested in Prof. Pen's paper. On the one hand, if the wage rise does not fully match the price increase, the implied fall in real wages is unlikely to be accepted by the unions. On the other hand, a rise in wages below the rise in productivity need not imply a fall in real wages, and might be justified by the need to achieve certain economic goals.

Mr. Weinberg said that he would like to answer Mr. Mattei's question of how the necessary investment will be financed if the share of wages in national income is rising. A recent study, made by Bert Hickman for the Brookings Institution, has shown that the productivity of capital, as well as of labour, rises and therefore that to achieve a given rate of growth, proportionately less and less capital will be required. This implies, moreover, that if full employment is to be achieved, government and consumer spending must rise faster than national income, and one way of ensuring the latter is to raise the share of the wage and salary bill.

Mr. Mattei replied that the Italian investment needs to which he referred were essentially non-productive social investments — hospitals and schools, etc.

Mr. Weinberg pointed out that such investments were financed out of taxes, not profits.

Mr. Mattei agreed, but stated that in Italy there was a need to raise the yield of direct taxes for this purpose, and an increase in profits would be useful to that end.

Mr. Weinberg, turning his attention to the question of escalator clauses, pointed out that he was associated with a union which for some years had negotiated long-term contracts that contained both escalator clauses and annual improvement factor provisions that are intended to reflect the economy's long-term rate of productivity growth. Long-term contracts can be successful only if they contain both types of provision. There is a question not only of protecting the workers' standard of living against rising living costs, but also of ensuring that the workers' share in national income does not fall during the life of the agreement. Mr. Weinberg added that upon the expiration of such agreements, the union is in a position to bargain for an enlargement of the workers' share.

Dr. Markmann stated that he was pleased that Prof. Pen's paper introduced non-economic factors into a discussion of wages and inflation. West German trade unions find that they must constantly remind the government that wage determination cannot be based only on certain statistical series, but must also take account of some very relevant social, political and psychological considerations. In contrast, employers are fully aware of the importance of such factors.

The German construction workers' union has taken a lead in tackling social tensions. They have done this, in the first place, by acknowledging along with the employers that changes in national productivity provide one important guideline for wage increases. In fact, by adopting this criterion construction workers have obtained higher wage increases than many other groups. Secondly, the union has persuaded the employers to transfer to workers sums of money in excess of the negotiated wage increase in the form of a share in capital formation, in effect a long-term savings plan. These shares cannot be cashed for at least five years and by this means it is hoped that there will not result an inflationary increase in consumers' expenditure. Some employers and the general public appear to favour such schemes, and great efforts are being made to encourage trade unions to modify their wages policies so that such schemes can be adopted. Union opinions are still divided, but it seems probable that the psychological — as opposed to the financial — advantage of this type of scheme, will eventually ensure its widespread adoption.

In conditions that favour large wage claims — full employment and a strong centralised union movement — the West German unions have been noted for the moderation with which they have exercised their power. This moderation has been recognised in the reports of the Council of Economic Experts and is partly responsible for the German economic 'miracle'. The unions have fully endorsed the need for concerted action to stabilise prices proposed by the Council of Experts, though unfortunately the authorities have not. In such circumstances, there seems to be little need for any German government to bring moral, or any other, pressure to bear on the union movement, as a condition for the success of an incomes policy; the present liberal system of collective bargaining would be quite compatible with its effective implementation.

The German trade union movement is at present opposed to the adoption of long-term contracts. It has had some experience with two-year contracts that have proved unsatisfactory on account of changes in the economic situation that have occurred after they have entered into force, and, particularly, because of subsequent rises in the cost of living. Yet the unions are unwilling to include escalator clauses in wage contracts on account of the sensitivity of the German public about any device that might contribute to hyper-inflation and because they might provide the government with an argument for administered price increases. It has been estimated that more than 50 per cent. of price increases are due to government measures in connection with food prices, housing rents, etc.

Prof. Giersch asked Dr. Markmann if it could be said that the system of 'co-determination' in the German coal and steel industry had helped to reduce social tensions and, furthermore, whether the type of co-operation that had developed between the unions and the German building industry, and which had resulted in special benefits for union members and a form of savings plan, could not be attributed to special factors; for example to the fact that the building trade is hardly exposed to foreign competition and to the likelihood that the additional workers' savings will sooner or later increase the demand for houses?

Dr. Markmann said that 'co-determination', the participation of workers' representatives in management decisions, had indeed been responsible for a lessening of social tensions in the German coal-mining and steel industries and for a restraint in wage demands. Coal-mining is in a very depressed condition, and given its concentration in the populous Ruhr area, the fact that social and political tensions have not been more pronounced must be attributed largely to the system of co-determination. Even with the help of state subsidies the mining industry is not in a position to grant wage increases equal to the average for the country as a whole and therefore the miners' union has negotiated a two-year contract that provides for a wage increase of only 4 per cent. per annum and has succeeded in persuading its members to accept these terms. Similarly the last contract in the steel industry was negotiated in the trough of a cycle, with the result that the co-determination system yielded a wage stop for a period of 15 months, though working hours were reduced and some social benefits were obtained for the labour force.

Dr. Markmann agreed with Prof. Giersch that special characteristics of the construction industry had favoured the introduction of the long-term savings plan. The employers are aware that one result will be an ultimate increase in the demand for houses, and the fact that the industry tends to be sheltered in some respects does set it apart from others. Nevertheless, it is desirable that such schemes be adopted more widely, if only for the psychological benefits that they confer.

Mr. Weinberg thought that whilst the system of co-determination may have played some role, the relatively low wage increases in the German coal and steel industries were more likely attributable to the depressed state of the industries. Also, it is possible that the savings scheme in the building industry will be inflationary to the extent that it gives rise to an increase in the demand for housing, since the construction industry is frequently a bottleneck in the economy.

Dr. Markmann pointed out that construction workers' savings need not be devoted to house purchasing; for instance, they can be used to buy shares or life insurance. In any case, the time is likely to come when a greater demand for houses will help to maintain capacity utilisation in the construction industry at an acceptable level.

Mr. Le Brun said that he agreed with most of the contents of Prof. Pen's paper. However, the formula proposed in the paper appears to be mathematically much too simple to describe the manner in which each of the chosen variables affects wage increases. Moreover it seems to be based essentially on the widely accepted idea that wage increases should conform to rises in productivity. In fact, Mr. Le Brun was not convinced that all wage increases in excess of productivity improvements are necessarily inflationary. Such increases tend to be accompanied by a rise of profits below the rate of productivity increase; and whether or not they are accompanied by demand inflation depends on how other expenditure categories — public consumption, investment and exports — change in relation to productivity. The only rational way of determining the necessary and permissible increase in wages, is to relate it to all the other major policies and policy objectives; in short to adopt the kind of technique used in France, a coherent and balanced development of the national economy within the framework of a plan couched in both volume and value terms. With this approach, wage increases will be larger the greater the rate of economic development and the smaller the weight attached to other objectives. They will also be larger the greater the rate of increase in productivity, but this does not mean that the two should be identical.

Long-term contracts are desirable provided, again, that they are integrated with a national economic plan and that their provisions are revised annually along with those of the plan. Escalator clauses are also desirable and may even have a disinflationary effect. In France they are used only in the printing and publishing industry. In this industry, however, they are strictly applied, with additional wage increases being granted according to the productivity performance of the industry. As a result, workers are rarely in conflict with the employers, but when they are it is to some effect. Wage increases are higher and more stable than in most other industries, productivity improvements are also greater and prices rise no more rapidly.

Mr. Le Brun fully shared Prof. Pen's scepticism about the value, in the present context, of schemes for profit-sharing, capital-sharing and investment wages. A more fruitful and less complex approach than that embodied in such schemes is to raise wages in order to increase workers' savings. Such savings could be encouraged, as previously pointed out, by changes in the fiscal system, and the resulting funds channelled, with the support of the unions, to investments provided for in the plan.

Prof. Pen, replying to Mr. Le Brun, said that his formulation of the variables affecting wage increases was intended to be a politically neutral classification of such factors.

III. LABOUR SHORTAGES AND COMPETITIVE BIDDING

A discussion on the basis of the papers prepared by Mr. Le Brun and Dr. Markmann, introduced by Prof. Sturmthal.

Prof. Sturmthal thought that a discussion of the causes of inflation revealed schizophrenic attitudes. One group of people point to the unions as being responsible, whilst a second group defend them from this charge. Yet if the question is asked whether or not the unions can raise wages above a level that the market prescribes, the former group allege that unions can do little for their members in this direction, whilst the latter group claim that they can and that unions are largely responsible for the rising living standards of the working population! In these circumstances, perhaps a rational approach to the problem is not easy.

It would be wrong to interpret the type of data presented in Mr. Saunders' paper as necessarily indicating that labour costs and the unions have been responsible for inflation in recent years. Such statistical series merely show that between two selected dates wages have risen faster than prices and output. By itself this proves little since, firstly, a choice of different dates might change the results, secondly, the anticipation of future economic events can influence current developments, and, thirdly, there is in any case nothing new in the phenomena that the statistics portray. A glance at the post First World War years reveals the same kind of inflationary phenomena and the same kind of lags that we consider to be particular to our time. In short, the empirical data can be interpreted in a number of ways.

The main basis of the cost-push theory of inflation is that despite a relatively high level of unemployment in the United States during the 'fifties, wages continued to rise contrary to what theory suggests. The usual explanation of this is that, like large companies, trade unions possess an oligopolistic power which allows them to maintain and even raise wages in such circumstances. But this is an inadequate explanation in that it fails to explain why the unions did not use this power previously; why it was only at a particular moment of time that it became effective. Did the union here retain power which it now released? If so, why? Have some elements in the situation changed? If so, which? It is logically difficult to explain a changing effect on the basis of a constant cause. It is important to know much more than we do about the actual causes and processes of inflation, otherwise ideological prejudice and the power of public opinion play too large a role in discussions of this problem.

Prof. Sturmthal said that it was important to realise that the discussions had revealed two types of inflationary problem : the short-term emergency situation — which may last for quite a while — and the longer-term problem. The United Kingdom for instance is confronted with an emergency problem associated with balance of payments difficulties. Such an emergency justifies measures which neither Mr. Aubrey Jones nor any of the participants would accept in the long run. But the longer-term problem is the more fundamental one, and it should be the primary concern of the Symposium. This problem is closely associated with the fact that whilst it is now understood how to maintain full employment, we do not yet know how to live with the implications of this happy state of affairs. It is also associated with the fact that whilst in the conditions of capital scarcity and ample labour supplies that characterised the last century we learned how to administer capital resources, we have not yet understood how to administer labour now that it too has become a scarce factor.

What sort of institutional changes does an incomes policy as currently understood require? If wage restraint and price stability are to be maintained over a period of years, it is necessary for individual unions to exercise greater control over wage rates and actual earnings at the plant level and for the central trade union federation in any country to have a greater degree of control over the actions of member unions. Whether or not such changes are desirable on wider grounds is another matter. But certainly they would represent a radical change in the union structure in many countries and it is difficult to believe that they would be readily acceptable. A greater degree of discipline on the part of employers is also required. Even in Sweden the employers' federation has not been singularly successful in controlling the actions of its members.

Yet the obstacles in the way of these changes are relatively minor compared with the question of how unions and management would manage to survive at all in a world from which the basic objectives of their activities have disappeared. Trade unionists would find it extremely difficult to recruit members on the strength of wage rises that might be even larger in the absence of unions. Nor would management find it easy to explain to shareholders that they had forgone certain profits in the interest of extraneous national objectives. Such actions may be acceptable in emergencies but not over longer periods. Yet, as pointed out, this longer-term problem of organising a full employment society is our primary concern, and if it is to be solved by means of permanent wage and price restraint then there is no room for the system of trade unionism and of enterprise as we know it. Moreover there is a danger of developing a society in which the leadership of all interest groups forms a coalition in favour of one cherished objective, price stability, but in which individuals both inside and outside of the relevant institutions in general have little influence upon their own fate.

In order to find a solution to this problem, we must know how the labour market functions. An OECD study has shown that wage differentials, and changes in wage differentials, are probably not as important in allocating labour supplies as we have been led to believe.[1] Mr. Crossley, of the London School of Economics, has shown that in fact the short-term elasticity of supply of labour is quite high. Neither study claims that the effect of changes in wage differentials is altogether negligible particularly in the long term. In fact, therefore, there is a need for wage differentials to change in the way determined by a labour market. Yet incomes policies may prevent these changes in wage differentials. The use of coercive devices such as wage and price restraints instead of the traditional use of changes in wage differentials would hardly be acceptable, especially on a long-term basis.

In Prof. Sturmthal's view the use of such devices should be limited to the short-term situation. In the case of the long-term problem, only a modest goal — a reduction in the rate of inflation — should be set, and pursued not by disciplining interest groups but by the implementation of active manpower policies. An active manpower policy seeks to promote and accelerate the required structural redistribution of the labour force in both the short run and the long run by measures that influence the schedules of demand and supply of labour. The schedule of demand can be influenced by the discriminatory use of fiscal measures (including subsidies), by restrictions on the location of firms and by many other methods. But it is measures that affect the supply side that are growing in importance in our attempts to administer labour resources as carefully as capital. Educational, training and retraining programmes are being reorganised and linked to improved skill requirement forecasting techniques. The mobility of labour is being increased by mobility premiums, resettlement allowances and the provision of living accommodation. Imperfections in the labour market are being tackled by measures to improve the effectiveness of employment exchanges and by the elimination of discriminatory hiring practices.

Against such a background, what role can wage and incomes policies play ? First they have a symbolic role, to reassure the public that the authorities are aware of the problems that exist. More specifically, wage

[1] OECD, *Wages and Labour Mobility, op. cit.*

and incomes policies may be needed to deal with short-term problems, since the fruits of an active manpower policy only appear to the full in the long term. However, there is a danger that, once introduced, wage and price controls become permanent. It is necessary therefore to attach deadlines to their operation.

Prof. Sturmthal said he was curious to know how the wage and price restraints used in France could be reconciled with the system of indicative planning that had also been adopted. In contrast to the 'dirigisme' of the inter-war period, did not indicative planning have the very commendable goal of operating on demand and supply schedules rather than directly influencing economic variables, such as wages and prices, that result from the operation of the market mechanism.

Mr. Massé replied that the French economy, while operating within the framework of a plan, remained essentially a market economy. In 1963, an emergency situation required the adoption of price controls only for a limited period ; they are now, in fact, being relaxed. As Prof. Sturmthal had rightly said, it is important that the introduction of such short-term measures be accompanied by a termination date, otherwise they tend to become permanent.

Prof. Sturmthal was pleased to hear that the operative word in Mr. Massé's reply was 'emergency'.

He said he would like to conclude his statement by drawing attention to three important aspects of the general problem. First the manpower policies that he had advocated need to be integrated with other economic policies, since all of them are essentially concerned with administering scarce resources. Secondly, experience in dealing with the problem of inflation will accumulate only gradually, and for some time it may be necessary, on occasion, to accept some rise in prices in order to prevent excessive unemployment, though in these circumstances the victims of inflation should be compensated in some way. Thirdly, as Prof. Giersch has pointed out, such a long-run anti-deflationary policy might be incompatible with a system of fixed exchange rates. In that case, and in view of the cost in human suffering and forgone output to which the alternative policy of deflation gives rise, the advantages of stable exchange rates seem to be insignificant.

Mr. Rehn thanked Prof. Sturmthal for very eloquently presenting much of the case for the active manpower policies now being preached by OECD.[1] The development of these policies could be aptly illustrated by Swedish experience. At a relatively early stage, the Swedish trade unions tried to show the government that, as Prof. Sturmthal has pointed out, union attempts to persuade their members to exercise restraint in wage demands during a period of full employment (achieved through a high and

---

[1] The OECD Council Recommendation on an Active Manpower Policy of 21 May 1964, presented with comments in the OECD *Observer* August 1964, was published in various countries in official publications.

in many areas excessive level of effective demand) are hardly likely to be successful, especially over a long period. The government was not convinced and, from feelings of solidarity with the Labour Government, the unions therefore tried to implement a policy of wage restraint. The result was that during the periods of restraint such pressure accumulated (for example, discontent among large numbers of wage- and salary-earners over the fact that profits or wage drift benefited only certain groups) that ultimately the policy collapsed and was followed by a wage explosion, the effects of which may have been as inflationary as if no restraint had been exercised. Indeed, this is a general feature of incomes policies : a period of success in their application seems almost inevitably to give rise to a relaxation of demand management and therefore to be followed by a counter-attack from the inflationary forces. The prevention of this counter-attack requires the persistent use of alternative measures which, in practice, often means a deflationary policy. But in turn such a policy gives rise to pockets of unemployment, to a cry for redeployment measures and, thereby, to the discovery of the need for an active manpower policy in two forms : the selective creation of employment in areas of labour surplus and measures to stimulate the adjustment of the labour force to the structure of labour demand — in order to maintain full employment without the need for excess demand over the greater part of the economy. Perhaps because Sweden experienced this sequence — wage restraint, the accumulation of inflationary forces, a consequent wage explosion and deflationary measures — at a relatively early stage, it was the first to experiment with an active manpower policy, though other countries, notably Canada and Norway — and more recently the United States, the United Kingdom, and France among others — have been moving along the same road.

A primary task of an active manpower policy is to promote a reallocation of labour resources in such a way that a moderation of the rate of increase in prices and wages becomes economically and psychologically possible — though unions and oligopolistic employers also have a role to play in achieving this. One way in which an active manpower policy can promote this goal is to facilitate efforts to change the structure of wages and prices, and thereby the levels of wages and prices, in the required direction. In particular it helps those trade unionists who take a broad view of the labour market situation to keep the wage structure as rational and equitable as possible. Because of the well-known imperfections in the labour market, attempts to attract labour to areas and firms with acute labour shortages by the use of wage differentials would require these differentials to be very wide and to change violently. This is not very practical. If such differentials (and changes in them) appeared, they would provoke attempts to restore earlier patterns, which would eventually cause large all-round increases in wages (wage-wage spirals) and therefore wage-price spirals. In fact, employers are frequently aware of this result and, therefore, try to avoid competitive bidding for labour — often in vain, however. Obviously other means are needed for redeploying labour as quickly as possible towards the bottleneck points in the economy; this is one task of an active manpower policy.

Mr. Rehn said that the size and difficulty of the task of steering a course between inflation and unemployment by means of an active manpower policy should not be underrated. The extent to which active manpower policies can be successful in this role is something no one can forecast. The direction in which to go is known, but so far there is insufficient experience of the ultimate quantitative effects of the various measures we group under the general heading of 'active manpower policy'. Some observations about the characteristics of the labour market and its functioning indicate the problems to be dealt with.

Whilst there are grounds for believing that elasticities of labour supplies are rather low, it is also true that there is a tremendous amount of mobility (or rather, turnover) in the labour market; although net labour flows between areas or sectors may be rather small, the gross figures from which they derive are very high. In order to ensure that the net movements are in the required directions there is a need, firstly, to reduce the unwanted flows and, secondly, to improve the quality of employment services and, in general, the information available to job changers so that the gross flows can be directed more effectively to where they are needed.

The large gross movements imply that financial incentives for labour mobility cannot and should not be paid to everyone who undertakes a move. On the other hand, society should not necessarily be reluctant to give financial compensation even to many persons who would have undertaken a move in the absence of such incentives. For the cost of such compensation does not represent a real charge on the resources of the economy, only a transfer of income from the community to individuals who experience the burdens and costs of mobility. It seems socially just that those who move in the desired directions are compensated by society; this would be analogous to an insurance system or a spreading of costs — and not an increase in real costs (except to a minor extent) — to be weighed against the benefits of a more efficient redeployment and of higher employment at a given level of (inflationary) demand pressure.

In this context we must also appreciate that some groups experience particular adjustment difficulties — in spite of the high gross turnover statistically registered. These groups, mainly the older workers, become a social and political problem as soon as certain areas experience a fall in the demand for labour which makes some of these workers redundant; this is an inevitable consequence of serious attempts to use fiscal-monetary instruments for creating a non-inflationary balance in the economy. To make such a policy psychologically acceptable a price has to be paid in the form of generous help for alleviating the particularly difficult circumstances of these groups.

Whether the cost of measures to help workers overcome adjustment difficulties and to stimulate movement in the most productive directions should be met by the taxpayers or employers is a relatively minor question. But it would seem desirable that these financial resources be administered by the employment service, since this agency is best placed for determining which labour flows are needed.

Are the measures for improving adaptability in the labour market, which have up to now been tried, efficient ? In the case of incentives for geographical mobility, no deep or detailed investigations have been made. However, on the basis of impressionistic evaluations, supported by elementary statistics, the authorities in countries where these measures have been used more extensively (Sweden, Norway, Canada) have found them worth while enough to be continued, and have provided larger resources for this purpose.

In countries where they have been used, retraining schemes also seem to be regarded as successful enough to warrant further — and rapid — expansion, although there is relatively little scientifically analysed evidence about their quantitative effects. Some cost-benefit studies have been made in the United States, but the results cannot be regarded as conclusive until the methods and the basic data are improved. However, there is a general impression that these schemes are advantageous to the economy. By this, some observers mean that their benefits are many times larger than their costs ; others question the validity of such statements — but nobody seems to suggest that the experiment should be discontinued. Rather intuitive evaluations of experience with adult retraining programmes in Sweden (where such programmes, having an immediate bearing on short-term changes in the labour market situation, and covering about 1 per cent. of the labour force annually, for an average six-month course, have been tried most) are so encouraging that recent plans envisage a doubling of their scope within five years. At the same time the coverage of the programme is being broadened by making everyone eligible — and not only the underemployed or persons with other employment handicaps — thereby rendering it possible to attract a larger number of workers more rapidly to areas of labour shortage. Similar developments, based on acquired experience, can also be detected in a number of countries where the programmes have so far been more limited in scope.

The question which is of particular interest in the context of this Symposium, namely to what extent can these and other labour market adjustment programmes help to prevent inflation, is, of course, a rather difficult one, both conceptually and empirically. How can we know the extent to which an improvement in the functioning of the labour market (a superior allocation of the labour force, achieved without large changes in wage differentials and consequent wage-wage spirals) helps to reduce inflation as opposed to raising the level of employment, and how much it helps in both these directions in relation to other possible impacts ?

When more experience is garnered and analysed it may be possible to say rather more about the quantitative effect of manpower measures upon labour flows towards bottleneck areas. It may prove possible to estimate the effect that this would have in the form of lower wage drift in these areas. But will it ever be possible to estimate the size of the inflationary effect (in the form of the contagious influence of such wage drift throughout the economy) which has been avoided by preventing certain wage-wage spirals by this means ? That these difficulties are encountered when estimating the quantitative effects that result from replacing excess demand by selective and adaptive manpower policies as a method of keeping full employment, does not mean that we must abstain from taking action that is expected, at least, to work in the right direction. (In technical terms, action to move the Phillips curve to the left and to make full employment and high rates of growth possible without inflationary profits forming the basis of capital accumulation.)

Raising the level of employment from, say, 94 per cent. to 98 per cent. *may* give rise to more inflationary pressures than measures to maintain the level of employment at 98 per cent. More precisely, when unemployment levels are high, so are employers' recruiting standards and it can be very difficult to persuade them to change their attitudes and lower these standards in order to reduce the level of unemployment. In contrast, once the level of employment has been running for some time at 98 per cent., employers' recruiting standards will be adjusted to this situation and there will be no need for measures to change them. The opposite view can also be argued, however ; during the process of raising the employment level from 94 per cent. to 98 per cent., there will be a lagged effect on wage and price determination procedures, and being linked with conditions of relatively high unemployment rises in these variables will still tend to be moderate. But when the level of employment has been at 98 per cent. for some time, individuals become more and more aware of the fact that the situation favours a faster growth in monetary incomes, and their demands increase accordingly. In our present state of knowledge, it is therefore difficult to say whether *maintaining* full employment without inflation is more or less difficult than *attaining* it without inflation.

There is another aspect to the role of an active manpower policy in conditions of full employment : it is very probable that with the level of general demand which cannot be exceeded if strong inflationary pressures are not to appear, pockets of unemployment will persist even though general unemployment is at an acceptable level. Therefore, in addition to fostering required labour mobility in conditions of full employment, active manpower policies should make provision for 'local' job creation, even if this means subsidising certain activities.

To conclude his statement, Mr. Rehn said that he would like to pursue quite a different line of thought. Imperfections in forecasting techniques mean that attempts to prevent fluctuations in the level of unemployment, by being wrongly timed, can accentuate inflationary pressures. Therefore it is desirable for people who are hit or threatened by unemployment to be so well cared for that the need for the manpower authorities and the other economic policy-makers to keep employment constantly 'full' is less pressing. Some of the active manpower measures of the adaptive type are, of course, of this kind. Some people may prefer to be 'unemployed' or, more correctly, to remain outside the queue of job-seekers, if they are provided with attractive retraining facilities and income maintenance during a period when there is a reduction in the demand for their type of labour. But it should also be possible to develop other acceptable means of varying labour supplies to make them conform with variations in demand. One example of such flexibility is the system of rotating rights to 3-month holidays in a 5-year period, which has been established in the American steel industry (instead of an equivalent reduction in the standard working week); by special agreement the workers can use these rights to take extra long intermittent holidays (they might even be called 'periods of fully paid unemployment') when demand for the products of the industry is slack, in return for avoiding this during boom periods.

If it is desirable to avoid both inflation and socially unacceptable forms of non-employment, a wider application of similar systems that provide for sabbatical periods should be sought, and more flexible pension systems than those currently used should be established. When, as can be foreseen, countries provide extended and collectively financed (or at least supported) education and training schemes for both adults and young people, an effort should be made to arrange for the utilisation of these schemes to be varied in such a manner that it accords with structural, conjunctural and other fluctuations in the demand for labour. This would lessen the need for maintaining employment (in the strictest sense of the word) so close to the theoretically possible maximum level each day in each area and each sector, a practice which makes inflationary bottlenecks unavoidable. Mr. Rehn was aware that, in view of the failure of incomes policies in conditions of widespread excess demand, some people draw the conclusion that the economic systems of Western Europe can be kept stable only with higher levels of unemployment than have prevailed in recent years. But before abandoning the commendable goal of avoiding unemployment, which most countries have accepted during the 1960s, other methods for avoiding unemployment should be attempted : selective and adaptive manpower policies, of the types referred to by Prof. Sturmthal and the OECD Recommendation, and those mentioned by Mr. Rehn. It is, of course, a purely terminological question whether the latter type of policy should be called 'maintaining full employment by varying the supply of manpower in accordance with variations in demand' or 'making deviations from full employment socially acceptable by income maintenance during periods of non-work'.

Mr. *Le Brun* expressed his agreement with the type of active manpower policy that had been advocated. Turning to his paper, he noted that he had already elaborated on its later passages. In the first part, statistics are presented to show that whilst plant-level collective bargaining does exist in France, it is not very widespread. Other data suggest that the reason for this is the insufficiency of industry agreements, either at the national, regional or local level which, in turn, can be attributed especially to an inadequate number of trade unions and the dissensions within the union movement.

Whether or not the terms of national or other higher-level contracts are applied at the firm level depends on the strength of unions in particular plants and also on the ability of the relevant service of the Ministry of Social Affairs to ensure that these terms are enforced. The paper also draws attention to the fact that in France actual wage rates are much higher than negotiated rates. This is hardly surprising when it is realised that wage rates negotiated for a whole industry must be low enough to be acceptable to all firms, including the least efficient. But the disparity is more than can be accounted for by this factor alone, and both the weakness and division of the trade union movement, and the restrictive policy pursued by the authorities in the last ten years with respect to the SMIG,[1] must also bear part of the blame.

Despite the shortcomings of the statistics, it can be estimated — after allowance has been made for the legal extension of provisions in some contracts — that little more than half the workers in industry, commerce and services are covered by collective agreements that contain wage clauses. In this circumstance it is difficult to believe that the wage negotiations that precede these contracts can play anything but a relatively minor part in the inflationary process.

In general, the French trade union movement prefers this system — or at least, the system as it was originally conceived in 1936 and operated immediately after its reintroduction in 1950. It is a system that is particularly valued for the decentralisation of decisions that it allows. Yet such a system could be reconciled with the operation of an incomes policy if, as suggested, the policy is formulated within the framework of an acceptable economic and social plan and thus be assured of the support of labour.

Dr. Markmann, referring to his paper, said that essentially it sought to examine the scope which existed for making wage bargaining more centralised and the possibility of rendering decentralised wage determination less prone to inflation, in the context of conditions in Western Germany. He pointed out that it was important to realise that the positive and constructive attitude that West German trade unions had displayed to economic problems hardly justified any restraint being placed on their freedom of action. More particularly, the unions were very sensitive about attempts to thrust a wages policy upon them when corresponding measures were not applied to other incomes.

[1] See Chapter 7.

The Labour Market and Inflation

Union opinions, both leadership and rank and file, are democratically reflected in collective bargaining negotiations in Germany, since union representatives on the collective bargaining commissions are chosen both from the enterprise level and from the trade union centres. By this means, labour requirements and economic conditions that obtain both at the national and 'local' levels are taken into account. Nevertheless, the unions believe that the bargaining procedures and machinery can be improved, though they are blocked in their attempts to effect such an improvement both by the employers and, to a lesser extent, by the Government. More precisely, the unions' attempts to shift the process of collective bargaining towards the plant level is frustrated by the employers who prefer centralised collective bargaining. For instance, the metal manufacturing employers' association, covering a sector employing three and a half million workers, refuses to participate in collective bargaining even at the branch or district level, so that the union's desire to take account of the variety of local conditions is ignored. German employers have also resisted union attempts to introduce more scientific methods of wage fixing, for which technological developments have meant there is a need in both industry and commerce.

There is no doubt that the existence of full employment puts the unions in a strong position, and despite the restraint and responsibility with which the German trade unions have exercised this power, the employers and the Government are very quick to protest that every new wage claim means the end of the German economic 'miracle'. Yet a much greater threat lies in the malfunctioning of the labour market and in the actions of employers. In the absence of a developed active manpower policy, labour supplies do not flow very easily to those expanding firms, industries and areas in the economy to which Mr. Rehn has referred. As a result, and in an attempt to attract these supplies, employers in the expanding firms increase their product prices, undertake competitive wage bidding, raise the earnings of their employees and, eventually, force other firms in the same locality to follow suit.

Prof. Sturmthal suggested that a rise in the market wage to attract labour to expanding firms indicates that, contrary to Dr. Markmann's opinion, the labour market is functioning satisfactorily.

Dr. Markmann maintained that imperfections in the labour market existed in the sense that the required labour mobility is absent, and that this gives rise to inflationary pressures via the sequence he had referred to.

Mr. Mattei said that the exchange between Prof. Sturmthal and Dr. Markmann had left him rather confused. He agreed with Prof. Sturmthal's earlier remarks that there was a need to make better use of labour resources, and he would have thought that the functioning of the German labour market as described by Dr. Markmann would, in fact, help to achieve this objective. That is, if a firm or industry can afford higher wages, it means that it is more efficient and therefore should pay higher wages ; and if the productivity of workers in the marginal firm is low, they

A Summary of the Discussion

should move to the more efficient, higher wage sectors. In any case, it is very important that further consideration should be given to the question of whether a decentralised market-guided wages system with its inflationary elements or a centralised wage determination system is more conducive to the efficient utilisation of manpower resources.

It is important that the unions abandon the illusion that full employment will be safeguarded in all circumstances. In Italy, a certain degree of unemployment has been chosen as a means of reducing inflationary pressures. And it seems that the United Kingdom Government has recently made a similar decision.

Mr. Mattei agreed with Prof. Giersch that the pursuit of incomes policies had implications for exchange rates and, more particularly, required that they be flexible. But are exchange rates, in fact, fixed ? The agricultural policy of the Common Market provides for a system of levies that vary with the level of international prices. Two years ago, the British authorities imposed a surcharge on imports ; and the new selective employment tax has the effect of discriminating between domestic market activities and export industries. Is it correct, therefore, to speak about fixed exchange rates when it seems that there is a movement towards the systems used in certain Latin American countries where different rates of exchange apply to different sectors and products ?

As Prof. Sturmthal had pointed out, an incomes policy can be used to deal with an emergency situation in order to allow time for long-run solutions to be found. But many emergencies are associated with balance of payments deficits and, as previously pointed out in the discussion, it is difficult to solve this problem by an incomes policy. For the value of incomes policies is severely limited by the fact that they can only restrain wage increases ; they cannot attempt actually to reduce wages without giving rise to unbearable social tensions. Other solutions must be found for remedying a balance of payments deficit and the terrible truth is that, at the moment, the only alternative is a deflationary policy with a concomitant rise in the level of unemployment. The major problem, therefore, is to find a substitute for this classical remedy.

Dr. Markmann said he would like to refer to a few further points in his paper. Both the unions and employers in Germany are uneasy about the nature and extent of wage drift, though the employers regard it as a means by which negotiated rates are brought into line with what individual enterprises can afford and need to pay. The existence of different methods of wage payment constitutes an important source of wage drift. There is a general tendency for piece earnings to rise continuously and automatically and the earnings of hourly-paid workers need to be increased accordingly if unacceptable differentials are not to appear ; often labour skills that are now required cannot suitably be remunerated by traditional means and, in the absence of modern wage-fixing methods, employers are returning to mixed systems of time rates and bonuses. Another cause of wage drift is an increase in the number of categories of workers provided for in wage contracts and in the systems used by individual enterprises. Differences in firm sizes, and in the consequent levels of wages paid, give rise to tensions and, in conditions of full employment, there is a tendency for wages in small and medium-sized firms to be raised to those in large firms, providing yet another element in wage drift.

It is very difficult to measure wage drift in West Germany, and consequently there is a dispute between trade unionists, employers and economists about the extent of the 'hard core' wage drift. Nevertheless, it has been estimated that 'hard core' drift accounts for about 10–15 per cent. of the industrial wage bill; and actual earnings in Germany appear to rise in about the same proportion as centrally negotiated wage rates, but the value of fringe benefits has perhaps risen faster. However, there is a remarkably clear short-term relationship between the degree of drift and the business cycle: in a boom, the gap widens, in a slump it narrows. Indeed, at the present time there is negative drift in the sense that earnings are rising more slowly than negotiated wage rates. Yet, the long-term trend is definitely towards a widening of the gap between earnings and wage rates. It should be said that both union and employer opposition to a degree of control of collective bargaining procedures is not lessened by the fact that the degree of wage drift is increasing in countries that implement something approaching an administered or regulated wage policy.

Dr. Markmann agreed with Prof. Sturmthal that incomes policy could be useful in an emergency situation, but he thought that there was real danger that a policy introduced for this purpose would in fact be retained for longer periods and he was opposed to the use of an incomes policy in this way. In the absence of any government guarantee about the claims and interests of the labour force, it was preferable to retain the existing system of free collective bargaining. In any case, the West German unions had proved themselves responsible and they take account of the national economic situation when negotiating wage increases. This is not to suggest that there is no room for rationalising wage determination procedures. In the last five years collective bargaining procedures have become progressively more complicated in West Germany with the result that the influence of the trade union centres has increased at the expense of that of shop stewards and the rank and file. A combination of this greater degree of centralised strength with a rank-and-file membership better informed about the wider economic situation, might lead to a position in which the lower levels of collective bargaining follow some centrally decreed wage guidelines.

Prof. Sellier agreed with Prof. Sturmthal's conclusion that there is a need for attention to be paid to the administration of labour resources. But to argue that the development of such a labour shortage derives from a rise in the price of labour relative to the price of capital, is largely tautological; this relative change is the result of technical progress and productivity as Kendrick has shown.

Prof. Sturmthal agreed with Mr. Mattei about the significant role that wage differentials can play in promoting required labour mobility. Does Dr. Markmann's concern about competitive wage bidding imply that he thinks that labour should be retained in the less productive enterprises rather than being attracted to the more dynamic ones ? The framework of the German collective bargaining system derives from measures taken during the First World War, and cannot be fully understood except in the context of the role and nature of the workers' councils. There is no doubt that the system needs to be reappraised and considerably changed in the light of current needs.

Prof. Sturmthal added to Mr. Mattei's examples of devices that circumvent fixed exchange rates. The United States military procurement system, under which the price of foreign supplies must be less than half of the price corresponding domestic goods before they are chosen, implies a dollar devaluation of 50 per cent.

Mr. Stein said that Prof. Sturmthal had implied that it is not possible to attract workers to a job that they regard as inadequately paid. Mr. Stein felt that this had to be put into perspective. Many studies about the motivations of people leaving and taking jobs showed, perhaps rather surprisingly, that financial considerations play what economists may feel is a depressingly minor role in their decisions. Prof. Sturmthal had cited the OECD report, *Wages and Labour Mobility*, to the effect that whilst it does not aver that the wage structure plays no role in the allocation of labour, it does claim that it plays a smaller role than had generally been thought. In this connection it is important, but difficult, to distinguish between the short- and the long-term situations. The study in question was concerned essentially with the short to medium term, that is up to about ten years, and showed that over periods of this length inter-industry wage differentials had been relatively rigid whilst industry employment changes had been very varied.

The experts responsible for the report had indeed drawn attention to some instances where the wage structure had changed, and to the evidence that industries with higher than average increases in earnings also tended to be those hiring more labour. This association, it was felt, however, might be an effect of the prosperity of these industries rather than of their need to attract manpower by raising wage scales. Generally speaking, labour force growth, together with the fact that new entrants tended to take jobs which were available because they were available, enabled expanding sectors to fulfil their labour requirements without undue concern about the structure of wage relativities. Another relevant mechanism in redistributing labour was the fact that a relatively rigid wage structure can contribute to putting a number of firms out of business, so releasing their workers onto the labour market.

The Labour Market and Inflation

Long-term developments had not been examined in detail in the report, though a section devoted to occupational differentials suggested that these had narrowed over the long term, 40 to 50 years, perhaps as a result of the relative scarcity of totally unskilled labour.

The implication of these considerations is that a short-term incomes policy, say for a period of less than five years, need not be unduly concerned, if at all, with provisions for changing the wage structure. The existing structure may or may not be 'satisfactory', but the fact is that it has undergone little change in the countries studied for 10 to 20 years. This has not prevented a substantial reallocation of the labour force, and there has been a considerable amount of economic growth during this time.

What, then, should be the objective of an incomes policy ? It would seem that an incomes policy is probably unsatisfactory as a means of dealing with an immediate balance of payments problem. And where there is a great deal of excess demand, there is probably no alternative to the use of traditional instruments — monetary and fiscal measures — to combat inflation. However, it has been observed that even when demand is not excessive prices continue to rise in periods of full, and even not-so-full, employment. It is to combat this that an incomes policy based on appropriate guidelines and used in conjunction with such other measures as an active manpower policy may have a role to play.

Mr. Aubrey Jones could not agree with some of the views expressed by Prof. Sturmthal. Measures to make the supply of manpower more elastic and to utilise labour resources to better effect are not sufficient ; and an incomes policy is not a measure that can be used to deal only with a short-term problem and then discarded — a longer-term policy is needed, for example, in the United Kingdom. Perhaps Prof. Sturmthal's views are a result of viewing the problem only in economic terms when in fact other considerations are equally important. As Prof. Sturmthal had pointed out, people act according to their expectations about the future. But future expectations are largely conditioned by past experience. And when a community has become accustomed to creeping inflation over a period of 10 to 15 years, a rather drastic form of incomes policy may be required. If it is accompanied by mere persuasion, people will act in the expectation of continued inflation and thereby undermine the policy.

Inflation is largely due to the way in which trade unions and oligopolies exercise their powers. These powers have grown considerably over time — unionism, for example, is spreading up the social scale — and given the general expectation of continued inflation, management and unions have exercised their powers at the expense of the interests of consumers. The answer is not to break up large organisations into smaller units — though much anti-monopoly legislation is based on this approach — but to seek ways of curbing their powers. Restrictions on their freedom of action can be justified on the grounds that we have inherited a set of notions about economic freedoms that were appropriate when the units in question

A Summary of the Discussion

were small but which are altogether too wide in present circumstances.

Mr. Weinberg thought that regardless of what the situation may be in other countries, recent price rises in the United States are not the result of the exercise of trade union power ; average hourly employee compensation (including fringe benefits) rose by 3·7 per cent. per year between 1960 and 1965, whilst labour productivity increased by 3·8 per cent. But Mr. Aubrey Jones' comments about oligopoly pricing, Mr. Stein's references to creeping inflation in the absence of excess demand and Mr. Massé's remarks on the use of price controls rather than wage controls in France prompt the question of why price stability cannot be sought by policies directed at prices rather than wages. If a rise in the price level could be effectively prevented, no special measures might need to be taken in respect of wages. For if employers do not have the financial resources to pay larger wage increases, unions cannot obtain them. Action on prices would also limit competitive wage bidding ; only the more efficient and profitable firms would be able to offer large wage increases and this would promote a desirable redistribution of the labour force. And if there were no rise in the cost of living, unions might be willing to accept changes in national productivity as a general wage guideline, subject to some very important qualifications. It is pertinent that, when Minister of Economic Affairs in the United Kingdom, George Brown said : 'there are some prices which play an outstanding part in manufacturing or export costs. Others have an important influence on the cost of living. There are very strong arguments for starting work with key prices of this kind. Successful work on prices will provide a firm basis for proceeding to deal with incomes.'

Mr. Massé said that the French view is that it is necessary to influence all the elements which bear on the inflationary process. The new Cost and Incomes Study Centre would certainly not confine its attention to wages, but would also examine profits and prices. And it should be noted that the United Kingdom Board, of which Mr. Aubrey Jones is Chairman, is concerned with prices and incomes.

Prof. Giersch pointed out that in West Germany during the last two years there had been excess demand for labour in the sense that the number of vacancies had been much above the number of unemployed ; the wage level rose substantially more than average productivity. Although the cost increases resulting from this could be fully explained by market conditions, public authorities and the general public largely supported the view that the trade unions and their wage claims were responsible for the unsatisfactory development of costs and prices. From this Prof. Giersch concluded that in all discussions of wage problems a clear distinction should be drawn between, on the one hand, situations of excess demand for labour accompanied by tendencies to hoard labour and, on the other, situations in which unemployment could be regarded as an indication that wages are too high rather than too low. If there were a choice, Prof. Giersch would vote for some excess demand for labour, or

The Labour Market and Inflation

what amounts to the same thing, for real wages somewhat below the equilibrium level. Compared with the opposite situation, a slight excess demand for labour has definite advantages in a growing economy. Shifts in the structure of employment would be brought about through the pull of industries seeking more labour, and not through dismissals from firms that are squeezed out of the market by a lack of demand.

One major difference in the two situations is that in a sellers' market workers have a greater freedom of choice of jobs. Moreover, the reallocation mechanism works more smoothly. In a sellers' market for labour, workers are pulled out of their jobs by more productive alternatives; but if structural change is to be brought about by the push of dismissals the question whether the workers dismissed are more useful elsewhere hardly receives any consideration. Hence it can be assumed that the disappearance of excess demand on the labour market is quickly followed by the appearance of frictional unemployment.

Mr. Meidner reported that calculations made by the Swedish Government showed that three cost categories — wage increases, larger direct taxes and increases in rents, import costs and agricultural incomes — had each contributed about 2 percentage points to price increases in recent years.

Prof. Pen said that he had made calculations for the Netherlands comparable to those carried out in Sweden. They show that during a seven-year period, which included the recent wage explosion, three-fifths of the price rise were accounted for by labour costs (wages rose by 77 per cent.), two-fifths by profit and interest margins (this element rising by 35 per cent.).

Mr. Weinberg thought that the results of such calculations did not affect the point he had made that inflation might be treated by measures relating directly to prices. In the absence of such direct action with respect to prices, calculations of the contribution of wage increases to price rises are not relevant to his argument.

Mr. Saunders said that, from the views expressed, he gathered that the general opinion is that wage drift performs the function of restoring the impact of market forces on a wage structure that is distorted in the process of collective bargaining. He was doubtful if this is, in fact, the effect of drift. Inter-industry comparisons suggest that wage drift — the difference between collectively agreed rates and actual earnings — does not greatly modify the wage structure, rather its effect is to stabilise inter-industry wage differentials over time.

Such a result can be interpreted as reflecting the essentially tripartite nature of the wage determination mechanism. First, unions agree with employers on a certain set of wage increases. Secondly, particular employers in their search for labour of the desired quality offer additional remuneration. Thirdly, and this is the factor that seems to predominate in the end, the worker's desire for equal pay for equal work — and in practice this seems to be a preference for existing differentials — is given effect, either formally through the unions or shop stewards or by informal pressures on employers, and the pre-existing differentials restored by a further degree of wage drift. Thus individual employers' attempts to attract labour by using wage drift to bid for labour is frustrated and the net effect is not a change in inter-industry wage differentials but an upward shift in the whole structure.

It is very difficult to prove that this is, in fact, the actual sequence of events or, indeed, to show that in a wider perspective drift does not influence the wage structure. In particular there is very little information about differences in drift among the various firms of a given industry. Suffice it to say that it has not yet been established that the efficient and progressive firms are responsible for most drift.

Mr. Weinberg pointed out that wage drift is essentially a European phenomenon and is not encountered to any great extent in the United States where wage negotiations relate to effective rates rather than to minimum rates as in Western Europe. A small degree of drift arises in the United States where piece rates are used, in circumstances of labour shortage (as in the steel industry), in non-union firms and where job evaluation is used — employees tending to be highly rated when the labour market is tight and classified in lower categories when it is slack.

Prof. Sturmthal noted that Mr. Stein had questioned Prof. Sturmthal's remarks about how workers can be attracted to jobs. Prof. Sturmthal had in mind experience with job evaluation systems which shows that often after the wage differentials have been 'scientifically' determined workers may not offer themselves at certain of the rates. In these circumstances, the employer must abandon the rates dictated by the system in order to obtain the necessary labour. Perhaps the apparent conflict of views with Mr. Stein about wage differentials is resolved by the fact that Prof. Sturmthal had in mind, primarily, long-term changes in occupational and inter-firm differentials rather than changes in inter-industry differentials.

Mr. Aubrey Jones had said that by Prof. Sturmthal's reckoning all that is needed is to make the supply of labour more elastic. While this is by no means all that is required, it would indeed be a very great achievement if Mr. Aubrey Jones' labours in the United Kingdom were to have this effect. For such a result requires fundamental changes in the structure of British trade unions and even of the community as a whole, changes which would encounter tremendous resistance. Prof. Sturmthal had expressed scepticism about inflation being attributable to the use of oligopolistic power, since such power had existed for some time and the cost-push theorists had failed to explain what new element had appeared to cause it to have an inflationary impact only at certain times. In this connection the fact that unionism, whilst it does not appear to have recently increased much in numerical terms in the United Kingdom or the United States, has, according to Mr. Aubrey Jones, tended to rise up the social scale, might be one empirical factor explaining recent developments, though there is yet no proof of this.

Prof. Sturmthal did not wish to create the impression that he has become a *laissez-faire* economist. He believes along with Mr. Rehn that it is necessary for economic policy to help the market to function smoothly, and at times this can involve a considerable degree of intervention by the authorities for speeding up structural changes and for alleviating the burdens that accompany them.

Mr. Eskilsson thought that in Sweden the degree of wage drift does differ between industries. But the reactions of the negotiating parties are such that in each round of bargaining wage rates are changed in such a way that they correct for the different degrees of wage drift, thereby creating a relatively stable wage structure.

Prof. Sellier drew attention to the paradox mentioned in Dr. Markmann's paper, that while wage negotiations in the West German metal industry are essentially at the industry level, negotiations are frequently conducted at the plant level in such other sectors as food, textiles, clothing, banking and commerce. The explanation of this is simply that the employers choose the national level in the case of the metal industry because at that level the metal trade unions are relatively less strong, and the plant level in the other sectors mentioned because that is where the unions are less powerful in these cases. That wage negotiations are conducted at different levels in different industries is a feature of all countries. In France the major negotiations in the metal industry are at an intermediate level, the regional level. The employers have chosen this level, in opposition to union wishes, because it is where, relative to the unions, they are strongest. Employers in the metal industry regard national wage bargaining with disfavour because, in effect, it means negotiating wages at the Paris level. They dislike branch-wise bargaining from a fear that the higher rates negotiated in the motor vehicle section might be used as a pattern-setter for the whole industry.

IV. The Inflationary Impact of the Wage Structure

A discussion on the basis of the papers prepared by Mr. Aubrey Jones and Mr. Eskilsson, introduced by Mr. Meidner.

Mr. Meidner, reviewing Mr. Aubrey Jones' paper, said that he would like to draw attention to some difficulties encountered by attempts to tie income increases to rises in national productivity. First, unions are not prepared to accept the existing distribution of income which this implies. In the long term they want a rise in the share of wages in national income and, in this connection, he noted that whilst in any given country labour's share appears to be very stable, it varies considerably between countries. Secondly, difficulties are raised by the fact that with the national productivity type of criterion prices must be allowed to rise in firms where pro-

A Summary of the Discussion

ductivity increases are low. Thirdly, productivity improvements resulting from structural changes towards high productivity sectors are reflected in the national productivity index but would clearly be inflationary if translated into a wage rise applicable to all the labour force. Fourthly, there is a timing problem to which reference has already been made. Currently, contracts are being made for as long as three years in Sweden. How can productivity changes as far away as that be forecast with any accuracy ?

Mr. Aubrey Jones distinguishes three elements that must be brought under a greater degree of control : union bargaining power, market forces and comparability criteria. Mr. Meidner thought that market forces are the primary determinant of the extent of union bargaining power, though unions are prepared to use the 'comparability' argument where it is useful. The paper deals essentially with the question of wage relativities in what seems to be an unbalanced economy. Mr. Meidner thought that in a balanced economy there is no need for an incomes policy whilst in an unbalanced economy it cannot be achieved.

There are indeed great disadvantages in the use of the 'crude comparability' philosophy, to which attention is drawn in Mr. Aubrey Jones' paper : it involves an endless wage-wage spiral and preserves irrational wage relativities. Making the wage structure more rational is an objective of Swedish trade union policy, as well as the British incomes policy, but what criteria can be used to replace the current principle of the preservation of existing differentials ? It is difficult to understand the British answer to this question. In his paper Mr. Aubrey Jones proposes that 'the factor to which more weight must be given is the national rate of productivity growth', but whilst this might have the effect of limiting the general rise in wages, the fact that it is the same for all groups would itself tend to preserve the existing structure of wages. The paper does qualify the statement by allowing that differential increases might be permitted where more 'refined comparisons' reveal that they are in the national interest and where productivity agreements lead to the abandonment of restrictive practices. In fact, neither of these two exceptions constitute acceptable criteria for reshaping the wage structure except in an emergency situation such as the one that the United Kingdom currently faces. If an incomes policy is to be a long-term one the whole concept of comparability needs to be reformulated.

Both Mr. Aubrey Jones' and Mr. Eskilsson's papers have, as a common point of departure, the need to limit wage rises to increases in national productivity. Whilst, however, Mr. Aubrey Jones considers the steps that a government can take when normal negotiating machinery has been superseded to minimise the inflationary impact of the wage structure, Mr. Eskilsson directs attention to the possibility of limiting wage drift by modifying the systems of wage payment adopted by the employer. A question raised by Mr. Eskilsson's approach is the extent to which — as Mr. Saunders has suggested — increases in basic wage rates and wage drift are complementary. Is it in fact true that there is a predetermined increase in earnings corresponding to each labour market situation and that action, on the one hand, by the negotiating parties and, on the other, by employers acting unilaterally can only determine how this total rise is distributed between changes in basic rates and drift, without affecting the total itself ? There seems to be some evidence that in Sweden a relatively small contractual rise, such as that in 1964, is followed by exceptionally high drift. If this is indeed the case, then Mr. Eskilsson's proposals for reducing wage drift cannot be expected to have much net effect.

Mr. Eskilsson's main thesis is that with a given degree of excess demand for labour, different wage systems give rise to different degrees of wage drift. More particularly, he believes that piece rates are a mainspring of wage drift, and therefore incentive systems should be used less widely in Sweden. Mr. Meidner supported Mr. Eskilsson's desire to reduce wage drift — it is also an objective of unions since drift distorts the wage structure they seek — and he agreed with efforts to reduce the use of piece rates in Sweden — their incentive effect has been exaggerated and they are not suited to modern production techniques — but he thought it unlikely that the former goal can be achieved by the latter means. It is not at all certain that wage drift in Sweden can be mainly ascribed to the use of piece rates. In some years' time rate earnings contained a larger drift element than piece earnings, and countries where incentive systems were used much less than in Sweden experience considerable drift.

For these reasons Mr. Meidner did not consider that the campaign of the Swedish Employers' Confederation against wage drift would prove successful. Job evaluation and merit rating systems of the type proposed by Mr. Eskilsson leave a margin of uncertainty in a rate that will always be affected by the state of the labour market. Referring to measures to improve the balance of the labour market and the economy as a whole, Mr. Eskilsson writes : 'it would be wrong to expect that wage drift could be altogether reduced by these means'. In fact, however, not enough consideration has been given to the possibility of obtaining beneficial results in this field by improving the equilibrium of labour markets and sub-markets. Such an approach would have more chance of success than measures to change wage payment systems and heroic resistance to market forces by groups of employers.

Mr. Aubrey Jones believed that his paper brought out a basic division of views that had been revealed in the discussions. On the one hand, Dr. Markmann, Mr. Mattei and Mr. Meidner seem to support the view that the roots of the problem being examined by the Symposium are essentially economic. On the other hand, Prof. Pen, Mr. Stein and Mr. Saunders appear to be leaning towards the opinion that it is, in a large part, a social and political problem. Mr. Aubrey Jones also thought that the problem is essentially social and political in nature, and whilst it is not possible to prove conclusively that these elements are more important than purely economic causes, some relevant illustrations can be cited.

The Prices and Incomes Board was requested to examine the pay of teachers in Scotland ; teachers in England and Wales had been granted a pay rise of 13 per cent. and Scottish teachers claimed the same. In fact the working conditions of these two groups of teachers are quite different. Teachers in Scotland must be graduates, so that their salary levels are higher, and the salary structure differs from that in England and Wales. Similarly when London busmen obtained a 6 per cent. wage increase, busmen in the provinces claimed the same amount. The Board discovered that conditions are quite different in the provinces ; in contrast to London, there is no shortage of busmen in such areas as rural Wales, mid-Cornwall and the centre of Scotland. In both these cases the basic problem was quite unconnected with the economic condition of the labour market. It was simply a question of concepts of fairness, each class, or group, trying to maintain its relative position in society. For the following two reasons, this problem is going to become worse rather than better.

Firstly, Mr. Aubrey Jones had already pointed out that unionism was moving up the social scale and that this is likely to make the problem more difficult. The Prices and Incomes Board, having been asked to review the pay of railway clerks and manual workers, considered that their position merited a wage rise above the national $3\frac{1}{2}$ per cent. norm, and recommended an increase of 5 per cent. Whereupon the railway managers, earning not less than £3,000 per year and whose position had not been referred to the Board, claimed a 5 per cent. rise, in an attempt to maintain their relative position in society. In fact, if as seems likely higher income earners become organised in trade unions and obtain percentage rises equal to those granted to low income workers, inequalities will become wider in absolute terms.

Secondly, individual groups are increasingly inclined to compare their position with that of corresponding workers in other countries. For example, British doctors having a language in common with North America can command a good salary on the international market. They are also now highly organised in a militant trade union and recently have used this potential on the international market to obtain a salary increase which, if it were not for the current freeze, would have had repercussions throughout the British trade union movement. Consider the implications of such actions in conjunction with each group's insistence on maintaining its relative position in society and all against a background of fixed exchange rates ! It is true that the relevance of the system of exchange rates introduces an economic factor into the problem, but basically it has social and political causes that are going to become worse.

There is the question of whether an incomes policy should only be used in an emergency situation. The United Kingdom has been faced by an emergency situation caused by wage inflation, against which a credit squeeze is not sufficient and which has given rise, therefore, to the wage freeze. At the time of the introduction of the freeze some settlements — one of 13 per cent. per annum already referred to — had been reached which, if they are allowed to come into effect after a freeze of, say, 12 months, will clearly have an inflationary impact given the reaction of other groups to maintain their relative position. It is not possible to say what the British authorities will eventually do about this but it would seem that there is a need for all existing settlements to be renegotiated. An incomes policy must be more than a short-term emergency measure.

The protagonists of a free labour market, that is the antagonists of government intervention by means of an incomes policy, seem to base their attitudes on the claim that the market ensures flexibility. In fact the market seems to be far from flexible in the case of wage relativities and so a degree of government intervention is needed to promote the necessary changes. In this connection it is pertinent that trade unions appear to have abandoned their early goal of a greater equality of incomes, and have become an instrument for perpetuating, and indeed aggravating, existing inequalities. The unions should resume their original concern with income distribution by prescribing priorities for the various wage claims.

Finally, Mr. Aubrey Jones stated that whilst Mr. Eskilsson's paper naturally related to only a small part of the whole problem, he agreed entirely with its contents.

Mr. Eskilsson said that the type of situation referred to by Mr. Aubrey Jones, in which salaried workers claimed rises as high as those sought by wage earners, is by no means unknown in Sweden. The Swedish school teachers had struck for a salary rise of the order of 15 to 20 per cent.

Referring to his own paper, Mr. Eskilsson pointed out that methods of measuring wage drift differ between countries. In most countries the difference between two indices measuring earnings and wage rates is called wage drift. In Sweden, where all wage increases are given with the actual earnings as a base, wage drift is measured as the difference between the increase in earnings and the calculated cost of the wage round.

The degree of wage drift varies with the situation in the labour market. Therefore it is important, if wage drift is to be reduced, that governments adopt appropriate policies with respect to the general level of demand. It is now accepted that these policies cannot be pursued in a disinflationary manner to a point where full employment is endangered, though given the imperfections of economic forecasting it may be necessary from time to time to have unemployment levels above those normally accepted, as a means of remedying previous policy miscalculations. However, Swedish experience has shown that even if excess demand for labour is removed, wage drift still exists. With a given level of demand for labour, the degree of wage drift varies with the nature of the labour market institutions and, in particular, with the type of wage payment system. In Sweden two-thirds of all working hours are paid by piece rates and it is known that

A Summary of the Discussion

incentive payment methods are more prone to wage drift than hourly rates. The paper contains some suggestions about how the wage payment system might be made more resistant to wage drift without diminishing incentives. By taking account of such factors as the difficulty of the job and the performance and capability of the worker, it should be possible to derive a set of acceptable wage differentials in a systematic way. The labour costs of a firm comprise three elements, contractual increases in wage rates, changes in social benefits paid to the worker and wage drift. Attempts to combat wage inflation must take account of the existence of all three elements. It is not sufficient simply to limit increases in contractual rates.

Prof. Pen drew attention to the fact that in the Netherlands university professors recently claimed a 50 per cent. salary rise in addition to their normal claim of 10 per cent. per annum on the grounds that their relative position has deteriorated since 1938. The doctors followed with a claim for an 80 per cent. rise, and the Queen for one of 400 per cent.! Despite the fact that certain difficulties attend its use, it seems that only a wide-ranging system of job evaluation offers any promise of breaking this wage-wage spiral. No doubt occupational wage and salary differentials, when judged by such a system, will be found to be too wide.

Mr. Weinberg, in reply to a point made by Mr. Aubrey Jones, stated that the unions had done much to correct unwarranted inequalities in wages. In Sweden there is the trade union 'solidarity' principle, and in the United States, unions had done much to eliminate wage differentials between men and women, to stop employment discrimination against Negroes and to promote minimum wage legislation. But it is not simply a question of redistributing wage and salary income among workers, but also between employment and property income. If, for instance, a steel-worker forgoes a wage rise, what assurance is there that it will be used to raise low wages rather than profits ?

Naturally, union leaders looked to the interests of their own members but when it comes to wider issues of social justice the basic traditions of the labour movement are such throughout the world that the notions of social justice they apply tend to be the right ones, and lead to improvements in the situation of distressed, disinherited or dispossessed individuals.

Dr. Kienzl believed that the implementation of an incomes policy required some adaptation of the labour-market institutions. This is very difficult to achieve, especially if it has to be done quickly. How can the British trade unions undergo the necessary adjustment in the short term ?

Dr. Kienzl agreed with Mr. Aubrey Jones that it is the duty of the trade union movement to establish priorities for wage claims and, thereby, the wage structure, and where there is a strong union centre this should be possible. Such a system is preferable (and more acceptable to trade unions) to government attempts to attain the same goal via the actions of a mediator. If a wage structure is to be obtained in this way, by discussions within the union movement, it is important that the union centre be guided in these matters by an official from a union whose members are exposed to foreign competition — a metal worker would be suitable — to help ensure that the wage structure, however determined, does not become out of line with the international market.

In principle, an incomes policy seems to be better adapted to dealing with a short-run emergency situation. The difficulty here is that action in such emergencies has to be quick, which assumes the pre-existence of machinery for implementing an incomes policy. The permanency of such machinery would not prevent a relaxation of the incomes policy at appropriate times — indeed this would be very necessary — and at such times budgetary and monetary policies designed to balance the demand and supply of resources would be the most important. In times of emergency, the necessary controls would be tightened and, as Mr. Weinberg has suggested, might be applied particularly to prices, since in addition to treating stability directly this would make an incomes policy more palatable to the trade unions.

Mr. Rehn emphasised that a strong centralised trade union movement could only have the beneficial results that Dr. Kienzl anticipated if general disinflationary policies are successful in removing excess demand for labour. For if there is excess demand for labour then any 'solidaristic' wage policy based on job evaluation or any other scheme will eventually fail as a result of employers bidding against each other and because of the actions of labour groups — university professors for example — outside the solidaristic union movement. Thus, on the one hand, it is important to realise that the existence of strong centralised union movements in Austria, Sweden and Norway is not sufficient to yield the desired results and, on the other, that economies in which there are no such centralised union structures should not necessarily regard these countries with envy.

Prof. Sturmthal wanted to reply to Mr. Aubrey Jones' assertion that an incomes policy should not be used only in an emergency situation and that Prof. Sturmthal was wrong in his belief that it should be limited in this way. A reconciliation of their views might be found in the fact that the current emergency in the United Kingdom is likely to last for a considerable time.

Mr. Aubrey Jones thought there was some evidence in the United Kingdom that systems of job evaluation are conducive to a greater stability of earnings, when applied within a given firm. What is not certain — though research is afoot in this field — is the practicability of extending a given system between firms and industries.

Mr. Aubrey Jones agreed that there exists no objective standard of social justice, and that it is frightening for any individual to have to act as an arbiter in these matters. Mr. Weinberg had responded to Mr.

A Summary of the Discussion

Aubrey Jones' earlier challenge by indicating that whilst no objective standard of social justice existed, the trade unions were perhaps best placed to make the necessary judgments. Dr. Kienzl had added that to make these decisions effective requires increased central control within the trade union movement, and also — as most other unionists agree — an absence of government interference. But this implies a certain contradiction with Mr. Weinberg's view that the introduction by trade unions of a scale of priorities for wages should not open the way for a rise in profits, since only the government, not the trade unions, are in a position to prevent this. If a major cause of price increases is, essentially, other price increases, this sequence cannot be suppressed solely by the government's manipulation of effective demand. What is required is something that trade unions are reluctant to accept, active intervention by the government in price and wage determination procedures.

Mr. Weinberg noted that whilst he had said that it was necessary to take direct action with respect to price increases this did not imply that no action would be needed in the case of wage increases. Under the UAW proposal referred to in Mr. Weinberg's paper,[1] price leaders in major industries would have to give advance notice of any price increases. A government board, plus a Consumer Council to represent the public interest, would then publicly examine these intended price increases in the light of all pertinent data and a cross-examination of witnesses from the corporation. If the latter based their claim on union wage demands, then union representatives would also have to answer to the board. Census data suggest that this procedure could be reasonably effective as regards the general price level even if it were applied to no more than a hundred corporations.

There would remain the question of whether public opinion, marshalled in this way, would be an effective deterrent. Nevertheless the procedure has the merit that it focuses attention on the crux of the problem, price increases. Whilst wage restraint is only required as a means of achieving price stability, action against wages rather than action aimed at the fundamental objective, prices, has hitherto always been taken first. The explanation of this seems to be that it has proved politically and administratively easier to attack on the wages front. But, firstly, attacks on wages have not succeeded, and, secondly, there is no reason why political views and administrative institutions should not be changed to yield the desired results.

Mr. Aubrey Jones replying to Mr. Weinberg said that a criticism levelled by some orthodox economists against the British prices and incomes policy is that during the first 18 months of its operation it had a greater restraining effect on prices than on incomes. This is true. A possible explanation of this result is that whilst businesses have become chary of taking action that injures the public interest, trade unions, as yet, have not.

[1] Chapter 3.

235

The Labour Market and Inflation

Because wages rose relative to prices, the government decided to introduce monetary and fiscal policies that would abate the inflationary raised prices relative to wages by the selective employment tax for example. The response of the unions was to prepare new wage claims. All this suggests that the question is more complicated than Mr. Weinberg makes it appear, though basically Mr. Aubrey Jones was in sympathy with his views.

Mr. Weinberg thought that because wages could rise relative to prices this suggested that profit margins might have been too large initially. In any case, it did not seem that the effect of the relative increase in wages had been to reduce employment.

Mr. Aubrey Jones said that he did not know whether or not margins had been unduly large at the outset.

Mr. Mattei thought that if costs increase but prices cannot, the result must be a fall in employment.

Mr. Weinberg replied that if there is effective price restraint then there are limits to the claims that unions can make and to the wage bidding that employers can indulge in, so that costs will not then necessarily rise.

Mr. Mattei recalled that Europe had had considerable experience of price controls during and after the Second World War. But, as Mr. Aubrey Jones pointed out, price freezing may not necessarily solve the problem, for there may come a time when in order to reduce real demand the government will wish to reduce the real wage by increasing prices. In any case, conditions in the United States differ from those in Western Europe, so that Mr. Weinberg's approach may be suitable only in the former country. In particular, the relatively small size of national markets in Europe and the ease with which goods can cross national boundaries, mean that price competition, and therefore limitations on price increases, are in any case stronger.

Mr. Weinberg agreed that prolonged price control leads to a deterioration in quality and the mal-allocation of resources and he would advocate price control only in an emergency. Nevertheless, he had heard no convincing argument why a direct attack on the inflation problem from the price side should not work more effectively than an indirect approach through wages. Conditions in the United States are not so very different from those elsewhere and, certainly, the economy is not insulated from foreign competition.

A comparison, over the past five years, of changes in employee compensation per hour and productivity in the United States reveals that there has been no pressure for price increases from the side of wages. Yet prices have increased, and whilst some increases can be attributed to certain scarcities in food supplies, the sizeable increase in wholesale prices relative to unit labour costs and in profit margins, reveals that this was by no means the whole explanation.

A Summary of the Discussion

V. Some Aspects of the International Co-ordination of
Incomes Policies and Collective Bargaining

A discussion based on papers prepared by Dr. Crijns and Mr. Weinberg. Mr. *Fehrs* introducing Dr. Crijns' paper recalled that Prof. Giersch had emphasised the very great importance of the international implications of incomes policies. It was with these implications and problems in mind that, as indicated in Dr. Crijns' paper, the European Economic Community had turned its attention to the question of incomes at the level of the Community. The major step to date is the inclusion in the first medium-term economic programme of certain general principles for the guidance of incomes at the Community level. In fact, this programme contained only a brief statement of principles, reflecting the fact that the Community has turned its attention to this question only very recently. In turn this is partly attributable to the speed with which the problem had to be considered and partly because the elements of this first medium-term programme, for the years 1966–70, are presented only in global, volume terms, thereby preventing any detailed analysis of the evolution of prices and incomes. However, it is very likely that the second programme, for the period 1971–75, will examine in much more detail income changes at the level of the Community.

In his paper Dr. Crijns emphasised, firstly, that an incomes policy at the Community level should relate to all incomes — to profits as well as wages, and also to transfer payments; secondly, it should seek to suppress inflationary tendencies by relating, in some fashion, income increases to productivity changes; thirdly, it should favour unduly low incomes, thereby modifying the income distribution; fourthly, it should be accompanied by a policy relating to the distribution of wealth; and fifthly, it needs to be accompanied by other measures necessary for its implementation — price, credit and fiscal policies.

In the latter connection, the Commission has emphasised that it would not seek to restrict the freedom of negotiation enjoyed by the parties. It would therefore be vital for the negotiating parties to meet regularly with the authorities both at the national and Community levels to discuss the problems associated with the incomes policy and its implementation. The success of the policy would depend crucially on the participation and support of each member country's government and its groups' representatives, the Commission itself being powerless to implement the policy without such support. Obviously the formulation and implementation of an incomes policy at the international level poses even more problems than at the national level.

Finally, Mr. Fehrs said that he wished to draw attention to certain relevant studies being carried out by the Community. One, now almost completed, whilst concerned primarily with methods of wage determination, in fact has many important implications for incomes policies. Others are concerned with wage drift and with worker participation in the achievements of the enterprise. All these studies will assist the formulation of an incomes policy for incorporation in the second medium-term economic programme.

Mr. Eskilsson thought that certain of the proposals in Mr. Weinberg's paper on the international co-ordination of wage bargaining [1] would lead to very inflationary results in some countries and encounter strong resistance from both employers and governments. Moreover, especially in developing countries they would be likely to retard the growth of employment — or even cause reductions in employment — and thereby severely impair the development process.

Mr. Weinberg replied that employer and government resistance to union goals was nothing new. Also, he did not agree that the effect of his proposals would be to cause inflation or hinder economic development. In reply to a request for information, the Venezuelan authorities had said that the lowest-paid employees of United States firms in the oil and iron ore industries in Caracas received wages twice as high as those in other industries. These high wages have not spread to other industries but, naturally enough, have caused some envy in other workers who are now keen to take advantage of a training institute to learn the not very complicated skills required in the iron ore and oil industries. Neither is the payment of high wages in cases like this likely to produce unemployment, since the wages would be geared essentially to the productivity of the relevant industry; there would be no question, for example, of trying to induce a small car assembly plant in Turkey, operating without modern production techniques, to pay wages equal to those in Detroit. The fact that such relatively less developed areas of the United States as the South are obliged to pay car and steel workers the same wages as in Detroit and Pittsburgh does not prevent car and steel plants from locating there. Not only does it seem unlikely, therefore, that development would be hindered, there are even grounds for thinking that it might be fostered. Firstly, as already pointed out, workers in developing countries would have an incentive to be trained. Secondly, funds that would otherwise be repatriated from the developing country in question would be retained in the form of higher wages.

In the latter connection, it must be acknowledged that experience has shown that economic development in under-developed countries cannot depend on imports of private capital from industrialised countries : such capital flows essentially to other developed economies or is limited to the extractive industries in under-developed economies. If the development of under-developed countries is to be accelerated, the necessary capital will have to be provided by the governments of developed countries, and in the form of grants rather than loans given that the time is approaching when debt

[1] Chapter 11.

repayments will transform developing countries into net capital exporters.

Prof. Giersch said he would like to comment on some of the points made by Mr. Weinberg. He thought it unlikely that problems which are difficult to solve on a national scale are made easier when approached at the international level. It is difficult to know how successful the harmonisation of wage policies in the European Economic Community will be, but it would be undesirable if the equalisation process were artificial in the sense that it ignored regional productivity differences that are attributable to location factors. To some extent locational disadvantages can be remedied by improvements in communications but the only way in which certain regions can compete with others is by paying lower wages. Southern Italy may be a case in point, but even in West Germany there are peripheral regions which manage to compete only by paying relatively low wages and thus by specialising in labour-intensive products.

Any attempt at the premature international harmonisation of wage levels is bound to give rise to problems of inter-regional resource allocation. Harmonisation policies that are not preceded by a co-ordinated development of the component regions causes labour to move to, and capital to stay in, the major centres. This creates a need for a regional policy that largely consists of a fiscal mechanism for redistributing income from the richer centres to the peripheral regions in order to compensate them for the burden of wages much above the equilibrium level.

Mr. Mattei agreed with the views expressed by Prof. Giersch, especially with his statement that incomes policies pose problems enough at the national level, let alone at the international level.

Whilst every country would like to be able to afford the wage level of the United States, it is very difficult to see how this can be achieved by individual enterprises paying United States wage rates. Perhaps a more effective method than that proposed by Mr. Weinberg would be for the industrialised countries to accept more immigrants from the less developed economies — a measure that would link with Prof. Sturmthal's plea for a more flexible supply of manpower in full employment societies. Mr. Weinberg had also suggested that the governments of developed countries need to help developing countries by giving them more assistance in the form of grants. Such international action would also have implications for national incomes policies. More precisely, the labour forces in developed countries would have to forgo some of their share of the national product in order to provide the necessary resources.

Prof. Pen disagreed strongly with Mr. Weinberg's proposals. The 'upward international harmonisation of wages' implies either inflation on an enormous scale for most countries or the abandonment of equal pay principles and job evaluation schemes. International trade union solidarity should not express itself in this way but in the acceptance by workers in developed countries of cheap imports from developing countries.

Mr. Weinberg replied to the comments on his paper. He agreed with

Prof. Giersch that regional productivity differences have an important bearing on wage differentials but he believed that inter-regional productivity differentials rapidly disappear with the spread of a common technology. Also, although the United States is larger and has more varied climatic and physical conditions than the European Economic Community, most of its industries have nevertheless been able to eliminate, or greatly narrow, regional wage differentials. The location of industry is now determined essentially by the geographical distribution of raw materials, power supplies and markets. In a given industry, productivity levels do not vary greatly from region to region.

In reply to Mr. Mattei, Mr. Weinberg said that the sharp contrast between developed and developing countries in living standards and material prospects is intolerable, and that it is necessary for all groups in industrialised countries, including workers, to forgo a part of their share in increments in national product in order to remedy this problem. Moreover, there exists sufficient idealism and generosity in every community to support such action. The Marshall Plan, which necessitated higher per capita expenditures in favour of the people of Western Europe than the United States is at present dispensing for the benefit of developing countries, was initially attacked by many United States politicians, yet it was supported by the community at large and therefore successfully carried through.

In the twentieth century it is not possible for economic development to be based on sweated labour in the same way that it was in the nineteenth century in America and Europe. Apart from other considerations, the existence now of an alternative political philosophy, Communism, prevents this. Developing countries are not going to be exploited, and their people will insist upon enjoying a fair share of the fruits of economic development and of modern technology. One United States automobile company has an automated engine plant in South Africa employing largely exploited Negro labour. Because of the limited size of the South African market, which cannot support an automated engine plant, these engines are probably being exported for incorporation into cars assembled by relatively high-paid workers employed by the same corporation in other countries. No trade union can accept such a situation without trying to improve the employment conditions of the South African workers.

Mr. Weinberg reminded Prof. Pen that the upward harmonisation of wages would need to proceed within the limits prescribed by productivity improvements. Also, he wanted to point out that the American trade union movement, by and large, has a good record in the field of trade liberalisation. For example, it had supported the Trade Expansion Act and had resisted proposals that car tariffs — which are low relative to those in Western Europe — be raised as a means of stopping incursions into the United States market by Western European manufacturers.

INDEX

INDEX

Page numbers in bold-face type indicate contributions by participants.

Index

Index